From Gangs to Gangsters
How American Sociology
Organized Crime,
1918-1994

From Gangs to Gangsters
How American Sociology Organized Crime, 1918-1994

Marylee Reynolds
Caldwell College

Harrow and Heston
PUBLISHERS
Guilderland, NY

Harrow and Heston, Publishers
1830 Western Avenue
Albany, N.Y. 12203

Library of Congress CIP:

Reynolds, Marylee
     From gangs to gangsters: how American sociology
     organized crime,1918-1994 / Marylee Reynolds
         p. cm.
     Includes bibliographical references (p.) and index.
     ISBN 0-911577-30-0

  1. Chicago school of sociology. 2. Sociology—United States—Philosophy. 3. Sociology—United States—Methodology. 4. Organized crime—Research—Illinois—Chicago. 5. Deviant behavior—Research—Illinois—Chicago. 6. Criminology—Illinois—Chicago. I. Title.
HM22.U5R49   1995
301' .01--dc20

                                  95-34255
                                      CIP

Contents

. . . Another difficulty is contained in the very term "social disorganization." The term is perhaps appropriate to certain types of behavior subsumed under it . . . It is ironic, though, to reflect that this term was supposed to refer to crime— and that was in Chicago in the 1920s!   Many of these phenomena are indeed highly organized.

—Peter L. Berger and Brigitte Berger

1

Introduction

Nature of the problem

A CRITICAL approach to crime and deviance theory in American sociology continues to develop. Crime and deviance theories have often been criticized for focusing on the deviance of the powerless (Turk 1969; Quinney 1970; Chambliss and Seidman 1971; Liazos 1972; Thio 1973; Taylor, Walton, and Young 1975); for focusing on the individual deviant while ignoring the structural conditions of society (Mills 1943; Snodgrass 1972, 1976; Cullen 1983); and for reinforcing capitalistic values (Schwendinger and Schwendinger 1974; Quinney 1974, 1977). However, one critical point that has not been systematically raised is the lack of literature on organized crime in American sociology. This is all the more important since racketeering, gangsterism, and organized crime in the city of Chicago coincided exactly with the development of American sociology in that same city.

In the 1920s, the city of Chicago was the crime capital of the United States. Beer wars, bombings, bootleg liquor hijackings, racketeering, and gang murders made national and international headlines. Al Capone was its notorious underworld chieftain. It is not surprising as Kurtz (1984) writes, that in such a city the Chicago sociologists would turn to the study of crime. What is surprising is that the Chicago sociologists, as this book will demonstrate, were not focusing on the organized crime in that city, but on Chicago's lower-class crime and delinquency. Studies of organized crime have played a marginal role in the development of American sociology, until relatively recently, particularly during the period of Chicago dominance, when that city was identified with bootlegging, racketeering, gang wars, and organized crime. The University of Chicago is where urban sociology and the sociology of deviance developed against a backdrop of organized crime—reminders of whose existence covered the daily newspapers and the movie screens.

This book addresses the discipline of sociology itself and what it is sociologists do or do not do. It brings into question sociology's traditional view of itself. It is only since the late 1960s that "the tools developed in the sociology of knowledge have extended to a 'sociology of sociology' " (Carey 1975, p. 5). Sociologists often find it difficult to study their past in an objective and detached manner (Carey 1975, p. 5). This book attempts to do this.

The central contention of this book, then, is the fact that a very important kind of crime, which we now call organized crime, was almost entirely ignored by American sociologists, even the Chicago sociologists, from the classical period of American sociology in the 1920s and for many decades afterwards. The following chapters will carefully document how American sociology, until relatively recently, has ignored a significant social problem, organized crime. The procedure and methods of study for the forthcoming chapters are introduced in the final section of chapter 1.

How can we go about studying this neglect of organized crime by American sociologists? We must first try and understand what organized crime is. The difficulty lies not in the term "crime" but in the term "organized." Society's members can easily determine if a crime has been committed; there are federal and state criminal codes which define crimes and their punishments. However, there is no consensus by society's members as to when a criminal group is "organized." Moreover, if criminal activity is organized it is not necessarily considered organized crime. A brief review of the history of the concept "organized crime" will help to clarify the term for the reader.

Understanding the concept of organized crime

The difficult problem of defining organized crime lends support to the claim that sociologists have ignored or minimized the problem of organized crime. One of the principal reasons sociologists have shied away from studying organized crime is because there is no consensus among sociologists, or the law enforcement community for that matter, as to what activities constitute organized crime. Dissenting definitions of organized crime probably have much to do with the ideological predispositions, theoretical differences, and methodological obstacles which confront those who wish to study organized crime. Organized crime is not easily available to scholarly inspection; it is often hidden and therefore misrepresented to the public, even by sociologists. Furthermore, organized crime has undergone changes over time; it has not remained static. The changeable nature of organized crime has contributed to the difficult problem of defining it.

There are currently three general models of organized crime in American society. The first model views organized crime as an alien conspiracy transported to America from foreign soil. According to this model early Italian immigrants imported organized crime to America. This model was given credence through the President's Crime Commission Report of 1967, and the classic work, *Theft of the Nation*, written by criminologist Donald Cressey in 1969. Cressey was a member of the Federal Task Force on Organized Crime, and used this data to prepare his manuscript *Theft of the Nation*. The problems inherent in using government sponsored documents as the basis for our understanding of organized crime are discussed in chapter 8. This model, often referred to as the Cressey model, is favored by the law enforcement community. The other two models focus on the ethnic pluralism and economic aspects of organized crime, and view organized crime as indigenous to, and as a function of American society. These models are often favored by academics, including sociologists (see Albanese 1989; Potter 1994). Definitions of organized crime often reflect the organized crime model one adheres to. As we examine the history of the concept organized crime we will come to see how these three models evolved over time, and how definitions of organized crime have developed and changed over time. It is interesting to note that all three of these models did not come into full view until the 1960s and afterwards.

The expression "organized crime" was not part of contemporary parlance until the 1920s and the Prohibition era. It was during this time that academics and newspaper editors began to use this term as a label for an old phenomenon (Woodiwiss 1987, p. 8). Like the term "racketeer," which is discussed in some detail in chapter 6, the origins of the term "organized crime" are not always clear. However, there is some evidence that its usage has undergone considerable change since its inception in the 1920s. Let us examine some of the earlier and later uses of this term.

Barnes and Teeters (1943) explain that organized crime refers "mainly to organized efforts to achieve bank robberies, and to organized swindling gangs, smuggling gangs, murder syndicates and the like" (p. 21). Barnes and Teeters (1943, p. 60) list the following activities as forms of organized crime: operation of murder rings, organized bank and train robberies, truck and warehouse robberies, fraud and swindling, blackmail, smuggling, dope peddling, and providing women for vice. According to Ianni and Ianni (1983), criminologists in the United States first "used the term *organized crime* to distinguish the professional from the amateur criminal" (p. 1095). Ianni and Ianni (1983) argue that with this distinction "any gang or group formally or informally organized to rob banks, steal automobiles, or pick pockets is part of organized crime. Over time, . . . governmental commissions, congressional committees, law enforcement agencies, and the media have used the term to describe a formally structured nationwide conspiracy involving thousands of criminals organized to gain control over whole sectors of legal as well as illegal activities" (p. 1095). In a similar vein Alfred Lindesmith (1941) defined organized crime as "usually professional crime . . . involving a system of specifically defined relationships with mutual obligations and privileges" (p. 119).

The first academic to focus on organized crime was Frederic Thrasher, a Chicago school sociologist, in his classic work *The Gang* (1927). The focus of Thrasher's work was on how gangs operated in an organized world. He noted the difference between the older, pre-Prohibition urban gangs and their more modern counterparts. Motive distinguished earlier gangs from contemporary criminal gangs. Earlier gangs were fighters; they fought to protect their turf and honor. The contemporary criminal gang had economic motives (Thrasher 1963, pp. 289-90).

Thrasher (1963) also distinguished between different types of criminal gangs "with reference to their resources, power, and potential to the community" (p. 297). For example, the master gang, with a chiefly adult male membership, was the most successful criminal gang. The major interest of the master gang was the illegal liquor industry, although these men were also involved in other illicit ventures such as vice, gambling, and robbery (Thrasher 1963, pp. 298-300).

The second landmark study of organized crime in Chicago, in the late 1920s, was John Landesco's *Organized Crime in Chicago*. John Landesco was also a Chicago school sociologist. Thrasher's comments on organized crime were, in a sense, an introduction to Landesco's work. Although Landesco never gave a specific definition of organized crime, Landesco took organized crime to be the urban environment in which gangsters carried out their criminal activities.

Thrasher and Landesco shared some common observations about organized crime. Both tied organized crime to its economic motive, not to ethnicity, and therefore not to any alien conspiracy theory. Further, both men spoke of organized crime as the environment or social world of the gangster or racketeer and not as a label for the individual criminal himself. Inciardi, Block, and Hallowell (1977, pp. 103-04) have suggested that this usage of organized crime was common among early writers. These early writers were interested in analyzing the urban social context within which organized criminal activities were carried out. Contemporary sociological discussions of organized crime have been preoccupied with the question "how organized is organized crime?" and have largely ignored the urban social context in which these crimes are carried out. As a result organized crime has lost its historical meaning as a term to describe certain types of crimes and has become a synonym for a monolithic criminal organization known as *La Cosa Nostra*.

For Thrasher and Landesco, then, organized crime was the environment in which gangs interacted and carried out their activities. The influence of environment as the cause of crime was popular among the members of the Chicago school. For example, an article in the *New York Times*, February 24, 1929, had the following headline, "Finds Environment the Cause of Crime," "Dr. Shaw Tells Psychiatrists of Effect of Chicago Loop on Delinquency." Clifford Shaw (1929), a Chicago school criminologist, held that "delinquency to a certain extent, reflects the community background in which the delinquent lives. Gang delinquencies are largely products of the social disorganization that results from the very rapid growth of the city" (p. 28).

During the period between Landesco's (1929) study of organized crime in Chicago and the President's Crime Commission Report of 1967, there appeared very little empirically objective research on the real nature of organized crime (Smith 1975, p. 306; cf. Albanese 1989, p. 94; 1991, pp. 203-04). The President's Crime Commission Report of 1967 was the first attempt to define and explain the problem of organized crime to the public. As already stated, Cressey published *Theft of the Nation* in 1969, based on the data he compiled while working for the Federal Organized Crime Task Force. According to Cressey (1969), organized crime is:

> A nationwide alliance of at least twenty-four tightly knit "families" of criminals. . . . The members of these "families" are all Italians and Sicilians, or of Italian descent, and those on the Eastern Seaboard, especially, call the entire system "Cosa Nostra." Each participant thinks of himself as a "member" of a specific "family" and of Cosa Nostra (or some equivalent term). . . .
>
> The "families" are linked to each other, and to non-Cosa Nostra syndicates, by understandings, agreements, and "treaties," and by mutual deference to a "commission" made up of the "families." (pp. x-xi)

This definition of organized crime, which has been disputed by scholars of organized crime, has shaped not only the public's perception of organized crime, but has also influenced much of the scholarly writing that has taken place since its publication. With this definition of organized crime, Cressey has identified several characteristics that have come to be associated with organized crime: (1) organized crime is made up primarily of one ethnic group, Italians; (2) each organized crime family has a formal hierarchical structure; and (3) organized crime is a nationwide crime syndicate known as La Cosa Nostra or the "Mafia."

During the 1970s, and afterwards, several empirical studies were undertaken by social scientists to ascertain the true nature of organized crime. Why this occurred is discussed in the forthcoming chapters. Suffice it to say that the findings and conclusions drawn about organized crime were quite different than the findings and conclusions of the President's Commission Report of 1967 and Cressey's *Theft of the Nation*.

A number of scholars of organized crime do not agree that the existence of organized crime in American society is attributable to the existence of a Mafia in the United States. Instead, these scholars, who have conducted primary research on organized crime, believe it is inherent in the social, political, and economic life of American society. Organized crime has evolved with urban living in America. A number of social historians have documented the successive movement of a number of different ethnic groups in and out of organized crime (Bell 1953; Tyler 1962; O'Kane 1992). The links between organized crime, politics, and minority status have also been well documented. Prohibition brought opportunities for success for Jewish, and eventually Italian racketeers. Prior to this, the Irish controlled the political machines in a number of major American cities. Today, a number of ethnic and racial groups (Cubans, South Americans, Asians, African Americans, Caribbean blacks, and others) have found organized crime to be a convenient avenue for upward social mobility. Social scientists who adhere to this view do not view organized crime as an alien conspiracy but as part of American social life, a way in which minorities can gain wealth and power, and eventually move into respectable positions within American society. Others who adhere to this view believe organized crime is made up of locally situated ethnic groups who often participate in joint ventures when profitable to do so. From this perspective, organized crime is not made up of a single formal organization but of several loosely structured social groups.

Other social scientists, including many economists, argue that organized crime operates like any other business in America. Goods and services that have been declared illegal by the government are in demand by the American public. The proceeds from these goods and services are used to finance a number of legitimate and illegitimate activities. The proceeds are also used to protect their criminal activities through the corruption of public officials. In this view organized crime is part of our capitalist economic system, differing only in its degree of illegality (Smith 1975; Smith and Alba 1979).

The model of organized crime which one adheres to—as an alien conspiracy, as ethnically pluralistic, or as indigenous to American society and economic values—is not only a matter of academic interest. The model of organized crime which one embraces will quite naturally dictate the strategies implemented for its control and eradication. Adherents of the alien conspiracy theory will argue for the eradication of the nationwide conspiracy through prosecuting and incarcerating leaders of organized crime. Those who view organized crime as ethnically pluralistic claim that prosecuting leaders will not be successful because there will always be others to replace the leaders. Instead they favor the legalization of consensual behaviors, and an understanding by the victimized community of the social costs of organized crime. It has been argued that the underground economy, in which organized crime operates, would be eliminated through the legalization of consensual behaviors such as gambling, narcotics, and prostitution. By the social costs of organized crime is meant those subcultural values that erode and weaken dominant social institutions such as the family. Finally, those who view organized crime as part of the market system favor economic strategies. These strategies include decriminalization or legalization of gambling, narcotics, and sexual behaviors; and a better understanding of the market forces that are conducive to organized crime (Albanese 1989, pp. 91-102).

Regardless of the model of organized crime one adheres to, it is possible to define organized crime without attempting to account for its origins or structure. All models of organized crime share certain assumptions about the nature of organized crime: it is organized, and whether it has a formal structure or an informal network of relationships its existence will continue beyond its individual membership. Unlike street crime its activities are planned and rational, not impulsive. Organized crime is protected through the corruption and cooperation of political officials. Finally, organized crime's primary purpose is to provide a wide range of services, legal and illegal, to the public (Ianni and Ianni 1983, p. 1096). If these assumptions of organized crime are correct, then organized crime can be defined as "a persisting form of criminal activity that brings together a client-public which demands a range of goods and services defined as illegal" (Ianni and Ianni 1983, p. 1096).

The primary focus of this book is on the illegal goods and services that were provided to the American public through organized criminal activities in the early part of the twentieth century. Therefore, for the purposes of this book organized crime refers to the illegal activities of racketeering and vice (bootlegging, illegal drugs, illegal gambling, usury, and prostitution) coordinated by two or more people, on a continuous basis, for economic gain and sustained through force and/or the corruption of public officials. This definition is based on the definitions formulated by Block and Chambliss (1981, p. 12) and Albanese (1989, p. 5). Racketeering, as defined by Landesco (1968) is "the exploitation for personal profit, by means of violence of a business association or employees' organization" (p. 149). During the early part of the twentieth century, which is the principal focus of this study, racketeering and vice in the forms of bootlegging, gambling, and prostitution were the most common organized criminal activities (see Haller 1971-72, p. 229).

This introduction has briefly outlined the difficulty of defining the concept of organized crime. We have seen how the meaning of organized crime changed from the environment in which gangsters interacted (from this perspective organized crime is indigenous to American society, based on American social and economic values), to professional crime, to an alien conspiracy. Today, most social scientists and members of the law enforcement community would concede that the concept of organized crime has lost its ethnic distinction. The label of organized crime is now applied to many more criminal associations. What remains are the "organizational characteristics that had first been identified as distinctive of Mafia 'families'" (Borgotta and Borgotta 1992, p. 1406). However, this does not mean that the law enforcement community has given up its view of organized crime as an alien conspiracy. This view of organized crime is now directed at Colombians, Motorcycle Gangs, Asians, Africans, and others that engage in organized criminal activities (Potter 1994, pp. 7-8). Potter (1994) in explaining the government's official view of new criminal organizations remarks, "All have 'alien' origins, are described in terms of some kind of culturally delineated 'family' structure that resembles a rational corporate bureaucracy, and are rapidly expansionist in organization size and market share" (p. 8).

Procedure and methods

The theory of social disorganization was developed by the Chicago school sociologists and used to explain lower-class crime and deviance in the city of Chicago. In chapter 2 it is introduced to the reader to explain the assumptions of the theory of social disorganization, to show how the theory was applied to lower-class crime and deviance, and to explain why the theory was not used to understand the presence of organized crime in the city of Chicago.

Theories of crime have focused on attempts to explain individualistic criminal behavior, not organizational criminal behavior. In fact, while sociologists have offered many theories to explain crime and deviance rarely, have these theories been directed specifically at organized crime. Theories developed by American sociologists to study crime, beginning with the theory of social disorganization developed by the Chicago school sociologists, have ignored or covered over the fact of organized crime.

As chapter 2 will demonstrate, the Chicago school sociologists studied crime from the framework of the social ecologists. Crime was an unnatural, disturbing feature of the social landscape—understood as abhorrent and therefore, "socially disorganized."

In fact, the epigram by Berger and Berger (1972), which appears at the beginning of this book, captures the ironic fact that given the historical and sociological nature of crime being "organized," in Chicago during the 1920s, it was studied through a concept of social disorganization. Not only have the Chicago school sociologists provided a theory of crime that explains abherrant street crime but the crime that was so overwhelmingly prevalent to the public at that time was what we today call "organized crime." The Chicago school theorists gave us a theory of crime that had little to do with the organized crime that was becoming such a familiar cultural object to the American people.

Chapter 3 presents a systematic story of how American sociology and organized crime developed together in the city of Chicago. There is a historical coincidence between the birth of American sociology at the University of Chicago in the 1920s, and the birth of racketeering and gangsterism in that same city. Racketeering and gangsterism were, in a significant way, in the minds of Americans; including the minds of American sociologists. Questions arise, such as "How much did organized crime and sociology overlap?" and "To what extent did organized crime exist in the minds of the sociologists who were studying street crime?" Chapter 3 answers these questions through the documentation of the history and evolution of organized crime in Chicago, in the 1920s, and through an examination of the published works of the Chicago school during this same period. In order to understand and appreciate the exclusion of organized crime from the curriculum and the published works of the department of sociology from 1918 to 1933, the writer examines how other topics were supported, sponsored, and treated by this generation of scholars. By presenting a chronological development of studies of crime and deviance by the Chicago school sociologists we will come to see that organized crime was not a topic that they studied or wrote about. The two chronologies presented in chapter 3, although seemingly unrelated, are related in time, location, and duration. While the Department of Sociology at the University of Chicago had a growing reputation as a center for academic excellence, the city itself had a growing reputation for gangsterism, racketeering, and vice. Yet the Chicago school sociologists, while studying lower-class crime and deviance in the city of Chicago, ignored or overlooked the organized crime that was so much a part of the public consciousness.

Chapters 4 and 5 examine the case of John Landesco. While searching for any significant works on organized crime of the period, the present author discovered a classic work, virtually unknown to people in the field of criminology and criminal justice, John Landesco's, *Organized Crime in Chicago* (1929). Why had scholars of criminology and criminal justice no knowledge of John Landesco or his classic work on organized crime? Chapter 4 traces Landesco's early history and academic career, including his association with the Department of Sociology at the University of Chicago during the 1920s. Through an analysis of the available literature, chapter

4 gives some plausible explanations for why Landesco, and his classic work on organized crime, were little known. Chapter 5 takes a closer look at the Landesco study itself. A description and analysis of the historical and sociological significance of Landesco's study on organized crime is given.

An important part of this book concerns the extent to which organized crime was a vital part of public opinion at the time that American sociologists seemed to be ignoring it. This is why it is so remarkable that American sociologists did not study it, until relatively recently. Chapter 6 documents the extent of public knowledge of and interest in organized crime through the review of newspapers, books, articles, and films of the period, which introduced organized crime to the American public.

When and how organized crime became part of the field of the sociology of crime and deviance are the subjects of chapter 7. The author briefly reviews the history of criminology in American sociology and examines the content of some earlier and later criminology textbooks to document when and if organized crime becomes a part of these textbooks.

Finally, chapter 8 concludes with some reasons—theoretical, methodological, and ideological—for the omission of organized crime, until relatively recently, from the history of American sociology.

2

The social disorganization paradigm of crime and deviance

IN THE introductory chapter the theory of social disorganization was introduced as the theory developed by the Chicago school sociologists to study crime and deviance in the city of Chicago. The theory was useful in explaining the crime and deviance of individuals in the lower social classes. However, the theory was not useful in studying the organized crimes and organized criminals that were so prevalent in the neighborhoods of Chicago during the 1920s. As this chapter will demonstrate, the theory was biased in its treatment of lower-class criminals and deviants because it ignored the criminal activities of the middle and upper classes. The creators and practitioners of the theory held a number of ideological, theoretical, and methodological assumptions about crime, human beings, and society which influenced their decisions about who and what were deviant. In the minds of the Chicago school theorists crime and deviance were equated with the individualistic street crimes of the lower classes and not the organized crimes of the middle and upper classes.

The sociology of deviance

We begin our analysis by briefly examining a subfield of sociology, the sociology of deviance. It has been said that there is a class bias in the sociology of deviance which can be traced back to the early Chicago sociologists (Mills 1943; Liazos 1972; Thio 1973; Taylor, Walton, and Young 1973; Pfohl 1985). An exception to this criticism of class bias in the sociology of deviance is Edwin Sutherland's now classic study of white-collar crime (1949). Sutherland (1949) argued that crime was just as prevalent among the higher classes as it was among the poor. In fact, Sutherland believed that the same theoretical principles could be used to explain white-collar, as well as street crimes. This is a significant observation. It was not that these early criminologists did not have theories to explain organized crime; they just failed to apply these theories to organized criminals. Chapter 8 will draw some conclusions about why this was so. A class bias exists not only in the theoretical attempts to explain deviance, but also in the research methods which are used to study deviance. In both cases scholars have looked at individual deviants in the lower social classes and their social environments (Thio 1973). Lacking is any analysis of the established power structure of the society. Thio (1973) defines deviance as "conduct that is in violation of rules made largely by the power elite of a given society or group" (p.1). What is significant in this definition is the concept of a power elite. The definition assumes societies are made up of two groups, those who have power and those who do not. Those who have power are able to enforce their will on the rest of society through the creation of laws which benefit the elite of a society (Thio 1973, p. 1).

The issue of class bias is raised in the widely cited 1943 article by C. Wright Mills entitled "The Professional Ideology of Social Pathologists." Mills examined a number of social problems textbooks of the 1920s and 1930s and related the typical concepts employed in the field of social disorganization to the structure of American society and the backgrounds and careers of social pathologists. A number of sociologists whom Mills (1943) refers to as "social pathologists," studied social deviants during the early 1900s; these theorists had common backgrounds which influenced their perception of who and what was deviant. The theorists were predominantly male, white, middle-class, Protestant, and rural. Mills (1943) maintains, "the relatively homogeneous extraction and similar careers of American pathologists is a possible factor in the low level of abstraction characterizing their work" (p. 166).

Social scientists, including disorganizational theorists, generally come from backgrounds which are white, male, and middle-class. These backgrounds often are confining and do not allow social scientists to experience worlds that are socially, culturally, or ethnically different. Instead, social scientists view these different worlds as abnormal or unnatural, and therefore as disorganized (Pfohl 1985, p. 167). These "social pathologists" also believed that deviance was the fault of the individual and that deviance was not related to the social structure of American society. Therefore, deviance was analyzed from a smaller, micro theoretical perspective rather than from a larger, macro level perspective. A macro theoretical perspective would have allowed the theorists to consider larger sociohistorical and political forces that may be responsible for deviance. Instead, these theorists believed that society was basically good and not responsible for the deviance in society. These theorists supported the status quo: society did not need to be reformed, the individual deviant needed to be reformed (Mills 1943; Snodgrass 1972; Pfohl 1985).

Often the social pathologists would view the individual deviant as one who has considerable difficulty in adjusting or being assimilated into American life. For example, the problems of immigrants trying to assimilate were often studied by social pathologists. Polish immigrants were the subject of study in *The Polish Peasant* (1918), which had a profound influence on the social disorganization perspective. The concepts employed in studying immigrant groups were often used to explain other "social problems" (Mills 1943, p. 180).

Some of the concepts utilized in the texts written by social pathologists include disorganization, maladjustment, abnormality, pathology, and inadequate or faulty socialization (Mills 1943; Thio 1973). The areas inhabited by hoboes, prostitutes, drug addicts, alcoholics, immigrants, the poor, the irreligious, and the like would be sought out by social pathologists who would then apply their concepts to these unfortunate citizens. Typically, "problems" concerned urban behavior. When "rural problems" are discussed they are found to be a consequence of urbanization (Mills 1943; Thio 1973). The focus by social pathologists primarily on the powerless members of society reinforced the public's stereotyped perception that the powerless are somehow more corrupt, immoral, deviant, or dangerous than the powerful. In fact, sociologists who studied crime and delinquency during the same period were also guilty of focusing on the powerless classes. In studying crime and delinquency the Chicago school criminologists—Thrasher, Shaw, and McKay—neglected the possibility that the powerful classes were partly responsible for the crime and delinquency in their midst (Thio 1973, p. 3).

It might be said that the preoccupation with lower-class deviants has diverted our attention from the deviant actions and behaviors of the powerful classes. So that the deviant actions and behaviors of the powerful go unnoticed. For reasons which will be considered in chapter 8, the sociology of deviance has not considered the deviant acts of the powerful part of their subject matter. Therefore, a class bias is inherent in the field of the sociology of deviance (Liazos 1975, p. 259). A class bias is even more obvious when one examines the treatment, or just as often, lack of treatment, by American sociologists when considering the issue of organized crime.

Theoretical image of social disorganization

Our analysis continues by examining a particular perspective on deviance popular until the 1940s, that of social pathologists or what is commonly referred to as social disorganization theory. The social disorganization perspective became a fully developed theory during the 1920s at the University of Chicago.

The early proponents of this perspective, often referred to as the "Chicago school," were active in the period following World War I and extending to the early years of the Great Depression. "The Chicago school may be considered a 'school' rather than a solidarity group committed to a particular point of view, in that it represented a vertically bonded network of practitioners located in and identified with a specific institution, all of whom shared near identical beliefs and ideas" (Thomas 1983, p. 390). Theorists of the Chicago school included such men as W. I. Thomas, Robert Park, Ernest Burgess, Clifford Shaw, and Henry McKay. Active during a period of rapid immigration, industrialization, and urbanization in American society, and trying to make sense of the social problems that accompanied urban living, these scholars studied the crime and deviance in their midst through an analysis of the urban setting. Employing an ecological model of the city, the Chicago school sociologists concluded that the areas of the city with the highest rates of crime and deviance also had the highest rates of social disorganization.

The focus of early disorganization theory was on apparent changes in American society during the 1920s, particularly changes in the areas of technological development, organization, and immigration. The theory of social disorganization was first conceptualized by W. I. Thomas and Florian Znaniecki. Later, Robert Park, Ernest Burgess, and their students applied the theory of social disorganization to the ecological aspects of social problems in the city. The specific writings of the Chicago school sociologists are the subject matter of chapter 3. For now, the author will review the origins of the Chicago school within its particular sociohistorical context.

The 1920s were particularly important to the development of American sociology. Middle-class managers and professionals, responding to the social changes that were taking place in the American social landscape, demanded that these changes be directed changes. The challenge to direct change technically and efficiently fell to a group of sociologists at the University of Chicago. These sociologists also had the political and financial backing of the elite of Chicago and of the nation. They responded to their challenge by developing the theory of social disorganization and applying it to the social problems of the city, which would be controlled through the theory of social disorganization (Pfohl 1985, pp. 136-137).

The changes of the 1920s were accompanied by considerable fear, tension, and anxiety. Yet those affected most adversely by change showed little visible signs of protest. Those most adversely affected included displaced rural laborers, immigrants, and minorities concentrated in urban areas. Postwar overproduction, mechanization, and an expanding class of white-collar workers negatively affected displaced rural laborers, immigrants, and minorities who were all competing in a difficult labor market (Pfohl 1985, p. 140).

The 1920s were almost entirely absent of organized labor strikes and violent collective outbursts, such as riots. The groups which suffered the most economically, displaced agricultural and industrial laborers, immigrants, and the urban poor, did not engage in violent protests. Pfohl (1985, p. 140) suggests that one possible explanation for this lack of collective violence during this period may be the fact that urban living had created an anonymity among people, who viewed their troubles as individual and not collective problems.

But expressions of collective violence were not absent from another large segment of the American population. This segment—white, Protestant, small-town America—clung to the values and ideals of a previous time. This segment of the American population was also deeply threatened by the increased urbanization, immigration, and technologicalization of social and economic life. Immigrants were perceived as strange and alien. The reaction of this segment of the population to the tensions and fears of rapid social change can be described as the politics of nativism (Carey 1975; Pfohl 1985). "Nativism is a term used to describe several strands of collective social action, each directed towards returning America to the good old days in which white, Protestant, small-town interests reigned supreme" (Pfohl 1985, p. 140). The nativist reaction included an opposition toward minority groups, a patriotic zeal, and the belief that certain internal enemies threatened national security. During the 1920s nativism was evident in a number of collective social movements. These movements included the passage of Prohibition, the Red Scare of 1920, immigration restriction, the growth of the KKK, and the ban on teaching evolution in the schools. Nativists shared an antagonism toward the city whose features and characteristics threatened the small towns of America. Uniting the Nativists was the slogan, "One hundred percent Americanism" (Carey 1975, p. 24).

Two groups had their power enhanced by the rapid changes of the 1920s. These two groups consisted of a business elite who controlled corporate America and a professional middle class. These new middle-class professionals were needed for their expertise in the management of society. Both corporate owners and professionals were concerned with profit making. Both groups shared similar views on how to deal with the consequences of rapid social change. Both groups desired a stable social climate in which to conduct business. While both groups acknowledged that rapid social change was a threat to stability, they, unlike the nativists, had no desire to return to the good old days of a past era. They understood that they were the beneficiaries of rapid technologicalization, urbanization, and immigration (Pfohl 1985, pp. 141-142).

There were short term gains and long term disadvantages of technologicalization, urbanization, and immigration. The short-term gains included work that could be made more efficient and centrally controlled, a concentrated work force, an expedient system of transportation, communication, and mass marketing, and a cheap pool of laborers. Disadvantages included cities that were characterized by high rates of crime and deviance. These problems were viewed by corporate owners and managers as social ills that demanded the attention of professional problem solvers. Professional problem solving would come from the University of Chicago sociologists and their newly developed theory of social disorganization (Pfohl 1985, p. 142).

Social problems and progressive reform

During the 1920s a new view of problem solving emerged. The idea was to manage social problems as one would manage any business or industry. Along with this new view of problem solving came a new American political philosophy—liberalism. According to liberals, social problems were the natural consequences of rapid social change. Social problems were devoid of moral or political meaning. Professional problem solvers would locate social problems and come up with rational solutions for their amelioration. The epitome of liberalism was the Chicago school and its theory of deviance as social disorganization.

The work of the Chicago school was supported by the elite of business and industry (Faris 1970; Carey 1975; Bulmer 1984; Kurtz 1984; Pfohl 1985). The financial wherewithal of the Rockefellers was an important vehicle for the founding and continued funding of the University of Chicago. Furthermore, there was a reciprocal relationship between the Chicago business community and the Chicago sociologists. The Chicago business community and the Chicago sociologists worked together to initiate social policies for the amelioration of social problems. Welfare workers, youth workers, and urban specialists, who were part of "a new generation of salaried governmental problem solvers" (Pfohl 1985, p. 143), also worked closely with the Chicago sociologists.

The theory of social disorganization proved to be useful to the elite of business and industry in Chicago. In fact, the theory was so useful that it helped the University of Chicago's department of sociology gain national recognition. The theory of social disorganization fit in nicely with the view held by America's new middle class, that social problems were naturally caused and technically correctable by professional problem solvers. The Chicago sociologists, business leaders, and government problem solvers all viewed social problems as apolitical. This ideological viewpoint conveniently dismissed the possibility that deviance was in any way related to the frustration and discontent of America's disadvantaged classes. Disorganization theory was also grounded in empirical research and based on statistical analysis; this also pleased America's new middle class.

The relationship between the theoretical perspective of the Chicago school and the desire for an apolitical view of social problems, during the rapidly changing 1920s, can be better understood if we take a closer look at the University of Chicago as an institution and the Chicago sociologists as a group. Others have described the conditions which were present that led to the growth of sociological inquiry at Chicago (Shils 1970; Carey 1975; Pfohl 1985). These conditions included available resources from wealthy donors, the openness of university administrators to new ideas, the contributions of students trained in public affairs to society, the exposure of key Chicago sociologists to the research model of German universities, the links between the Chicago school and the local government business elite, and the links between the Chicago school sociologists and other social scientists made possible through the Local Community Research Committee (an organization established at the University of Chicago to encourage interdepartmental studies on the ecology and cultural life of the city). All of these things operated as institutional supporters for the stability of problems related to rapid technologicalization, urbanization, and immigration.

The final factor to be considered is the background of the Chicago sociologists themselves. These men came from the same class backgrounds as the emerging liberal middle-class professionals. They both agreed as to what was considered a social problem: crime, delinquency, alcoholism, mental disorder, and family breakdown. They also agreed that through the application of the perspective of social disorganization social problems would be managed and controlled (Pfohl 1985, p. 145).

It is necessary to examine the ideals of the early sociologists and the social environment from which they were drawn to understand their responses to the existing social problems of their time. Bramson (1961) has noted that American sociology was born into an atmosphere heavily infused with the spirit of reform. The rise of American social science can be linked to four movements: the Social Science movement, Populism, Progressivism, and the Social Gospel. But it is the Progressive movement, more than any other, that influenced the lives of the Chicago sociologists. While different interpretations of the movement have been suggested, the interpretation that the movement was "committed to liberal-individualist goals in its attempt to reverse the trend toward bigness" (Bramson 1961, p. 77) can be easily applied to the Chicago sociologists. Given the rural, midwestern, and religious backgrounds of the early sociologists it is not surprising that urbanism and industrialization became the focus of their approach to "social problems." These sociologists viewed the erosion of small-time values as a negative consequence of the rapid social changes taking place in urban America (Bramson 1961, pp. 78-79).

The leaders of the Progressive movement were well-to-do capitalists and Progressive reformers who embraced the existing social order. Society did not need to be reformed, individuals needed to be reformed. The professions did not criticize Progressive reforms because so many of them "benefited from their new role as consultants and experts in the emerging welfare state," and because their view of society and social change was "limited, elitist, and constrained by their own class outlook" (Platt 1977, p. xxvi).

Progressives were sensitive to the negative consequences of rapid industrialization and urbanization on American society. Yet they did not oppose modernization. Instead, they sought to create a society which would reflect their own values and interests. Progressives were optimistic about solving social problems and creating a suitable world. They believed they could do this by implementing new laws and institutions. Regardless of the task at hand, Progressives had confidence that legal and bureaucratic institutions could be found to improve existing conditions (Kyving 1979, p. 8).

The chief sponsors of sociological research in the 1920s were the Chicago reformers. On this point Carey (1975) explains, "The research projects sponsored by the Local Community Research Committee and partially supported by local groups reveal the interests of salaried professionals in civic, welfare, and criminal justice associations" (p. 138). For example, the Illinois Association for Criminal Justice, an organization made up of lawyers, court personnel, and police leaders, was partially responsible for the investigations made by Thrasher (1927), Shaw (1929), Landesco (1929), and Reckless (1933). These investigations were also aided by the Juvenile Protection Association and the Council of Social Agencies. These agencies were predominantly concerned with helping the families of delinquent children.

It should be noted, however, that the input from professional sociologists was used only sparingly in implementing recommendations for reforming the criminal and juvenile justice agencies. In fact, the Chicago Crime Commission (an organization concerned with organized crime in Chicago) was not responsive to sociological insight at all. The organization saw its role more as an overseer of the courts. If sociological talent was to be used at all it was usually in the form of hiring graduate students as investigators, who, because of their legal training, could gather evidence to be used in some type of adversary hearing. Reformers often kept a close watch on police links with vice activities. "If an investigator could gather evidence to show that police were being paid by houses of prostitution to allow them to operate illegally and this evidence led to indictments then the investigation was an unqualified success" (Carey 1975, p. 140).

It should be understood that the reformers were often in disagreement with the local political machines. Therefore, it was often difficult for the reformers to initiate change. It was extremely difficult for reformers to implement any changes in the adult criminal justice system. This was because citizens often desired the services provided by organized criminals. Organized criminals were linked to the political machine through ethnic and class loyalties, and organized criminals had deep and penetrating relationships with politicians in the city. More important, however, was the fact that the class backgrounds and life experiences of reformers were so different from the politicians and employees of criminal justice agencies. Reformers were mainly white, native American Protestants, and those who were employed in the criminal justice agencies were white ethnics of varying backgrounds. Reformers lived in the well-to-do areas of Chicago, the Hyde Park and Woodlawn areas surrounding the University of Chicago and the Gold Coast along Lake Michigan. Reformers, in contrast to the politicians and employees of criminal justice agencies, had different values and life experiences. Reformers were outsiders to the very communities they wished to change. It was much easier for them to achieve suitable law enforcement in their own communities than in the rest of the city. It was also much easier to achieve success in the juvenile court than in the adult system. Reformers knew little of the relationship between crime, justice, and politics (Haller 1970, pp. 625-26, p. 635).

Although all the reformers were in agreement that municipal incompetence and corruption should not be tolerated, not all the reformers agreed which reforms were the most important. Some reformers were concerned with sustaining moral values and others were more concerned with focusing on personal and property crime. The reformers interested in sustaining moral values were upper-class individuals who thought reform could be achieved by enforcing liquor laws. The reformers interested in concentrating on personal and property crimes were mostly business leaders. Crime and delinquency problems were confronted differently by business leaders and the lawyers who supported them than by social workers and their church supporters (Carey 1975, pp. 140-41).

At first glance, one would not think there was any observable reason for the reformers to use academic expertise. However, further examination reveals that there were social forces operating which suggest good reason to utilize academic expertise. University sponsored research projects carried more weight with government officials and the news reading public. Local researchers were persuasive in convincing those who controlled the financial resources that there was a need for a better trained, larger police force, and for increased funding of the Chicago Crime Commission (Carey 1975, p. 141).

Reform leaders knew that the University of Chicago researchers were there to assist them. There was an overlapping membership between some members in the crime-fighting organizations and the University of Chicago Board of Trustees. Hence, shared interests existed between reformers and academics. Finally, the

University of Chicago had its own funds which were provided by the Local Community Research Committee, and wealthy donors often matched these funds (see e.g., Carey 1975; Kurtz 1984; Bulmer 1984).

While the reformers usually agreed that sociological or criminological expertise was important and would help in getting recommendations implemented, not all reformers were anxious to utilize this expertise. Business reformers would be hesitant to use sociological or criminological expertise if there was a need for scant moneys and the end result was uncertain. In these instances reformers would rely on in-house investigations. Those trained in business or law were often desired. Social workers and ministers believed that the family was an important influence on crime causation. Therefore, they generally favored the use of sociologists, who would reinforce their own position. However, the presence of Ernest Burgess often determined whether sociological expertise would be used. Burgess was an active member of both the Chicago Crime Commission and the Juvenile Protection Association. Burgess had close alliances with both business leaders and social workers. He attended all meetings of the Chicago Crime Commission and Juvenile Protection Association and pushed enthusiastically for their reliance on sociological assistance (cf. Carey 1975, pp. 142-43; Kurtz 1984; Bulmer 1984).

The Chicago reformers often had already made up their minds about how social problems could be improved. It did not matter what the findings of the research reports they commissioned had found. For example, many crime-fighting groups, including the Illinois Association for Criminal Justice, believed that the crime problem could be resolved if the criminal justice apparatus was more efficient. The members of the Illinois Association for Criminal Justice hired John Landesco, a graduate student in the Department of Sociology at the University of Chicago to study organized crime. Landesco found that organized crime was not caused by administrative deficiencies but by community conflicts. Recommendations included increasing the membership of immigrants on community organizations and in employment, preventing juvenile gang members from advancing into organized criminal gangs, and separating the political machine and organized criminals. Yet these recommendations were ignored in Arthur Lashley's (1930, pp. 558-605) report. Lashley instead focused on how the criminal justice system operated inefficiently and how "loopholes" in the law allowed criminals to go free (cf. Lashley 1930; Haller n.d.b.; Carey 1975, p. 148).

As one historian has pointed out, "research results most eagerly accepted by the reformers were those which suggested administrative changes in the court or police" (Haller 1970, p. 627). This type of data was utilized the most and led to the greatest success by the reformers. The reformers were least likely to accept sociologists' views about the causes of crime and delinquency. Ideas about poverty and broken homes as causative factors in crime seemed unsophisticated to many reformers. Yet concepts such as "culture conflict" were misconstrued by most reformers. As previously indicated, reformers were outsiders to the world of criminal justice. Their values and expectations were in stark contrast to those who staffed the system of criminal justice.

Because of this, reformers were often unmindful of the impact of their reforms and often misinterpreted the entire criminal justice system. Reformers had no idea what was meant by Thrasher (1927) when he said that delinquency and crime could be attacked by reducing economic inequalities and reorganizing the neighborhood. Reformers did not go as far as the sociologists when attempting to redirect social and economic life. Sociologists agreed that the role of the government in attacking crime and delinquency should be increased; reformers were not so sure (Haller 1970, p. 619; cf. Carey 1975, p. 144-46).

In sum, a small group of reformers were the key sponsors of sociological research in the 1920s. This group included a diversity of people. Some reformers were from old established families, some were newly arrived businessmen, and some were professional people. Their interest in reform and the role of sociological expertise can only be understood within the structure of the new professional middle class that emerged during the 1920s. There was a vested interest shared by both the elites and the sociologists to make the urban environment an agreeable place to work. Sociologists and elites moved in the same social circles and were comfortable with each other. The working relationships which were forged between sociologists and local policy makers were not without their problems. The sponsors of sociological research often determined what would be studied, how it would be studied, and how the data would be interpreted. These problems of research scholarship are still present when sociological knowledge is used to address social and political problems (Carey 1975, p. 145).

The origins of social disorganization theory: The legacy of William I. Thomas, Robert E. Park, and Ernest W. Burgess

Social disorganization theory was initially conceptualized by the University of Chicago sociologist William I. Thomas. What began as a conceptualization of the problem of disorganization grew into a full-blown perspective during the 1920s. The development of the Chicago school owes more to Thomas than to any other scholar (Kurtz, 1984, p. 3; Pfohl 1985, p. 145). Thomas was typical of the early American sociologists in that he came from a Protestant, rural and religious background. His father supported the family by farming and preaching.

The most concise statement of the social disorganization perspective appears in the classic study by William I. Thomas and Florian Znaniecki, *The Polish Peasant in Europe and America*. Social disorganization was defined as "a decrease of the influence of existing rules of behavior on the individual members of the group" (Thomas and Znaniecki 1975, p. 35). *The Polish Peasant in Europe and America* focuses on the lives of rural polish peasants who had migrated to the United States in the early twentieth century and settled in American cities. Thomas and Znaniecki, through an analysis of the letters, diaries, and other personal documents of Polish immigrants, discusses how rapid social change lessens the impact of social norms. Changes brought about through immigration and the transportation of a rural people to an urban environment cause social disorganization. These immigrants no longer have social norms to guide them in their everyday behavior. This causes the immigrants to become confused and disoriented and to drift into the types of deviant behaviors which were studied by the Chicago school sociologists.

There were many reasons why Thomas and Znaniecki selected the Poles for their analysis. For one thing, they were the largest and most discernible ethnic group on the South Side of Chicago. In addition, the Poles were considered a "social problem" in Chicago.

Thomas often liked to combine his intellectual and social concerns. Social problems linked to assimilation were easily perceptible in the Polish American community. Thomas was interested in the often violent and explosive nature of crime by many of the young Polish boys and girls. These young people, who were conforming and law-abiding most of the time, would suddenly, without any apparent motive, engage in violent and explosive actions (Janowitz 1966, pp. xxiv-xxv).

Thomas also collected a huge amount of materials on the Poles in Europe. Thomas was able to collect these materials with the help of Polish intellectuals and immigrant protective associations. Thomas met Florian Znaniecki in Europe, in 1913. Znaniecki was a Polish philosopher and proved to be a most useful collaborator. It was Znaniecki who persuaded Thomas to include the "Methodological Note" in one volume of the work. The "Methodological Note" encouraged the use of subjective experiences in sociological research (Janowitz 1966).

Thomas (1966) states that the concept of social disorganization "refers primarily to institutions and only secondarily to men" (p. 3). Thomas (1966) continues, "Social disorganization has no explicit connection whatever with individual disorganization, which consists in a decrease of the individual's ability to organize his whole life for the efficient, progressive and continuous realization of his fundamental interests" (p. 3). Individual disorganization and social disorganization are unconnected. "In other words, social organization is not co-extensive with individual morality nor does social disorganization correspond to individual demoralization " (Thomas and Znaniecki 1927, p. 1129; Thomas 1966, p. 5). Since the two phenomena are distinct, individual pathology should not be used as an indication of social disorganization.

While it is true that Thomas was intrigued by the shift from a simple agricultural society to a complex industrial one, it is not true, as some critics have suggested, that Thomas longed for the good old days of a past era. Thomas was urban and sophisticated and therefore was unlike the rural-born sociologists who viewed the social changes of the urban landscape as problematic. Thomas never embraced the philosophy of German sociologist, Ferdinand Tönnies who described the transformation from traditional communities (Gemeinschaft) to modern communities (Gesellschaft). In Thomas's view, the thinking of Tönnies was too confining (Janowitz 1966, p. xxx; Carey 1975, p. 99).

Thomas believed that disorganization could result if there was too much rapid change. Disorganization may be a consequence of a rapid increase in the volume and density of a population, a sudden decline in population, rapid changes in technology or material culture which may generate a temporary state of disorganization, sudden booms, depressions, crisis and natural disasters. A crisis, whether technological, personal, social, or political could create the necessary conditions for disorganization.

In *The Polish Peasant in Europe and America* social disorganization was discussed as either family or community disorganization. Thomas and Znaniecki (1927) state that family disorganization referred to the "decay of the institution of economic family solidarity. . . . actual common ownership of property and common use of income" (p. 1138). When peasants make contact with the outside world, their world becomes disrupted. The peasants are exposed to new goods and services and learn new patterns of spending. As a result, new values are internalized, including new types of economic organization. A shift from "we" to "I" marks the final phase of family disorganization; this is usually proceeded by some type of reorganization.

For Thomas and Znaniecki the lack of public opinion is an indicator of community disorganization. Community solidarity and the institutions which support the community are weakened when public opinion is absent. Thomas and Znaniecki saw society as undergoing a process of organization, disorganization, and reorganization. Disorganization is but one stage in a three-stage process.

Robert E. Park was influenced by the disorganizational perspective laid out by Thomas. The Chicago school is well-known for its classical studies of ecological disorganization introduced by Robert E. Park and Ernest W. Burgess. Park, Burgess, and their students, borrowing from the plant and animal ecologists, developed a theoretical framework to study urban social life. From the perspective of human ecology the human community experiences a number of competitive and accommodative processes which affect spatial and temporal distributions. In sum, then, the initial framework for an ecological theory of the city was based on plant and animal ecology and Darwinian and Spencerian notions of web of life and evolution (Kurtz 1984, pp. 21-22).

Identifying the "natural areas" of the city absorbed the minds of the Chicago school sociologists. Burgess and Bogue (1964) maintain that it was "assumed that the city had a characteristic organization and way of life that differentiated it from rural communities" (p. 7). Like rural communities, however, "it was composed of natural areas, each having a particular function in the whole economy and life of the city, each having its distinctive institutions, groups, and personalities" (Burgess and Bogue 1964, p. 7). Some "natural areas" were high in deviance and others were low in deviance. According to Burgess and Bogue (1964, p. 7) the "natural areas" of the city could be studied by mapping the physical arrangements of the city and studying its cultural life—modes of living, customs, and standards. It was this first aspect, the mapping of the physical arrangements of the city, that gave rise to ecological studies.

Burgess (1926, pp. 3-18) discusses the city as developing according to a pattern. The pattern consisted of common urban areas which could be geographically located and spatially defined. Park designated these areas as natural because they came into being without design and tended to go through predictable cycles of development. Each natural area had its own specific function within the urban community.

However, sometimes the function of an area was undesirable, as in the case of the slum. Each natural area also had its own unique population. As previously mentioned, some of these areas were high in deviance and some were low in deviance. High deviance areas were characterized by a disproportionate amount of mental illness, suicide, crime, delinquency, alcoholism, drug addiction, and family discord. The turfs of some of these natural areas were identified by their ethnic groups, red light districts, and bohemias.

Ecological processes were central to the ecological model. Roderick McKenzie made the fullest statement on the "processes" of the ecological model. By ecological process he meant "the tendency in time toward special forms of spatial and sustenance groupings of the units comprising an ecological distribution" (Burgess 1926, p. 172). There are five major ecological processes: concentration, centralization, segregation, invasion, and succession (Burgess 1926, p. 172).

To understand the relationship between the ecological organization of the city and the growth of the city we turn to Burgess's zonal hypothesis. Burgess (1967, pp. 50-58), writing in the 1920s, suggested that urban expansion causes the modern city to assume a pattern of concentric zones, each characterized by a typical land use. Burgess based his writings on the knowledge of the structure of the city of Chicago at that time. These zones, according to Burgess, were idealized concepts. No city conforms absolutely to this scheme.

Burgess (1967, pp. 50-58) proposed that any city or town expands radially from the central business district. The inner zone ("the Loop") is also known as the central business district or downtown area. Burgess (1967) states, "In the downtown section of every large city we expect to find the department stores, the skyscraper office buildings, the railroad stations, the great hotels, the theaters, the art museum, and the city hall" (p. 52). The inner zone is essentially an area of retail trade, light manufacturing and commercialized recreation. Surrounding the downtown area there is normally an area in transition, which is being invaded by business and industry. This area has been referred to by Burgess as the zone of deterioration. Burgess (1967) explains:

> In the zone of deterioration encircling the central business section are always to be found the so-called "slums" and "bad lands," with their sub-merged regions of poverty, degradation, and disease, and their underworlds of crime and vice. Within a deteriorating area are rooming-house districts, the purgatory of "lost souls." Near by is the Latin Quarter, where creative and rebellious spirits resort. The slums are also crowed to overflowing with immigrant colonies—the Ghetto, Little Sicily, Greektown, Chinatown— fascinatingly combining old world heritages and American adaptations. Wedging out from here is the Black Belt, with its free and disorderly life. (pp. 54-56)

It should be noted that the zone of transition often contains some high-cost luxury housing, "The Gold Coast." A third area is inhabited by those workers who desire to live within easy access to their work. Burgess calls this area the zone of workingmen's homes. This area is "an area of second immigrant settlement" and is "the region of escape from the slum" (Burgess 1967, p. 56). Beyond the zone occupied by the working class is an area occupied mainly by professional people and owners of small businesses. Burgess refers to this zone as the residential zone. In this area are single family dwellings and high-class hotels and apartment buildings. "Still farther, out beyond the city limits, is the commuter's zone-suburban areas, or satellite cities-within a thirty-to -sixty-minute ride of the central business district" (Burgess 1967, p. 50).

Burgess and his students gave empirical support to the zonal hypothesis. They did this by investigating the city of Chicago and presenting sociological data which confirmed that, in passing from the central business district to the outer limits of the city, delinquency rates, sex ratios, and percentages of foreign-born persons tended to decrease, while home ownership tended to increase.

Park and Burgess are well remembered for their empirical studies, yet it was Roderick McKenzie who synthesized what he learned from Park and Burgess and developed a systematic theory of human ecology. In any event, the field of urban ecology owes a lot to the foundation laid by Park, Burgess, and McKenzie.

Critical assessment of the social disorganization perspective

A number of scholars have criticized disorganization theory (Alihan 1938; Martindale 1957; Taylor, Walton, and Young 1973; Carey 1975; Hunter 1980). However, the present discussion is limited to those criticisms which shed light on why the Chicago school sociologists ignored or minimized the problem of organized crime. There are two principle criticisms of disorganization theory which help to explain the Chicago school's neglect of organized crime: first, the Chicago school focused on lower-class crime and deviance; second, the Chicago school sociologists failed to incorporate a Marxist analysis into their work. Each of these criticisms will be discussed below and tied to our thesis that studies of organized crime have played a marginal role in the development of American sociology.

As previously stated, the Chicago school sociologists have been criticized for focusing on lower-class crime and deviance (Mills 1943; Liazos 1972; Thio 1973; Pfohl 1985). Significantly absent from their work are any studies which address the crimes of the powerful, the so-called "respectable" members of society. Disorganizational theorists held ideological assumptions regarding who and what was deviant. Crimes of the powerful, including organized and white-collar crimes, were not considered acts of deviance. These crimes were committed by the well-to-do, the inhabitants of the protected commuter zone. The deviant acts and behaviors of the lower classes were carried out in the zone of transition and included street crimes, alcoholism, mental illness, drug addiction, delinquency, and the like. Those who engaged in these acts and behaviors were often of the lower classes and had little or no power in the larger society. Because the theory of social disorganization was directed only at lower-class criminals and deviants, it made no attempt to explain why organized crime or organized criminals existed. It is because of this class bias that the theory of social disorganization is limited in its explanatory potential.

Furthermore, the Chicago school sociologists neglected to consider the social and economic inequalities that existed between social classes and how these inequalities contributed to deviance. The system of social stratification was immune from investigation. Residents of the transition zone were victims of social change, not victims of social, political, and economic inequalities. The Chicago school theorists viewed the slums where people resided as "natural areas." Slums were naturally created, not socially created areas. Slum dwellers engaged in deviance because they were products of social disorganization, not products of an unequal system of social stratification. The central business district was a "natural area." Neglected was the fact that the central business district also housed some of the most powerful and well-to-do who often took advantage of the powerless classes. There is no examination by the Chicago school theorists of the social, economic, and political forces that allow some people to dominate others. A Marxist analysis would have allowed for this type of examination. More important, it would have acknowledged the relationship between organized criminal activities and the capitalistic market forces of supply and demand that allows organized crime to flourish. If a Marxist analysis had been invoked, the network of relationships (organized criminals, law enforcement agents, and the political machine) that sustains organized crime would also have been examined more closely.

In short, the theory of social disorganization saw crime as disorganized, lower-class street crime. The theory did not provide for the analysis of capitalistic market forces or for the analysis of social institutions that might influence criminal behavior. The powerful were immune from investigation and were somehow viewed as morally superior to the powerless. Individuals engaged in crime, not organizations. It was the individual that needed to be reformed, not society. Society was good and a good society could not have something as evil as organized crime. Perhaps the Chicago school theorists felt it was better to leave this demon alone and move on to more "workable" problems. To the crimes and criminals that they could control and understand. To problems that were defined for them by their research sponsors. Who could get close to organized criminals anyway?

3

Early organized crime in Chicago and the development of American sociology: A chronology

Introduction

CHAPTER 3 presents a systematic story of how racketeering, gangsterism, and organized crime and American sociology grew up together during the decades following World War I. They even shared the same locale, the burgeoning Midwest city of Chicago where the population grew from 1.5 to 3.3 million from 1900 to 1930. The University of Chicago is where studies of crime and deviance developed against a backdrop of organized crime. Despite these common links, the two existed side by side with little official recognition of one for the other, as if representing two entirely distinct social configurations. Yet it is more than remarkable that the group of sociologists whose perspectives were intently focused on the life of the city and its streets, including its seamier sides of life, neglected almost entirely the particular phenomenon known today as "organized crime."

In this chapter, two chronologies are presented, one documenting the history of organized crime in the city of Chicago (chapter 7 will look at organized crime as a pervasive American cultural object) and one documenting the topics which were studied and written about by the Chicago school sociologists. These chronologies confirm that organized crime was present during the period of the Chicago school and American sociologists were studying and writing about topics other than organized crime. (Why this was so is examined in chapter 8.) This chapter also raises a number of important questions: for example, How much did the Chicago school know about the environment of organized crime that they were working in? and To

25

what extent was organized crime in the minds of the Chicago school sociologists?

The early history of Chicago's organized crime

Several writers have agreed that documenting the history of organized crime in America is not an easy task (Albini 1971; Homer 1974; Nelli 1976; Moquin and Van Doren 1976; Abadinsky 1981a). Organized criminals do not carry out their activities in the open for all to see. The very success of organized crime in America depends upon its secrecy. Practitioners of organized crime do not boast about their membership to the press or public. Very little field research has been done on organized crime. Therefore, most of what reaches the public comes from journalists, the law enforcement community, and government agencies. Often what is published for public consumption is fictitious. Journalists, law enforcers, and government agents are not as constrained by the rules of careful scientific investigation as are social scientists. The organized crime literature is so filled with contradictions that the public, as well as researchers of organized crime, are perplexed. Often the terms "Black Hand," "Mafia," "Outfit," "Syndicate," "Unione Siciliane," and "Cosa Nostra," are used interchangeably, without much regard for their true meanings. Most Americans have come to accept the dominant view that the Mafia and organized crime are one and the same in America. This belief has much to do with the fact that Italians have dominated organized crime since the 1920s. From 1890 to 1920 the terms Mafia, Camorra, and Black Hand were all used interchangeably to refer to criminal activities in the Italian communities. Since the televised Kefauver Hearings (1950-51) the term Mafia became a handy usage for journalists and the law enforcement community. The use of this term has suggested that only Italian Americans are participants in organized crime. This myth has been perpetuated because the Mafia had its origins in Sicily and it is often easier to blame domestic social ills on foreign-born enemies than on conditions inherent in American society. In fact, this chapter will document that organized crime in America does not consist solely of Italian Americans, nor does the organization referred to as the Mafia control all of organized crime in America today.

The history of Chicago's organized crime is as much a local history as it is a vital piece of our national history. Therefore, the present discussion will not be confined to the city of Chicago. The history of Chicago's organized crime was closely tied to the history of crime in the Italian community in that same city (see Nelli 1969; 1976). A logical starting point for our discussion then is with the crime in the Italian immigrant community, often referred to as the Black Hand. The author will trace the growth of Black Hand activities and the origins of Italian involvement in syndicate crime from 1890 to 1920. Syndicate crime refers to illegal economic activities such as bootlegging, gambling, prostitution, usury, narcotics, and racketeering. These syndicates were established by American-born Italian criminals who worked with other ethnic groups in order to make a profit from their illegal activities (Nelli 1976, p. xii). Finally, the role Prohibition played in the rise and eventual success of Italian criminals will be examined.

Adherents of the Eighteenth Amendment felt that its passage would encourage citizens to live clean and sober lives. However, this did not happen. Instead, Prohibition provided the opportunities for success which young ethnics were seeking. These young men would become a dominant part of American entrepreneurial crime. The passage of the Eighteenth Amendment persuaded many Americans to change their attitudes toward organized criminals. No longer were organized criminals necessarily viewed as deviant or evil people. Organized criminals were now providing a service which many upstanding Americans demanded. Opportunities for success did not end with the repeal of Prohibition. During and after Prohibition criminal entrepreneurs not only engaged in the profitable business of bootlegging but also in the highly profitable activities of gambling, narcotics, prostitution, and racketeering.

The men who came "from Southern Italian criminal societies" (Nelli 1976, p. xi; cf. Albini 1971, p. 212; Moquin and Van Doren 1976, p. viii; Lupsha 1981, pp. 3-24) prior to 1920 had a low level of status in Southern Italy. Once in America these men operated in the Italian communities. On the other hand, members of the criminal syndicates of the 1920s and 1930s were either American born, or more typically, came to America as infants and children. They learned American values and business practices. They grew up in urban environments which admired success, and success was sought at any cost.

THE BLACK HAND

Italian crime in the United States prior to 1921 meant the Black Hand or Mafia. The Black Hand was a method of extorting money from Italian peasants living in America. It's origins are in Sicily but it was transported to American shores during the wave of Italian immigration during the latter part of the nineteenth century. The Black Hand was not an organization, as some have believed, nor was it synonymous with the Mafia, the Camorra, the Unione Siciliane or any other secret society (cf. Landesco 1968, p. 108; Albini 1971, pp. 191-94).

The crime that began in the early Italian communities had long-lasting significance. First, Italian dominance of Chicago's organized crime began prior to the enactment of the Eighteenth Amendment. Further, Italian crime in Chicago prior to 1920 involved more than just Black Hand activities. Lastly, early Italian crime in Chicago consisted of two separate and distinct areas of criminal activity: the Black Hand activities which were confined to the Italian community and its residents and the crimes which took place in the larger American community. With the passage of Prohibition Italian crime moved into the larger American community, in the form of bootlegging. Bootlegging propelled many Italian criminals to the top of the organized crime hierarchy (Nelli 1969, pp. 373-91; cf. Albini 1971, pp. 177-200).

An incident in New Orleans in 1890 had important consequences for the Italian community in Chicago. On October 15, 1890, the New Orleans superintendent of police, David C. Hennessy, was murdered. Hennessy had previously arranged for a crackdown on crime in the Italian community. Because of this many citizens believed the Sicilians were responsible for Hennessy's death. While hundreds of Italians were arrested for the crime only nine were actually brought to trial. Six of the nine defendants were found "not guilty" and the jury could reach no verdict on the other three. The American community was outraged. They suspected bribery and intimidation of witnesses. In the end, with the support of the local community, a mob went to the prison and grabbed eleven Italian prisoners and lynched them. The American community had gotten their revenge (cf. Nelli 1969, 1976; Albini 1971; Kobler 1971; Homer 1974; Smith 1975).

Prior to 1890 the term Mafia had received scant attention in the press regarding the city's Italians (Nelli 1969, p. 374; cf. Albini 1971, pp. 159-67; Smith 1975, pp. 27-45). The New Orleans incident changed all this. Now the term Mafia appeared more frequently in the Chicago newspapers of the period. Americans were convinced that the Mafia existed wherever "Southerners" (Sicilian and mainland Italians from the areas south of Rome) could be found.

By 1891 there were many "Southerners" in Chicago. Italians took offense at the way they were portrayed in the press. They were a proud people and wanted to be accepted by American society. Many Italians denied the existence of the Mafia in Chicago. "Oscar Durante, editor and publisher of Chicago's *L'Italia*, insisted that it did not exist even in Italy" (Nelli 1969, p. 375).

Italians wanted Americans to understand that old-world criminal patterns were not being transplanted to America. After the turn of the century Italian language newspapers referred to crimes in Italian neighborhoods as Black Hand activities. Both American and foreign-language journals now favored this term. Crimes perpetrated by Italians against other Italians were considered Black Hand crimes not crimes of the Mafia. This usage of the term remained in place until the 1920s. As time went on an increasing number of crimes were attributed to the Black Hand by the press. Even the newspaper *L'Italia* conceded that the Black Hand was responsible for a number of bombings, blackmailings, and murders (Nelli 1969, p. 375).

As the number of Chicago's "Southerners" increased they became an inviting target for Black Hand crimes. Because of the reputation of the Mafia in Sicily, the "Southerners" were easily intimidated by Black Hand threats. The Hennessy murder in New Orleans prompted American newspapers to claim that crimes in the Italian communities were acts of the Mafia (Nelli 1969, p. 376).

Angered by the derogatory publicity that Black Hand crimes brought upon Italians, the White Hand society was formulated. The White Hand society consisted of Italians who wanted to put a stop to Black Hand crimes and to improve the reputation of the Italian people. Their example was followed in many cities. They hired attorneys and private investigators to assist the authorities in arresting and subsequently convicting a number of Black Hand criminals. Although the White Hand society was responsible for ridding the city of ten of the most dangerous Black Hand criminals, its impressive start was short-lived. Black Handers who were brought to justice were set free after giving bribes to law enforcement officials. For various reasons the membership of the society began to dwindle, and by 1913 the

Black Handers were freely terrorizing the Italian citizenry (Kobler 1971, p. 56).

Black Hand activities seemed to disappear in Chicago by the 1920s. Nelli (1969, p. 380) cites three factors which contributed to this decline. First, immigration legislation, passed in 1914, reduced the supply of victims. A second factor was the passage of a federal law prohibiting the use of the mails to defraud. This meant that Black Hand extortion notes would now have to be delivered in person. The element of secrecy would be gone. Black Handers would be recognized. A third factor which led to the decline of Black Hand activities was the passage of Prohibition. Prohibition provided resourceful young men with the opportunity to reap large monetary rewards. Criminals left their former occupations as robbers, murderers, burglars, thieves, and blackmailers for the more profitable work offered through Prohibition. Former Black Handers also followed the profitable path of Prohibition. Immigration restriction, federal legislation, and Prohibition led to the decline of Black Hand activities and the movement of Italian criminals into organized criminal opportunities in the larger American community.

The Early Syndicates

Several writers have given comparable historical accounts of the early crime syndicates in Chicago (cf. Peterson 1952, 1963; Landesco 1968; Nelli 1969, 1976; Albini 1971; Kobler 1971; Abadinsky 1981a). The origins of Chicago's organized crime can be traced back to the actions of Michael Cassius McDonald in the 1870s. During the mayoral election of 1873 McDonald organized the gamblers, liquor interests, and brothel keepers into a strong political power. The alliances between crime and politics in Chicago had a solid foundation under the leadership of McDonald. The first real political machine was established by McDonald and crime was more organized than it ever had been.

"King Mike" McDonald, as he was called, became a successful gambling operator. Not only did McDonald control the bookmaking syndicate in Chicago but he also owned "The Store," a place where both gamblers and politicians practiced their trades. "The Store" was located in the Levee, Chicago's infamous vice district in the First Ward. With McDonald's approval, the "Lords of the Levee," were the team of John "Bathhouse" Coughlin and Michael "Hinky Dink" Kenna. Abadinsky (1981a) describes Coughlin as a "powerfully built six-footer" and Kenna as a small "organizational genius" (p. 73). Coughlin was born in 1860 and made contacts with the rich and influential of Chicago through his job as a rubber in the select Palmer House Baths. These contacts helped him when he opened his own bathhouse. Among those who patronized his establishment were politicians, and Coughlin soon became a "Democratic captain" (Abadinsky 1981a, p. 74). On April 5, 1892, Coughlin was elected alderman of the First Ward. A politically corrupt city council was all but guaranteed.

Coughlin eventually joined up with "Hinky Dink" Kenna. Kenna was nicknamed after the waterhole he swam in as a youngster. Kenna was born in the First Ward in 1858. He began as a hardworking newsboy, and became a successful saloon keeper and politician. Kenna and Coughlin, in 1893, established a profitable

business whereby gambling and brothel operators paid for protection. Members of
the organization who got arrested were defended by two lawyers who were on the
payroll. The members of the organization operated with complete immunity. The
foundation for the infamous Capone gang was laid with the success of Kenna and
Coughlin (Peterson 1963, p. 31).The success of Kenna and Coughlin was simultaneous with the fall of McDonald. McDonald had accumulated a great deal of wealth,
and by the time he died in 1907 his interest in ward politics had faded. In addition
to Kenna and Coughlin, other prosperous gambling entrepreneurs included Mont
Tennes[1] on the North Side, James O'Leary on the South Side, and Alderman Johnnie
Rogers on the West Side. Tennes, who ruled until the 1920s, had acquired most of
McDonald's gambling operations. Subsequently, the Torrio-Capone gang seized
control of Tennes's operation. Although most of the wealth of Italian criminals was
accumulated after Prohibition, they did have a head start under the tutelage of
"Diamond Jim" Colosimo during the first two decades of the twentieth century.

Colosimo was a small boy when he left Calabria to come to the United States
in the 1890s. As a street sweeper in the First Ward he organized his fellow sweepers
into a successful political block. Colosimo eventually grew to be a powerful political
presence in the First Ward and Kenna and Coughlin made him a "precinct captain."
In addition to his political influence within the ward, he also owned the nationally
known restaurant called Colosimo's Cafe. The cafe was frequented by such notables
as Enrico Caruso and George M. Cohan. Nelli (1969) writes that "By 1914 'Big Jim'
and his associates had built a 'syndicate,' the first one organized by Chicago Italians,
based on vice operations, especially prostitution and gambling" (p. 385).

Colosimo brought Johnny Torrio from New York in 1910. Colosimo had been
receiving Black Hand extortion threats and felt Torrio could offer him protection.
Peterson (1952) notes that Torrio was once the "leader of the James Street Gang which
operated along the waterfront of the East River in New York City" (p. 107). During
this period Torrio developed qualities of leadership and organizational ability.
While under the supervision of Colosimo, in Chicago, Torrio quickly learned about
the city's politics and politicians. Torrio also captured the Levee market with the
Torrio-Van Bever slave ring. Torrio was once arrested when he and his compatriots
transported a dozen girls from Saint Louis to Chicago. While the others who were
involved received minor sentences, Torrio was freed because the prosecutor's star
witness, Joe Bovo, refused to testify against Torrio. Bovo was the pimp who delivered
the girls. Colosimo was not even questioned, he was protected by Kenna and
Coughlin (Kobler 1971, p. 53).

Colosimo divorced his wife Victoria Moresco sometime during the first months
of 1920. Colosimo had fallen in love with Dale Winters who was a singer in his cafe.
On April 20, 1920, the couple married. After the marriage Colosimo's life centered
around his new bride. Torrio was busy making plans of his own. Torrio had set Big
Jim up to be killed. Torrio told Colosimo to expect two truckloads of illegal whiskey
at exactly 4:00 p.m. on May 11th. The liquor never arrived. Instead, Big Jim was killed
by a gunman who vanished as suddenly as he appeared. Speculation has it that the

gunman was Frankie Yale, imported from New York by Torrio to do the job (Peterson 1952, p. 108).

Colosimo's funeral was a tasteless affair. It showed just how tightly woven crime and politics were in Chicago. Sociologist John Landesco (1968) writing in the 1920s on the funerals of gangsters remarks:

> The funerals of gangsters have invariably attracted wide attention, partly because of the great pomp with which they are celebrated and partly because of the extraordinary variety of persons—gunmen, politicians, and people promi-nent in public life—which there assemble to assist in the ceremony. These ceremonies are at the same time an exhibition of wealth and the influence of the men themselves, and a revelation of the intimate relations between politics and crime.
>
> The funeral of no man in Chicago ever brought together in all probabili-ty, as complete and picturesque a representation of the Chicago that lies outside of the "Gold Coast" as that, in 1920, of James (Big Jim) Colosimo, overlord of the old levee district. Among the honorary pallbearers were alderman, judges, congressmen, noted singers of the Chicago opera company, leaders of his immigrant group and his associates in underworld activities. (p. 191)

Johnny Torrio succeeded Colosimo as leader of the Chicago underworld. A four-story building known as the Four Deuces served as Torrio's headquarters. The building was located at 2222 South Wabash Avenue in Chicago and housed a saloon on the first floor, gambling operations on the second and third floors, and a brothel on the top floor. The building was often frequented by criminals, politicians, and political fixers. It was rumored that at least twelve unsolved murders had taken place at the Four Deuces. Yet this number pales in comparison to the murders that were to follow in the Torrio-Capone gang wars (Peterson 1952, p. 110).

Al Capone, the infamous New York gangster and principal actor in Chicago's heyday of racketeering, was Torrio's first lieutenant. With the installation of Capone the syndicate became even more powerful throughout Cook County, Chicago. In 1925, Torrio gave up his position of power within the organization and fled to New York. In New York Torrio socialized with well-known gangsters like Frank Costello, Charles "Lucky" Luciano, Meyer Lansky, Benjamin "Bugsy" Siegel, and others. Al Capone took over the underworld throne and the notorious organization he headed became known as the Capone gang. Italian dominance of organized crime made a strong beginning.

PROHIBITION AND THE RISE OF THE CAPONE ORGANIZATION

The Eighteenth Amendment and the Prohibition Enforcement Act (Volstead Act) went into effect on January 16, 1920. The passage of the Eighteenth Amendment was the culmination of earlier efforts by the antisaloon and antiliquor forces. The legislation prohibited the manufacture, sale, transportation, import or export of intoxicating liquors.

Writers of the period often portrayed the earliest efforts of the antisaloon and antiliquor forces to do away with the liquor business as a rural versus urban conflict.

The temperance movement was one of three movements, along with abolition and nativism, which emerged during the 1840s and 1850s. The term "temperance" is an unusual name for a movement which preaches total abstinence from alcohol. Sociologist Joseph Gusfield (1963, p. 5), in his classic work *Symbolic Crusade: Status Politics and the American Temperance Movement*, explains that the term was applied to the movement in its early years before the philosophy of the movement became so fanatical. Reacting to the immigrant, urban poor in their midst, reformers believed that temperance legislation would somehow assert the dominance of native American Protestant morality. Immigrants were mainly urban, Catholic, and poor. This contrasted sharply with the reformers who were mainly rural, Protestant, and middle class. The reformers saw the Eighteenth Amendment as a way to establish "the victory of Protestant over Catholic, rural over urban, traditional over modernity, the middle-class over both the lower and upper strata" (Gusfield 1963, p. 7).

The Eighteenth Amendment was an attempt by "moral entrepreneurs," to establish their values and interests through legislation. The Drys (antisaloon and antiliquor forces) firmly believed that by regulating behavior through legislation they were preserving the American way of life. Instead, the Drys unwittingly gave fuel to the organized crime activities in their midst. For immigrants, including Jews, Germans, Italians, and Irish, alcohol played an important part in their cultural activities. They had no taboos against drinking. Instead, Prohibition presented a vast number of opportunities for immigrant youth to become involved in the illicit liquor trade. Immigrant youth who resided in the urban slums of major American cities were easily recruited into organized gangsterism. Naturally, immigrants were now more widely viewed as criminals, and the native American Protestants were more determined than ever to force their morality upon the immigrants (Higham 1963, pp. 267-68).

The greatest supporters of Prohibition were the suburban middle class. These middle-class reformers wanted to gain control of the heart of the city, an area heavily populated with immigrants and controlled by the corrupt political machine. Reformers were correct in their belief of a strong relationship between the ward boss, the political machine, and the saloon. In order to destroy the boss system it was necessary to destroy the saloon, the foundation of his operation (Nelli 1976, p. 144).

The reformers hoped Prohibition would "uplift the lower classes," make "working men more moral," "improve the racial stock," and "increase industrial efficiency" (Nelli 1976, p. 144). But legislation alone was not enough to accomplish these things. There was conflict and confusion over whether the federal or state government had the primary responsibility of enforcing laws. Also, the word "intoxicating" was used in the Volstead Act. In court it was difficult to prove "intoxication" as opposed to the mere presence of alcohol. Finally, and probably most important, the general public desired alcohol. A majority of the citizenry demanded the services of organized criminals. Organized crime had customers not victims. The public accepted the services of organized criminals and in doing so acknowledged that these organized criminals were not deviants. It is difficult to have unpopular laws enforced when the illegal activity in question has the support of the upper and middle classes.

Prohibition also brought extensive changes in the internal structure of organized criminal groups. The most significant change was that illegal goods and services were now being distributed nationally. Prior to Prohibition most criminal activity was local in scope, often confined to the ethnic community. After Prohibition, organized criminals expanded their control of illegal activities to cities or even regions (Homer 1974, p. 33).

Before Prohibition, illegal activity was centered around several districts in the cities. In Chicago, the Levee was the district for illegal activities. "Bounded north and south by twenty-second and eighteenth streets and east and west by Clark and Wabash, the Levee had one of the world's heaviest concentrations of crime and vice" (Kobler 1971, p. 38). While some vice activities found in the Levee (such as prostitution) catered to upper-class and middle-class customers, most people still considered the Levee "the other side of the tracks." Prohibition changed this and liquor became available to everyone in the United States. According to journalist Kenneth Allsop (1968), "In Chicago alone, in 1930, Federal officials estimated that ten-thousand speakeasies were operating, each buying weekly six barrels of beer at $55.00 each, thus giving the gangs a weekly $3,500,000 revenue" (p. 34).

In short, the universal demand for alcohol led to the process of nationalization of organized crime. The illegal liquor industry was an unregulated market system. This meant that many groups could violently compete for their share of the market. Like any legitimate business, the illegal liquor business obtained a supply of the goods, transported the goods to a marketplace, and sold the goods at a price for a profit to be made. Unlike legitimate business, the government had to be kept in the dark about these activities. Bootleggers also faced the possibility that their liquor supply would be hijacked. Hijacking was an easy and cheap way to obtain a supply of goods. Victims of hijackings could not turn to legitimate law enforcement agencies for assistance. Nor could the bootleggers expect the government to intervene on their behalf regarding monopolistic business practices or price regulations. Therefore, bootleggers developed their own ways to deal with competition and the marketplace. The bootlegging wars and gangland murders, which made newspaper copy all over the world, were, in a real sense, one way to deal with business problems. Many young urban immigrants saw Prohibition as a way to escape poverty. While many paths to economic opportunity and success were closed to these youths, Prohibition was one path which was open. They were willing to do anything to protect their interests, including violence and murder.

Other forces were also at work during Prohibition that contributed to the nationalization of organized crime. Developments in transportation and communication encouraged citizens to travel to benefit from the services of organized crime and also allowed gangsters to organize on a national level. In addition, gangsters were now able to purchase weapons of wholesale slaughter, like the Thompson Machine Gun, with little difficulty (Homer 1974, p. 35).

From 1920 to 1933, bootlegging provided the chief source of income for the gangs; the Torrio-Capone gang grossed from $60 to $240 million a year (Nelli 1976, p. 150). As many have observed (Nelli 1976, p. 162; cf. Landesco 1932, p. 125), Prohibition was a big business operation in the grand tradition of United States capitalism, a crime of considerably more status and esteem than most other forms of crime.

Soon after the Volstead Act went into effect Torrio began operating breweries and a convoy of trucks. Torrio remained in control during the Republican administrations of mayor Thompson (1915-1923). As several writers (Landesco 1932, 1968; Peterson 1952, 1963; Haller 1970; Nelli 1976) have observed, agreeable politicians were necessary for the successful operations of bootlegging, gambling, prostitution, and narcotics. Torrio bought the cooperation and protection of police and politicians in order to carry out his illegal activities. As Landesco (1932) noted, "The relative immunity to punishment of gangsters engaged in organized crime has its counterpart in the huge amounts of graft received for protection by police and politicians" (p. 127). Like today, most of those who appeared before the courts for official processing were from the lower social classes. These included common street thugs, juvenile delinquents, wife beaters, and drunkards. Other criminals, including racketeers and participants in organized crime, rarely made appearances in court.

After Thompson's reign ended, William Dever, a Democrat, was elected as mayor of Chicago. Dever and his chief of police, Morgan A. Collins, refused to cooperate with Torrio. Torrio's reputation as syndicate chieftain was damaged and his ability to protect his associates was destroyed. On May 19, 1924, Chief Collins directed a victorious raid on the Sieben Brewery. Torrio, along with other gang leaders and several underlings, was arrested. The arrest and subsequent conviction of Torrio were proof that the syndicate no longer had the power to control the new city administration. This meant that rival gangs could challenge the Torrio-Capone gang.

By 1924 there were several established bootlegging gangs. The composition of gangland organization was based largely, but not entirely, on ethnic origins. Irish gangs were located on the West Side and South Side. William "Klondike" O'Donnell and his cohorts and the Valley Gang headed by Terry Drugan were on the West Side. Another group of O'Donnells, Steve, Walter, Thomas, and Edward were on the South Side. "Pollack" Joe Saltis was in charge of an Irish and Polish gang located southwest of the stockyards. Dion O'Banion, an Irishman, coordinated the group located on the near North Side. Included in this group were Poles like Earl "Hymie" Weiss and George "Bugs" Moran; Jews like Jake Zuta, the Gusenberg brothers, and "Nails" Morton; and an Italian, Vincent Drucci. The Italian gangs, in addition to the Capone organization, included the Gennas and the Aiellos (cf. Haller 1971-72, p. 219; Abadinsky 1981a).

Many of the associates of the Capone gang were known to them when they were poor slum kids in the South Side vice district and they rose to wealth together. The Capone organization was not entirely Italian. Frankie and Terry Drugan, Irishmen, helped in the brewing of beer and Jake Guzik, a Jew, was the business manager for the organization. The Capone organization proved to be the most feared and deadly organization during the bootlegging wars of the 1920s. The wealth accumulated by the Capone gang in the 1920s allowed them to branch out into other legal and illegal activities during and after Prohibition. In short, bootlegging propelled many Italians through business acumen and gangland violence to a position of power and dominance within the Chicago underworld (Haller 1971-72, p. 220).

Several writers have given standard accounts of gangland murders during Prohibition (Peterson 1952; Landesco 1968; Allsop 1968; Kobler 1971; Nelli 1976; Abadinsky 1981a). What follows is a condensation of these accounts. In 1924, Dion O'Bannion, florist and boss of the North Side gang, began feuding with the Gennas. At this time O'Bannion had also swindled Torrio and Capone. O'Bannion owned a share of the Sieben Brewery with Torrio and Capone. O'Bannion sold his share of the Sieben Brewery to Torrio and Capone for $500,000 because he knew the brewery was about to be raided. O'Bannion bragged about what he had done and was subsequently killed in his flower shop by three hired killers, Albert Anselmi, John Scalise, and Mike Genna. This began a war that lasted over four years culminating in the notorious St. Valentine's Day Massacre. Although the three men were never identified as the actual killers by law enforcement agencies, it was suspected that the killers were aligned with the Genna clan or were hired gunmen paid by the Torrio-Capone gang.

Polish American Hymie Weiss (born Earl Wajciechowski) was Dion's successor. Weiss vowed he would avenge the death of O'Bannion. In 1925, Weiss and his men attempted to kill Capone. After this incident Capone began driving in an armored Cadillac limousine. Torrio was hoping to avoid the battle by seeking haven in prison and pled guilty to his part in the Sieben Brewery affair. Before Torrio could begin serving his sentence, he was critically wounded by O'Bannion gunmen. After recovering from his wounds and completing his sentence, Torrio left Chicago and handed over the reins to Capone.

The O'Bannion gang continued to pose problems for Capone just as it had for Torrio. On October 11, 1926, Hymie Weiss was murdered. Soon after the murder a truce was called. The meeting for a truce was initiated by Saltis. Saltis was secretly aligned with Weiss although he pledged loyalty to Capone. Capone knew this but wanted peace more than revenge and so the meeting was held. At the meeting the city of Chicago was divided up among gang chieftains. The Capone and O'Bannion gangs received the largest shares. Also present were representatives of the McErlane-Saltis gang and the Sheldon gang which was now an ally of Capone. The truce lasted until April 4, 1927, when Vincent "the schemer" Drucci was killed by police officers. While Drucci was head of the O'Bannion gang he abided by the peace settlement. Now with Drucci out of the picture Bugs Moran was leader of the O'Bannion gang and had no intentions to honor the peace agreement. After a relatively long period of calm the gang war progressed. The climax was the bloody St. Valentine's Day Massacre.

The St. Valentine's Day Massacre was an event widely reported in the literature on organized crime and even made its way into American film history in Billy Wilder's *Some Like it Hot*. On St. Valentine's Day, February 14, 1929, several men dressed in police uniforms entered the premises of 2122 North Clark Street, a garage which served as the headquarters of Bugs Moran. Present were seven of Moran's associates who were awaiting the arrival of their leader. The uniformed officers told the seven Moran associates that they were under arrest and to face the wall with their hands up. The seven Moran associates did as they were told; a brush with the law was considered a mere nuisance in gangland, something to be expected and tolerated in their line of work. Suddenly the uniformed officers shot and killed their rivals with machine guns. The incident was open testimony to the rampant lawlessness in the city of Chicago. Like most Chicago gangland murders during the 1920s, the incident was never resolved. Although it was widely known that Moran was an enemy of Capone, Capone was never charged with the murder (Peterson 1952, p. 145).

One social scientist noted that the murderers were members of the Egan's Rats of Detroit and Saint Louis with whom Capone had connections (Abadinsky 1981a, p. 85). Allsop (1968, p. 140) maintains that the operation was arranged by a Capone gunman, Jack McGurn. Although Moran was the real target, he was not present at the garage that morning. In any event, Moran was frightened enough by the incident to flee Chicago for the east coast. Moran returned to more traditional criminal activities and was subsequently sent to prison for robbery of a tavern employee. Moran died on February 26, 1957, and Torrio died on April 16, 1957 (Abadinsky 1981a, p. 85).

The activities of the Capone organization angered the gangsters in New York, who did not appreciate the media coverage and governmental scrutiny that the St. Valentine's Day Massacre generated. Therefore, Capone was ordered to a meeting in Atlantic City, New Jersey, by Torrio, who was acting on behalf of a syndicate of eastern mobsters. Mob leaders from a number of American cities met to discuss the violence and bloodshed of the bootlegging wars. The wars were bad publicity for the business of organized crime. The gathering was the first major gang convention ever held. It was a futile attempt to get the mobs to cooperate with each other in carrying out their illegal activities.

A second convention was hosted by Capone at the Congress Hotel in Chicago late in 1931. The meeting was held under the chairmanship of Charles "Lucky" Luciano. Plans were made for the ending of Prohibition, the ending of gang wars, expanding gambling operations, and the recruiting of non-Italians into the ranks of organized crime.

Capone's income was greatly reduced with the onset of the Great Depression. Furthermore, a special team of federal investigators, under the leadership of Elliot Ness, began moving against Capone distilleries, breweries, and liquor shipments. In addition, a 1927 United States Supreme Court decision stated that even unlawful income was subject to income taxes. This decision led the Internal Revenue Service to move against the Capone organization.

As is common knowledge today, the "Feds," Ness and his men, were finally able to have Capone indicted for income tax evasion charges and conspiracy to violate the Volstead Act. Yet it was not Ness and his men who brought down Capone but Internal Revenue agents. Ness loved publicity and this proved detrimental to his cause. Each time he was to raid a Capone brewery he would inform the press. Cameramen would arrive at the scene and undermine the whole operation. On the other hand Internal Revenue agents operated in secrecy, and one agent was able to pose as a gangster and infiltrate the Capone organization.

Capone was brought down primarily by the efforts of one man, Special Agent Frank Wilson, who led the investigation against Capone. After investigating bank records, Western Union records, and interviewing hundreds of people, it was revealed that Capone, while in Florida, was receiving regular payments from Jake Guzik. Capone stood trial and was found guilty of income tax evasion. Capone's income from 1924 to 1929 was $1,038,654 and he never paid a cent of income tax. Capone was released from prison in 1939; good behavior allowed him early freedom. Suffering from an advanced stage of venereal disease, he died on January 26, 1947 (Abadinsky 1981a, p. 88).

Capone was considered a hero and admired by many ethnic immigrants and working-class Americans. Capone gained a reputation as a philanthropist and also assisted many politicians in his community to get elected to office.

In 1933, the Twenty-First Amendment was passed which repealed Prohibition. Bootlegging was no longer the prosperous business enterprise it once was and new avenues for success were found in the so-called victimless crimes of gambling and prostitution. Such criminal activities as gambling, prostitution, business and labor racketeering were being cultivated all during Prohibition.

The organization that Al Capone had worked so hard to build did not fall when he was convicted of income tax evasion. Three Capone associates kept the organization going, Frank Nitti, Jake Guzik, and Ralph Capone, Al's brother. Guzik directed gambling and vice operations, Ralph saw to the mob's bootleg liquor interests, and Nitti, once the enforcer, later became the financial advisor (Nelli 1976, p. 168).

NATIONAL EVENTS IN THE EARLY HISTORY OF ORGANIZED CRIME

Although the focus of this book is the city of Chicago during the "Golden Age" of the Chicago school, it is still useful to discuss some of the earlier events in the national history of organized crime. These events have helped to shape the public's perception of organized crime. However, it should be noted that these events are discussed here only for purposes of historical documentation. The significance of these events on the public's perception of organized crime will be the focus of chapter 6.

After the conference hosted by Capone at the Congress Hotel in Chicago in late 1931, there were several other similar gatherings to improve the business of crime. In 1934, a meeting was held at the Waldorf Towers in New York, under the direction of Luciano, Lansky, Costello, and Torrio. At this meeting a board of directors or national commission was named. The various mobs were given territories with the neutral regions up for grabs (Moquin and Van Doren 1976, p. 113).

The so-called apalachin convention took place on November 14, 1957, at the home of Joseph Barbara in upstate New York. Joseph Barbara had invited guests to his home for a barbecue. Several of these guests had out-of-state license plates which aroused the curiosity of local officials. Local officials responded by setting up roadblocks. News of the roadblocks reached the guests and many of them began to flee. Among the guests arrested by local officials were Vito Genovese, Stephen Magadino, Joe Bonanno, and Joe Profaci. The incident brought widespread publicity to organized crime. The syndicate was now in the spotlight. The public was reminded that organized crime existed in the United States on a grand scale. Those men who lived in "relative immunity as middle class, respectable businessmen were now considered to be something else" (Moquin and Van Doren 1976, p. 114).

Two additional events are worthy of mention, the Kefauver committee hearings (1950-51) and the testimony of Joseph Valachi in 1963. In 1950, under the chairmanship of Senator Estes Kefauver, a special committee was set up to look into organized crime in interstate commerce. The events of the Kefauver committee hearings were televised and Americans had their first opportunity to view senators, lawyers, and gangsters. Television interest focused on Frank Costello, who was the alleged head of the organized crime family formally headed by Vito Genovese and Lucky Luciano. It was discovered by the committee that many different ethnic groups were in charge of the syndicates and that these syndicate leaders were in contact with one another on a frequent basis. "It was only in reporting of subsequent events and in concentration on nuclear Italian families that people began to identify totally Italians with organized crime" (Homer 1974, p. 41; cf. Smith 1975).

The Kefauver committee concluded that there was indeed a nationwide crime syndicate known as the Mafia. The Kefauver committee also implied that the New York and Chicago syndicates were connected through Mafia links. However, neither Kefauver nor his state crime committee presented any real evidence that the Mafia existed (see Moore 1974; Woodiwiss 1987).

In 1963, Joseph Valachi, a low-ranking member of the Genovese crime family, testified on national television before the Senate Permanent Subcommittee on Investigations. The subcommittee was chaired by Senator John McClellan. The testimony that Valachi gave was considered by many to be the truth about the national Mafia. While many scholars and journalists were skeptical about what Valachi had to say, much of the public and law enforcement community believed his testimony.

The Influence of American Values and Culture on Organized Crime

Political scientist Peter Lupsha (1981) asked, "What is American about American organized crime?" His reply is it is a reflection of American economic and political institutions (p. 20). We can trace the American roots of organized crime to the street gangs of ethnic neighborhoods in the late nineteenth century (Thrasher 1927; Tyler 1962; Landesco 1968; Haller 1971-72; Nelli 1976). These gangs protected their ethnic neighborhoods while at the same time victimizing them. Organized crime provided an opportunity for young immigrant men who were reared, raised, and socialized in ethnic slum neighborhoods to achieve economic success. The leadership of organized crime in Chicago in the 1920s was primarily Italian, Irish, and Jewish. There were no native white leaders of organized crime (Haller 1971-72, pp. 210-11). Organized crime chieftains were primarily American born or raised. Organized crime was not a product, as some have argued, of Italy, Ireland, Sicily, Germany, Russia, or Poland. Organized crime is an American-made product. Organized criminals were home grown in the ethnic urban neighborhoods of America. The activities in which these organized criminals engaged were influenced by the American economic and political landscape of their day.

Italian and Sicilian immigrants who became organized criminals in America were not necessarily criminals in their native lands. Both native-born and Italian and Sicilian immigrants grew up in the same urban environments which influenced many of them to turn to organized crime. Colosimo came to this country as a young boy and rose to organized crime fame through his connection with the urban political machine. The Mafia was not transplanted from Sicily, and Colosimo, Torrio, and Capone did not come from Sicily. Colosimo was born on the mainland of Italy, Torrio was born in Naples, and Capone was born in Brooklyn, New York (Albini 1971, p. 212). Ethnicity was the historical factor that cemented the ties of the early syndicate leaders to the corrupt political machine. Today ethnicity is still a strong factor in determining organized crime constituents. Yet despite the varying ethnic backgrounds of syndicate leaders they have all used violence, secrecy, and protection to maintain their illegal operations (see Albini 1971, pp. 212-13).

The syndicates are exemplary of American free enterprise and their goals and methods resemble that of the early robber barons (see Moquin and Van Doren 1976; Abadinsky 1981a). They do whatever it takes to eliminate the competition and control the market. Their ultimate goal is to make money. They make their money by offering the public the goods and services they desire.

Contrary to the idea that organized crime is largely an imported institution, grounded in Italian and other ethnic roots, many (Tyler 1962; Landesco 1968; Albini 1971; Homer 1974; Smith 1975; Nelli 1976; Lupsha 1981) argue that organized crime is thoroughly rooted in American values and culture and has paralleled the development of American economic and political institutions. Organized crime "has evolved into a diversified multinational conglomerate, franchising criminal markets and firms" (Lupsha 1981, p. 22).

CONCLUDING REMARKS

Before leaving this discussion of the early history of Chicago's organized crime two points need to be made. First, organized crime as it existed during the 1920s and 1930s is no longer possible. Big, organized city crime of the 1920s and 1930s was dependent upon the economics, politics, and ethnic groups present during that particular period of American history. Changes in all three of these areas have changed the nature of organized crime in America today. Second, this historical presentation of Chicago's organized crime is highly selective. The historical events of Chicago's organized crime presented in this book are adequate for the task at hand.

Should readers wish a further examination of the early history of crime and politics in Chicago, they are referred to John Landesco's (1968) *Organized Crime in Chicago* and Virgil Peterson's (1952) *Barbarians in Our Midst.*

Contributions to the Chicago school of urban sociology: a chronological development

Introduction to the Monographs

As documented in the first half of this chapter, organized crime in Chicago evolved, from the late 1800s to the 1930s, into a lucrative business. At the same time the sociology department at the University of Chicago was evolving into the most dominant department of sociology in the country. Yet the two were evolving without any official recognition of one by the other. The Chicago school sociologists, whose very reputation was based on a number of important monographs[2] published during the 1920s and 1930s, on urban crime and deviance did not publish one monograph on the organized crime that was so prevalent in their neighborhoods. In order to understand and appreciate the exclusion of the topic of organized crime from the curriculum and the published works of the department of sociology from 1918 to 1933, it is worthwhile to point out how other topics were supported, sponsored, and treated by this generation of scholars. By presenting a chronological development of studies of crime and deviance by this generation of scholars we will come to see that organized crime was not a topic they studied or wrote about. More significant, it will establish just how similar the development of American sociology and organized crime were in location and duration.

Robert Park and Ernest Burgess guided the research for the many monographs that were published by their students during the 1920s and 1930s. The monographs shared a common focus upon the city and a theoretical framework which focused on social disorganization and human ecology. It can be said that these monographs gave substance to a field of sociology identified as urban sociology. Not only did these monographs make contributions to urban sociology but also to other fields of sociology, including criminology, deviance, social problems, and the family.

Under the directorship of Beardsley Ruml, a former psychology instructor at the University of Chicago, the Laura Spelman Rockefeller Foundation agreed to make funds available to various universities for social science research. The University of Chicago was one of the first universities that was awarded a grant from the foundation for social science research. The seed money, $25,000., was used to establish the National Social Science Research Council at Chicago and to fund subsequent and on-going projects. The funding lasted for a decade. Each year, contingent upon the University of Chicago raising matching funds from the community, the foundation would contribute moneys beyond the initial grant (Burgess and Bogue 1964, pp. 6-7).

Burgess and Bogue (1964) write, "It was understood that in Chicago, because of the beginning we made in the study of the city, the research would be concentrated and limited to the studies of the community" (p. 7). Henceforth the University of Chicago established the Local Community Research Committee (LCRC). The LCRC was comprised of an interdisciplinary team of faculty which included Dean Leonard C. Marshall, head of the economics department, Charles Merriam from the political science department, Dr. Edith Abott from the social services administration, and Marcus Jurnigon from history. Burgess was the representative from sociology. Leonard Marshall was made head of the committee. The research projects, which came to be identified with the Chicago school of urban research, were supported by the committee. As already stated (see n. 2), many of the studies were published by the University of Chicago Press in its Sociological Series. Ruth S. Cavan (1983, p. 417), a graduate student in the department during the 1920s, notes that the published monographs were often the Ph.D. dissertations of students. The students received full credit as authors but the monographs, in a larger sense, really represented the intellectual thinking of Park and/or Burgess. Park and Burgess, who guided the research projects, would often write the preface to each monograph. When the foundation no longer gave grant money to the LCRC for community research projects the monographs came to a halt. Although some books were still published in the 1930s by commercial publishers. These books, although not part of the Chicago Sociological Series, were still representative of the research methods, theoretical thinking, and research techniques of the Chicago school (Cavan 1983, p. 417).

The monographs selected for representation of the Chicago school have been separated into two groups. The first group will cover various studies of disorganizational deviance; the second group will cover studies dealing specifically with crime and delinquency research. Among the former are *The Hobo* (Anderson 1923), *Family Disorganization* (Mowrer 1927), *The Ghetto* (Wirth 1928), *Suicide* (Cavan 1928), *The Gold Coast and the Slum* (Zorbaugh 1929), *The Negro Family in Chicago* (Frazier 1932), *The Taxi-Dance Hall* (Cressey 1932), *The Pilgrims of Russian-Town* (Young 1932), *Vice in Chicago* (Reckless 1933), and Norman Hayner's *Hotel Life*, published in 1936 by the University of North Carolina Press.

The latter group will include Thrasher's *The Gang* (1927) and a number of monographs in criminology disclosing the research results of work at the Institute of Juvenile Research where Burgess was a key figure. These will include an ecological study by Clifford Shaw and his associates, *Delinquency Areas* (1929), two life histories edited by Shaw, *The Jack-Roller* (1930) and *The Natural History of a Delinquent Career* (1931), and Shaw and McKay's classic work *Social Factors in Juvenile Delinquency* completed for the Wickersham Crime Commission in 1931. Also included is the research of Edwin H. Sutherland who received his Ph.D. from Chicago in 1913 and returned in 1930 as a professor. Members of the Chicago school had a tremendous influence on Sutherland's intellectual thinking. Sutherland's *Twenty Thousand Homeless Men* (1936) and *The Professional Thief* (1937) will be discussed here. While these works were not published as part of the Chicago Series, they are still representative of the classic works of the Chicago school.

The monographs selected for illustration (with the exception of the works of

Sutherland) have all been written by graduate students in the Department of Sociology at the University of Chicago in the 1920s.[3] All of the monographs were jointly funded by the Laura Spelman Rockefeller Foundation and local welfare and civic agencies. Through an analysis of the works we can see what the Chicago school defined as a social problem, how and why specific problems were or were not studied (including organized crime), and the methodological, theoretical, and ideological assumptions the Chicago school held which encouraged them to or discouraged them from studying certain social problems. In short, we can come to understand how the Chicago school sociologists viewed the world around them.

Before discussing the monographs selected for illustration, it is necessary to give recognition to *The City* (1925), this book lays out the theoretical and methodological foundation for subsequent works written by the Chicago sociologists. *The City* published while Park and Burgess were already engaged in urban research, includes many of the research interests of the Chicago school during this period. Its first three chapters discuss what the Chicago school has since become identified with; research on the city employing a human ecological model borrowed from plant and animal ecology. In chapter 1 Park gives a general introduction to the city and explains how and why the city should be studied; topics include Park's ideas on human ecology, the neighborhood, segregated areas, vocational types, group mobility, the role of social institutions in social control, commercialized vice, party politics, and the moral region. Many of these same topics recur throughout the writings of the Chicago school. In chapter 2 Burgess introduces his ecological model of the city, including a discussion of concentric zones. Chapter 3 introduces McKenzie's ecological approach to the study of the human community, including a discussion of ecological processes.

Throughout the monographs published by the Chicago sociologists can be found two distinct sociological research traditions in their study of social disorganization. The collection of statistical data on deviance from official agencies (the police, the criminal courts, hospitals, and mental institutions) and subsequently plotting the known presence of these deviant populations throughout the various regions of the city represented one tradition. Statistical data and map plotting allowed the researcher to view in what "natural" areas various forms of social disorganization were most prevalent. The second tradition included the securing of personal documents and the life histories. Through the use of personal documents and life histories one was able to get at the subjective side of social life. It was a way to understand social life as experienced by the subjects themselves. This method included in-depth interviews as well as participatory and nonparticipatory observation and the securing of life histories.

STUDIES OF DISORGANIZATIONAL DEVIANCE

The Hobo (1923), by Nels Anderson, is the first in the series of important studies published by the University of Chicago Press in its Sociological Series. The study is one of the early classic ethnographic monographs and a forerunner of the human ecology studies. Ethnography means to literally write about culture; its customs, habits, and traditions. Often this writing is based upon participant observation in which the student lives with and shares in the experiences of the group he or she is studying.

Anderson was well suited for his research on homeless men. As he indicates in his introduction to the 1961 edition of *The Hobo,* he had been a migratory worker for several years; visiting several hobohemias in the western United States. For Anderson (1961), "the role was familiar before the research began" (p. xiii). Anderson had already written term papers on the hobo for his sociology classes that were well received. Because of this he had the opportunity to meet people who were interested in the homeless problem in Chicago. Initially, a small fund came from these interested parties for Anderson to continue his research. Subsequently, additional funding came from the Chicago Council of Social Agencies and the Laura Spelman Rockefeller Foundation.

Anderson's (1923) study of the hobo was partially financed by the Committee on Homeless Men, which "was organized by the Executive Committee of the Chicago Council of Social Agencies on June 16, 1922, to study the problems of the migratory casual worker" (p. xxvii). The purpose of Anderson's study was to help social agencies to understand and to deal with the problems of homeless men (ibid., p. xxvii).

The Hobo is typical of the tradition of Chicago sociology. Several sociological themes, introduced to Anderson by Park and Burgess, are included in *The Hobo.* For example, the area where hobos congregate is called hobohemia, it is a so-called "moral region," a segregated area.

Anderson (1961) remarks, "Every large city has its district into which these homeless types gravitate. In the parlance of the 'road' such a section is known as the 'stem' or 'main drag'" (p. 4). Anderson (1961, p. 4) goes on to say that the hobo, no matter what type (aged, veteran, homeless, drunkard, or radical), always has a friend in hobohemia; someone who will sympathize with and understand the hobo. Hobohemia is located close to the Loop and consists of four parts; west, south, north, and east. Hobohemia, "the 'stem,' is Chicago to the down-and-out" (Anderson 1961, p. 4).

Anderson (1961, pp. 248-49) focuses on the mobility and detachment of the hobo; concepts previously written about by Park. Unlike men who have wealth, homes, material possessions, and families the hobo is without these things. The hobo has no reason to remain stationary. The hobo is not fit for organized social existence and protects himself by moving on when difficulties arise. The hobo is full of wanderlust, "a longing for new experiences" (Anderson 1961, p. 82). This longing results in mobility, change, danger, instability, and social irresponsibility.

Also noteworthy is Anderson's (1961, pp. 87-106) discussion of the various types of homeless men. The hobo is a migratory worker, the tramp is a migratory nonworker, and the bum is the ultimate misfit, inept in every way. In describing the various types of homeless men Anderson has described one of the many urban social worlds which has come to be identified with the type of research carried out by the

Chicago school. In describing a social world the researcher "attempts to portray life as it is experienced by participants in a particular group, community, or institution" (Short 1971, p. xxxv). Like most of the monographs written by the Chicago school there is no detailed explanation of the research methods employed by Anderson. However the method employed by Anderson is known today as participant observation. As Anderson (1961) comments, "I took a room on Halstead Street near Madison, the heart of Hobohemia, and continued my research" (p. xii). In addition, Anderson interviewed hobos and used numerous written sources for his study. Typical of the monographs in the Chicago Series, Anderson's study ends with a summary of his findings and recommendations directed to the agency which funded the research.

Studies of family disorganization presented another focus for urban social research. Mowrer's *Family Disorganization* matches family types to the ecology of the city. Mowrer examines the social disorganization of family life in selected urban areas as well as divorce and desertion rates according to family type and urban area.

Burgess became the department specialist on the sociology of the family. Mowrer one of Burgess's students, undertook his study of family disorganization for his doctoral dissertation, completed in 1924, and subsequently published as *Family Disorganization* in 1927.

Mowrer (1964, p. 500) found five types of areas in Chicago in relation to the nature of the family: nonfamily areas, emancipated family areas, paternal family areas, equalitarian family areas, and maternal family areas. Nonfamily areas are composed of male transients. Emancipated areas are those of casual contacts; rooming-house and hotel residents. Paternal family areas are comprised of immigrant and lower income families where the father is the dominant figure. Equalitarian family areas are comprised of middle-class professionals where equality is a fundamental feature of family living. Maternal family areas are those in which the income-earning father commutes to the central business district where he works and subsequently returns to his suburban residence. Mowrer then placed these areas in the same concentric zones proposed by Burgess. The zone in transition is principally a nonfamily area, the zone of workingmen's homes is a paternal area, the residential zone is an equalitarian family area, and the commuter zone is a maternal family area. Emancipated families follow the line of transportation and therefore cut across all areas. Mowrer also found that the highest rates of desertion (a poor man's divorce) were among the lower classes found in the disorganized areas of the city (the zone in transition). In essence, Mowrer uses statistical data and mapping to document the distribution of family areas with reference to location within the city. These, again, are methods typical of the Chicago school.

There are a variety of racial, ethnic, and religious groups which can be found in the "natural areas" of the city. These so-called ghettos and immigrant colonies are often isolated and segregated in order to cling to their own values, beliefs, and traditions. In the early part of the twentieth century a variety of immigrant groups came to America and settled in the industrial cities of the Northeast and West. These were principally agricultural peoples who departed Europe for the urban cities of America. The Chicago school sociologists were intellectually curious about these immigrant peoples and made them the objects of scientific investigation.

The Jewish communities were of particular interest because they contrasted so vividly with most other ethnic groups. Many European Jews were accustomed to living in large cities in Europe. Therefore, they did not experience the transition from agricultural to city life that was found to be so disorganizing among other nationality groups. Jews, with their centuries of experience living in European ghettos, had developed customs and institutions to insulate themselves from the outside world. They sought to maintain their cultural heritage. Many of their traditions, customs, and institutions were transplanted from Europe to America. Wirth (1928, p. 19) comments that the first Jewish ghettos were voluntary; the Jews believed that by being physically separated and socially isolated it would be easier to practice their religion, customs, and traditions.

Louis Wirth published *The Ghetto* in 1928. Wirth's dissertation was on the same subject. Wirth (1928, p. ix) notes that both Park and Burgess played a major part in his undertaking the study. The book traces the history of the Jews in Europe and their subsequent experiences as immigrants in America, particularly in the city of Chicago. From the standpoint of the Chicago school the Jewish ghetto is significant because it represents one of the "natural areas" of the city. "The ghetto illustrates another phenomenon in local community life, a phenomenon which underlies also the segregation of vice areas, of bright light centers, of bohemias and hobohemias in modern cities" (Wirth 1928, p. 284). Therefore, Wirth undertook his study because it could help to answer questions of sociological interest to the Chicago school. Matters such as the origin of segregated areas and how cultural communities evolve. According to Wirth (1928, p. 4) the ghetto is of interest to sociologists because it is an example of social isolation. It is an attempt on the part of a people to live peacefully among the dominant population. It is, in a sense, a from of accommodation between dominant and subordinate groups. The ghetto also serves as a form of social control. In *The Ghetto*, then, we see a number of the sociological concerns of the Chicago school being addressed.

It was during the 1920s that E. Franklin Frazier commenced his investigations into the sociology of the Negro family. Frazier's first book, *The Negro Family in Chicago*, published in 1932, was developed from Frazier's doctoral dissertation which was supervised by Robert Park.

One objective of Frazier's study was to educate social scientists and the public about the true nature of disorganization of Negro family life. Earlier explanations for the disorganization of Negro family life were felt to be inadequate by Frazier. According to Frazier (1964, p. 404) explanations offered from the biological, sociological, and anthropological schools were inadequate. Biological explanations focused on the sexual desire and childlike mentality of the Negro. Sociological and anthropological explanations blamed African cultural heritage and lack of morality as the causes of Negro family disorganization. Frazier insisted that only through an understanding of the social and cultural history of the Negro family could one understand the true nature of Negro family disorganization. The Negroes were not a homogeneous group. Some were free before the Civil War and some were slaves and an agricultural, rural people. Emancipation, which brought many Negroes to the cities, was a difficult transition, as it was for many European immigrant groups.

The hypothesis which Frazier (1964) tested was that "family disorganization among Negroes was an aspect of the selective and segregative processes of the urban community" (p. 410). To test this hypothesis he employed "Burgess's theory concerning urban expansion which he demonstrated could be measured by rates of change in poverty, home ownership, and other variable conditions for unit areas along the main thoroughfares radiating from the center of the city" (P. 405). In Chicago, the Negro community had expanded southward, from the central city along a main thoroughfare, State Street. This expansion cut across several of the concentric zones introduced by Burgess. It was assumed by Frazier that the process of selection and segregation found in the larger community would also be present in the Negro community. The Negro community, on the basis of census tracts, was divided into seven zones which marked the expansion of the Negro community. Frazier used census tract data and the records of several organizations which provided him with demographic and social characteristics of Negroes in the seven zones. In addition he based his study on interviews and observations of Negroes in these zones. Frazier found that generally as one moved outward from zone I to zone VII family disorganization decreased, thereby confirming his hypothesis.

Related to the research by Wirth, Anderson, and Frazier is that of Pauline V. Young. Like Frazier, Young was influenced by Park. Under Park's guidance Young studied the cultural life of an isolated religious cult in Los Angeles, the Molokans. The Molokans emigrated from a Russian agricultural environment to an American city. Young examines the difficult process of assimilation to American life, including the culture conflicts between the first and second generation of Molokans. Young also traced the process of community disorganization and reorganization among the Molokans (Young 1939, p. 61).

Although Young's approach was essentially descriptive, it involved what has come to be known today as participant observation. This meant that she was to take part in the lives of the members of the community. At the same time she was to remain detached enough as to be objective in her descriptions of and observations of the Molokans. In this way she would gain a complete understanding of the Molokan culture, social world, and inner life (Faris 1970, p. 71).

According to Young (1939, p. 60) the same social situations, social processes, and social problems that confronted other religious and rural groups when emigrating to America were assumed to confront the Molokans. As did Wirth, Young found that social isolation among the Molokans protected them against the disorganizational influences of modern city life. The Molokans, similar to the Amish of Pennsylvania and Ohio today, maintained as much as possible their own dress, language, religion, and customs.

The Pilgrims of Russian-Town, like Anderson's *The Hobo* and Wirth's *The Ghetto*, describes an isolated and segregated social world; also similar were her methods of data collection: participant observation, interviews, statistical data, and the use of historical documents.

Suicide (1928), by Ruth Shonle Cavan, was another important study of disorganization in the 1920s. Influenced by both Park and Burgess, Cavan completed a study on the ecological distribution of suicide in the city of Chicago. Cavan had written several papers on suicide for her sociology classes before completing her doctoral thesis on the same topic. A principal finding of the study was that suicide rates in Chicago were highest in the disorganized areas (hobo and rooming-house districts) and lowest in the most stable areas (residential districts).

Influenced by previous studies of suicide, Cavan believed there was a causal connection between social disorganization and suicide. The question which concerned Cavan was, "Why does an individual commit suicide?" Cavan concluded that individual suicide might be caused by any one of the following three factors: (1) crisis in the life of the individual (e.g., death, divorce, or career failure); (2) weak social controls operating against suicide (e.g., having no close personal attachments to friends, relatives, or the community); and (3) a personality factor that may encourage one to be self-destructive (e.g., the difference between the person who gives up in the case of failure and the person who chooses to move on and try again) (Faris 1970, p. 85). *Suicide* is typical of the Chicago school monographs in that it looks at suicide, a social problem, as a consequence of social disorganization. Furthermore, suicide was found to be ecologically distributed throughout the five concentric zones outlined by Burgess.

Under the guidance of Park, Harvey Zorbaugh published *The Gold Coast and the Slum* in 1929. The book was a best-seller in Chicago. It describes an area of central Chicago known as the Near North Side. The Near North Side is an area of inescapable contrasts (Zorbaugh 1929, p. 6). "The Near North Side has the highest residential land values in the city, and among the lowest, it has more professional men, politicians, more suicides, more persons in Who's Who than any other 'community' in Chicago" (Zorbaugh 1929, p. 6). In the Near North Side there are contrasts between what is native and what is foreign, between wealth and poverty, between vice and respectability, and between the conventional and the bohemian. What Zorbaugh has done throughout his book is give a detailed description of each area in the Near North Side. The first area was the Gold Coast. It is an area of great wealth along the lake shore. Many of these families were listed in the *Chicago Social Register*. These families live and interact among themselves, highly aware of their role in society. Families form cliques and a true sense of "community" is lacking. What binds these families together is an awareness of class. Expensive hotels line the streets in this area.

Behind this wealthy area is the rooming-house area. This location is run-down. Many of the buildings were the former homes of Gold Coast residents. The population is a transient one; where boarders and keepers of rooming-houses change often. Rooms are let to people who are strangers, unconventional folk with no community ties. People do not dine or sit together. Rooming-house keepers do not share in the lives of their boarders. Anonymity is common and social control is lacking. In an environment such as this "there can be no community tradition or common definition of situations, no public opinion, no informal social control" (Zorbaugh 1929, p. 82). To the south the rooming-house area merges with the slum.

Towertown or the Latin Quarter, a bohemian district, is situated to the west and south of the Gold Coast. It is frequented by artists, writers, students, and others who have the freedom to be themselves here. Perhaps in a slightly negative and moralistic tone Zorbaugh (1929) writes of this population as "egocentric poseurs, neurotics, rebels against the conventions of Main Street or the gossip of the foreign community, seekers of atmosphere, dabblers in the occult, dilettantes in the arts, or parties to drab lapses from a moral code which the city has not destroyed" (p. 92). Homosexuality, promiscuous sex, and free love are all part of the reputation of the Latin Quarter.

Bordering on the slum district is the area occupied by hobos or what Zorbaugh called the "Rialto of the half-world." During the day this area just offers cheap stores but it becomes animated at night. In the evening one can see neon-lighted restaurants, pawn shops, cigar stores, cabarets, and dance halls. This is the playground for the hobo, prostitute, peddler, beggar, and small-time criminal. This is the area that Anderson (1923) described as hobohemia and that caters to the needs of the homeless man. Secondhand clothes shops, resale shops, and cheap restaurants were found here.

Finally Zorbaugh describes the slum itself. It is the district which has consecutively housed each new wave of immigrants, the Irish, the Germans, the Swedes, the Sicilians, and the Negroes who were then migrating from the South. Although Zorbaugh's study did not contribute much in the way of human ecology, and social disorganization, he did discuss the natural processes of the slum introduced by Park: expansion, invasion, and succession.

Similar to Wirth and Young, Zorbaugh focuses on the isolation and segregation felt by religious and racial groups and the comfort they experience in being with their own kind. Zorbaugh (1929, p. 141) writes that in the immigrant community the needs and desires of the residents are met through their participation in social and recreational activities. The immigrant who ventures outside the colony feels uncomfortable, like a stranger in an unfamiliar world. Zorbaugh's longing for a much simpler, earlier time also comes through in his discussion of the Near North Side. He writes that the school, church, and political organization have failed to function as proper community institutions. The school and the church have little influence on local life, and political meetings amount to no more than taking orders from a ward boss (Zorbaugh 1929, p. 132).

Zorbaugh used several techniques of investigation in his study of the Near North Side. Like most of the Chicago school he spent little time describing his research methods. Nevertheless his methods included life histories, interviews, official records, observations, and census data.

In *The Taxi-Dance Hall: A Sociological Study of Commercialized Recreation and City Life*, Paul G. Cressey describes the subculture of the taxi-dance hall. Cressey was a caseworker for the Juvenile Protection Association when he undertook his study. The research began in 1925 and the book was published in 1932 (Short 1971, p. xxxv). While a special investigator for the Juvenile Protective Association, he was asked to report on the new phenomenon of what eventually became known as the taxi-dance hall. The taxi-dance hall is a dancing establishment which attracts male patrons who desire social compatibility with a female dance partner. Women dance partners are expected to dance with any patron who pays for their services. Women dancers collect tickets from their patrons and are paid on a commission basis for each ticket they collect. The dance hall served primarily nonfamily men of the rooming-house areas and transients of the city. The dancers were young girls who had little or no employable skills, and who desired the material goods displayed in the shop windows (Cressey 1971, pp. 204-05). Cressey (1971) writes that the taxi-dance hall "is a distinct social world, with its own ways of acting, talking, and thinking. It has its own vocabulary, its own activities and interests, its own conception of what is significant in life, and—to a certain extent—its own scheme of life" (p. 193).

One of the most interesting aspects of the taxi-dance hall is referred to by Cressey (1971, pp. 199-200) as "schemes of life." The schemes of life of the taxi-dance hall are unique to that establishment because of its structure and the interests of its personnel. Schemes of life are representative of what dancers and patrons think are significant, that is, what they want out of the relationship. It is the blending of commercial and romantic interests in the exploitation of the opposite sex. The hall is viewed as a market-place where the dancer will do whatever is necessary to achieve her objectives; generally these include the accumulation of money and personal gifts, whereby the dancer engages in romantic behavior and sensual dancing, if need be, to commercially exploit the men. On the other hand the male patron wants an attractive woman with whom he can socialize with and not necessarily get involved.

Additional topics which fill the pages of *The Taxi-Dance Hall* include the vocabulary of the dance hall establishment, types of alliances with patrons, the exploitation of Oriental men, and the dominance of the taxi-dancer in the hall. As already stated, although Cressey did not use the term, he was describing the subculture of the taxi-dance hall. Subculture is certainly a term familiar to contemporary sociologists. Many fascinating studies have been undertaken by sociologists of deviance on homosexual, prison, police, drug, delinquent, and prostitute subcultures in America. Cressey, like his contemporaries, described life as it was experienced by the participants. Cressey did this through observations, interviews with patrons and dancers, and case records of the Juvenile Protective Association.

Norman Hayner's doctoral thesis "The Hotel: The Sociology of Hotel Life," was the accumulation of a number of term papers on the subject. Park was so pleased with Hayner's work that he encouraged him to publish it as a book, and in 1936 Hayner published *Hotel Life*. The book focuses on the mobility, detachment, and transience of hotel dwellers. In many ways the description of hotel dwellers is similar to Anderson's portrayal of hobos as mobile and detached. For example, Hayner (1964,

p. 314) writes that the hotel dweller is a stranger, isolated and socially distant from the other guests. Hayner also spends a good deal of time describing the various types of hotels and hotel dwellers. His data are based on observation, interviews, and census data. The book gives substance to Park's thoughts on the consequences of mobility and detachment on behavior. Park (1967, p. 40) writing about mobility in the city states that new developments in communication and transportation have made it easier for the city dweller to have contacts with others, but they have also made it easier for these relationships to be casual and temporary. On the other hand relationships in smaller communities are more intimate and personal.

The research undertaken by Walter C. Reckless was closely related to the research on crime and delinquency. Conducted during the 1920s and published as *Vice in Chicago* in 1933, the Reckless research focused on organized prostitution as a social problem, describing the social world of the prostitute and the natural areas in which the prostitute operates. For example, Reckless uses such subtitles as "The Slum as the Habitat of the Brothel," "Unorganized Prostitution in Rooming-Houses," and "Immoral Flats in Apartment-House Areas" to describe the natural areas of the city where commercialized vice (prostitution) takes place.

Reckless notes that vice is a morally isolated activity. Because of this vice has been forced to hide from the moral order of society (Reckless 1971, p. 240), so that it can survive. Vice is found in nonfamily areas where the moral attitudes which condemn it are not found. Areas of commercialized vice can be found in two principle locations within the city, the center and the periphery. The center includes the central business district and the zone of transition, the periphery includes apartment houses as well as single homes. According to Reckless (1971, p. 240), vice meets with little opposition in these areas because the inner city is a disintegrating one which can not fend off the invasion of vice resorts and the periphery has few settlers, clings to a rural culture, and is unorganized—all of which makes it a suitable area for commercialized vice.

Like his colleagues, Reckless framed the study of vice within the assumption of social disorganization. Commercialized vice was found to exist where other social problems such as poverty, suicide, divorce, and desertion were found. "Indeed, these problems, considered ecologically, indicate the areas of greatest social disorganization within the city" (Reckless 1971, p. 246). Therefore, in keeping with the tradition of Chicago sociology, Reckless is interested in the spatial and ecological distribution of prostitution in the natural areas of the city (Reckless 1971, pp. 239-51). The association between organized commercialized vice and organized crime was not a principal topic of the Reckless research. However, he does pay some attention to the fact that commercialized vice and crime are both forms of activity that "are legally and morally isolated and consequently must hide in the disorganized neighborhoods in order to thrive" (Reckless 1971, p. 246). The distribution of crime and vice within the urban community are generally identical (Reckless 1971, p. 245).

Reckless's data collection methods were typical of his colleagues: archives, newspapers, newspaper files, and records of various agencies that dealt with vice and prostitution.

STUDIES OF CRIME AND DELINQUENCY

The Chicago school of sociology included four leading criminologists: Frederic M. Thrasher, Clifford R. Shaw, Henry D. McKay, and Edwin H. Sutherland. Their perspectives on delinquency were influenced by the sociologists who were at the University of Chicago prior to and during the time that these men were conducting their research. For example, Thrasher, Shaw, and McKay were heavily influenced by the theory of social disorganization introduced by Thomas and Park's notion of ecological processes in the expansion of the city. Sutherland, however, was influenced by only some aspects of the Chicago school and therefore has a distinct place among the Chicago school sociologists. Because Sutherland completed his doctoral dissertation in 1913, before Park came to Chicago and before Thomas completed his work on *The Polish Peasant in Europe and America*, Sutherland was less influenced by them. Yet, as a teacher at Chicago from 1930 to 1935, Sutherland was influenced by Wirth's notions of culture conflict as a cause of crime and Shaw and McKay's notion of social disorganization. Thorsten Sellin, a non-Chicagoan also influenced Sutherland's thinking. Together Sutherland and Sellin published *Culture Conflict and Crime* in 1938 (Kornhauser 1979, pp. 27-28).

Sociologist Karl Schuessler (1973, pp. x-xi), a former student of the late E. H. Sutherland, and others (cf. Hall 1950; Mueller 1950; Vold 1951; Snodgrass 1972; Gaylord 1984) have provided academic histories of Sutherland's career. Sutherland received his bachelor's degree from Grand Island College (Nebraska) in 1903. In 1906 he enrolled as a graduate student at the University of Chicago. At the University of Chicago Sutherland was under the influence of Charles Henderson, Albion Small, and W. I. Thomas. In Sutherland's theory of criminal behavior (differential association) we can see a hint of Thomas's interactionist sociology. Sutherland's research methods are also representative of the Chicago school of sociology. Sutherland received his doctorate in sociology in 1913. He returned to Chicago in 1930 as a professor/researcher, where he remained until 1935. He then moved on to Indiana University as head of the sociology department.

Sutherland is well-known among sociological criminologists because of his criminology textbook *Principles*, his theory of differential association, and his concept of white-collar crime. Sutherland's official entry into the field of criminology is marked by his publication of *Criminology*, as the first edition of *Principles* was titled (Schuessler 1973, p. xii). However, in keeping with the subject matter of this chapter, we will discuss Sutherland's publications while he was an active member of the Chicago school.

Edwin H. Sutherland and Harvey J. Locke conducted a study of men on relief and produced *Twenty Thousand Homeless Men: A Study of Unemployed Men in Chicago Shelters* in 1936. They looked at men who were housed in abandoned schools, warehouses, and factories during the Depression. The study was authorized by the Illinois Emergency Relief Commission on January 15, 1934. It was a rather large study comprised of eight sociologists, four psychiatrists, two statisticians, and nine clerks and stenographers. Sutherland was the director of the project. Salaries were paid by the Illinois Emergency Relief Commission. Additional expenses were paid by the Social Science Research Committee (Sutherland 1936, p. v).

Life histories were obtained from men housed in the shelters. The life histories resembled the "own story" format favored by Chicago school criminologist Clifford Shaw. Some of the researchers lived in the shelters with the men. Speaking about the data collection methods, Sutherland and Locke (1936) comment, "Because verbatim reports are an indispensable means of securing insight into attitudes, such records occupy a considerable part of this book" (p. vi).

The book is principally a description of shelter men, their backgrounds and experiences and the consequences of "shelterization." The authors offer little in the way of analysis and do not address possible solutions to the problem. In this respect the book was not like most of the monographs written by the Chicago school, which offered recommendations for the amelioration of the problem under investigation.

Sutherland received funds from the Social Science Research Committee to conduct an investigation of the professional thief. *The Professional Thief* was published in 1937 and is a well-known work in the field of criminology. Sutherland was the author of *The Professional Thief* in much the same way Shaw was the author of *The Jack-Roller*. The subjects wrote down their experiences for the authors. Shaw's objective was to produce the Jack-Roller's "own story." However, this objective was not shared by Sutherland in *The Professional Thief*. Sutherland utilized "Chic Conwell," not to create an autobiography or case study, but to produce a monograph about the profession of theft. Sutherland (1937) writes:

> The profession of theft is more than isolated acts of theft frequently and skillfully performed. It is a group-way of life and a social institution. It has techniques, codes, status, traditions, consensus, organization. It has an existence as real as that of the English language. It can be studied with relatively little attention to any particular thief. The profession can be understood by a description of the functions and relationships involved in this way of life. (p. ix-x)

Thus, Sutherland was not concerned, as much, with his subject's background and entrance into a world of crime, as he was with describing professional thieves' activities, techniques, argot, and social world. In fact, Sutherland (1937) described the book as a "document" which "is a description of the profession of theft as experienced by one professional thief" (pp. vi-vii).

Sutherland was aware that his subject may have been biased in his reporting and therefore supplemented his experiences by submitting the manuscript to four other professional thieves and two former detectives. Without submitting the manuscript he also discussed the ideas and problems of the book with several other professional thieves and several other police professionals. According to Sutherland (1937) "these supplementary sources did not even hint at disagreement with the manuscript on fundamental issues" (p. viii).

Pages 222 through 226 of Sutherland's book discusses how social disorganization perpetuates the profession of theft through graft and collusion. This was a strong admission to make at the time, criticizing the society of which one is part. But his criticisms came more from the right of the political spectrum. Sutherland's rural Baptist roots aligned him with the right, not the left. Perhaps otherwise he would have challenged the structure of a society which would allow graft and corruption to perpetuate crime. Furthermore, Sutherland believed that crime was unrelated to class and economic conditions. In other words, crime could be found among all social classes. Poverty was not the only cause of crime!

Although Sutherland's theory of differential association was not completed at the time *The Professional Thief* was published, Sutherland does discuss this concept in the book. Sutherland (1937, pp. 206-07) writes that professional thieves are recognized and defined as such by other professional thieves and thus are defined by their differential associations. Although these professional thieves are segregated, they are at the same time, part of the larger social order.

Sutherland, like many of the Chicago sociologists, was describing a social world, made up of contacts and relationships. The similarities with the Chicago school ends here. As previously indicated, Sutherland was not as interested in the boy's "own story" as was Shaw. Sutherland's book seemed to lack the subjectiveness which is needed to tell the boy's "own story."

Under the guidance of Park and Burgess, Frederic Thrasher undertook a study of adolescent gangs in the city of Chicago. The study, completed in 1926, became Thrasher's doctoral dissertation and in 1927 was published as *The Gang: A Study of 1,313 Gangs in Chicago*. The study has been referred to as a "classic." Thrasher was interested not only in the gang per se, but in "gangland," that is, the environment in which gang boys hang out and interact. In the editor's preface Park (1963) comments, "The title of this book does not quite describe it. It is a study of the gang, to be sure, but it is at the same time a study of 'gangland'; that is to say, a study of the gang and its habitat, and in this case the habitat is a city slum" (p. vii). It was thought that gangs, like other forms of human association should be studied in its natural habitat. The slum is the habitat of a variety of individuals; hobos, gang boys, and immigrants all dwell here. Thrasher (1963) gives the following definition of gang:

> The gang is an interstitial group originally formed spontaneously, and integrated through conflict. It is characterized by the following types of behavior: meeting face to face, milling, movement through space as a unit, conflict and planning. The result of this collective behavior is the development of tradition, unreflective internal structure, esprit de corps, solidarity, morale, group awareness, and attachment to local territory. (p. 46)

Thrasher's focus was predominantly on juvenile gangs. Utilizing Burgess's chart showing the development of the city, Thrasher notes that gangs were predominantly found in the zone of transition. "The central tripartite empire of the gang occupies what is often called 'the poverty belt'—a region characterized by deteriorating neighborhoods, shifting populations, and the mobility and disorganization of the slum" (Thrasher 1963, p. 20). According to Thrasher (1963, pp. 20-21) gangland is a product of human ecology. As individuals abandon this area for better homes in the residential area and as business and industry encroach upon the area, the gang forms as one indication of the economic, moral, and cultural frontier which marks the interstice (the empty spaces between one area and another).

Thrasher believed that social disorganization (the weakening of social controls) made ganging possible. Like others in the theoretical tradition of the Chicago school, Thrasher explains that rapid social changes have taken place without the corresponding controls, and therefore the social order is upset. No longer is there a social code agreed upon by all members of society. Rapid changes, including urbanization, industrialization, immigration, and mobility have resulted in a high degree of disorganization which manifests itself in vice, crime, political corruption, and other social ills. These societal ills are either located in the suburban fringes or in the poverty region where they can go on without the control that is found in other areas of the city. Ganging is one manifestation of community disorganization. "Disorganized conditions do not directly produce gangs, but the gang is an interstitial growth, flowering where other institutions are lacking or failing to function effectively" (Thrasher 1963, p. 342). In the boys' gang the boys find the human needs that are not met in the community (fellowship, status, excitement, and security).

Thrasher's study is also significant because it was the first effort by a sociologist to describe and explain the nature of organized crime. The other important study of organized crime during this period was John Landesco's *Organized Crime in Chicago*, the focus of chapters 4 and 5. Although the principal focus of the Thrasher study was on adolescent gangs, he did include one chapter on "The Gang and Organized Crime." Thrasher's interest in organized crime centered on how youths became adult members of criminal gangs. According to Thrasher, youthful criminals were adult criminals in the making. The adult criminal's career had its beginning in the boys' gang. Thrasher (1963) explains that "The adult criminal gang, which is, as a rule, largely composed of men in their early twenties, carries on traditions thoroughly established in the adolescent group. . . . It is clear, therefore, that crime, in so far as it is facilitated by the gang, can only be understood by following it to its roots and beginnings in the boys' gang" (p. 281).

According to Thrasher (1963, pp. 287-88) the members of the adult criminal gangs were often the criminal residue of boys' gangs; meaning that while some young men who were members of boys' gangs become reincorporated into family and community life, a good number of these boys do not. Thrasher (1963) explains that these boys are "victims of peculiar combinations of circumstances which make social adjustment difficult" (p. 288). Generally, it is because these boys possess criminal records and have experienced institutionalization that they gravitate toward crime. These boys become "habituated to a life of crime" and "continue to attach themselves to criminal groups" (Thrasher 1963, p. 288). "Organized crime, manifesting itself in gangs . . . , may be regarded as the result of a process of sifting and selection whose final product is a criminal residue" (Thrasher 1963, p. 288). It is this residue that constitutes a large part of the criminal community (the underworld).

Some significant conclusions can be drawn from Thrasher's observations: (1) individuals become criminals because of life circumstances and not by choice; and (2) organized criminals are products of their environments and not products of Italy, Sicily, Ireland, or Poland. In other words, ethnic roots are not a deciding factor in criminality. As the criminologist Dwight Smith remarks in his *The Mafia Mystique* (1975, p. 76), Thrasher did not identify ethnicity as a master trait of the organized criminal. It is also important to note that Thrasher (1963) identified organized crime as "an area of life and activity characterized by the absence of ordinary conventions" (p. 284). Organized crime is a criminal community, a moral region, which could be identified by the hangouts of the gangs: street corners, poolrooms, roadhouses, saloons, and cabarets (Thrasher 1963, p. 285). When Thrasher spoke of organized crime he was not referring to a specific group of identifiable people but to the environment or social world of the gangster or racketeer. As indicated in chapter 1, above, definitions of organized crime have changed over time. Thrasher's original meaning of organized crime has been lost. Today, for most ordinary citizens, organized crime is tied to identifiable ethnic groups and is defined more by the activities of these gangsters than by where these gangsters hang out. As chapters 4 and 5 will document, Landesco shared many of Thrasher's liberal theories in respect to organized crime Thrasher (1963, p. 285) felt that the organization of the criminal community was fluid. New alliances and alignments were easily made for criminal exploits and were just as easily broken when parties no longer shared the same interests. This view is remarkably similar to some contemporary scholars who have concluded that organized crime is made up of locally situated ethnic groups who come together when they share a particular interest and break apart when these newly formed alliances are no longer expedient (cf. Albini 1971; Ianni 1972; Abadinsky 1981). Yet Thrasher also noted a certain degree of organization among the criminal community. Organization in the underworld consisted of a division of labor. At the top were the criminal entrepreneurs—the gangsters. Criminal entrepreneurs depended on functional middlemen who performed special services for the gangs. Thrasher (1963, p. 286) includes fences (those who deal in stolen goods), doctors, hospitals, political fixers, shrewd lawyers, corrupt officials and obligated bail bondsmen as those who may be called upon for special functions.

Thrasher (1963, pp. 289-91) also noted the difference between the earlier gangs and the more contemporary criminal gangs. Earlier gangs were interested in protecting their turf while contemporary gangsters were interested in economic motives and business technique.

Thrasher's (and Landesco's) analysis of organized crime is significant because it did not blame organized crime on ethnicity or on any alien conspiracy theory, but on economics. Organized crime did not have a formal structure but was made up of an informal network of relationships. The views of Thrasher and Landesco are still being debated in academic circles today. Their views on organized crime were not popular among law enforcement officials at the time and are still not accepted by this community today. Finally, Thrasher (1963, pp. 297-300) distinguished between the various types of adult criminal gangs. There were many ordinary gangs who engaged primarily in ordinary robberies and burglaries. And then there were the powerful master gangs. It was the master gangs who were predominantly interested in the illicit liquor industry, vice, and gambling.

Thrasher's interest in "The Gang and Organized Crime," then, lies predominantly in the transition of young gang members into adult gang members and the role of the gang in promoting organized crime. It is through the gang that members are trained, mobilized, and organized. The adult criminal gang is often just an extension of the adolescent gang. Thrasher (1963) writes that "The gang, . . . , while it is not the only element in organized crime, plays an important part in the mobilization of the criminal and the organization of the criminal community" (p. 291).

Thrasher, like most of the Chicago school sociologists, did not elaborate on his techniques of data collection. However, we do know that he used observation, personal documents collected from gang boys, and census and court records in his analysis of adolescent gangs. His book gave substance to the usefulness of the human ecology and social disorganization perspective in explaining how gangs evolve.

Clifford R. Shaw and Henry D. McKay were both born in the rural midwestern part of the United States. These two farm boys hailed from Indiana and South Dakota respectively. After graduating from small sectarian colleges, they came to the University of Chicago in the 1920s to undertake graduate study in sociology. The two men became collaborators in delinquency research at the Institute for Juvenile Research where Shaw was research director. Prior to the 1920s juvenile delinquency had been little studied. The work of Shaw and McKay gave substance to an empirical American sociology.

Shaw and McKay examined crime and delinquency within the Park-Burgess ecological model of the city. Shaw and McKay combined both quantitative (statistical) and qualitative (life histories) methods in their work. At the time there was an ongoing debate about which methods produced the best research results, and the work of Shaw and McKay demonstrated how both methods complemented each other. These two methods involved plotting the geographical distribution of delinquents in urban areas on maps and the collection of life histories from individual delinquents. "The life-history is the person's own account of his experiences, written as an autobiography, as a diary, or presented in the course of a series of interviews" (Burgess and Bogue 1964, p. 600). Such documents are recorded in the first person, in the subject's own words.

Shaw and his colleagues published *Delinquency Areas* in 1929. It is a classic in the study of social disorganization and delinquency. The research was based on 55,998 juvenile court records compiled over a period of approximately thirty years. There were two principal findings in *Delinquency Areas*: (1) the highest rates of delinquency were found in the zone of transition (slums) and these rates decreased as one moved outward toward the commuter zone; (2) regardless of the changing ethnic or racial composition of the zone of transition it consistently had the highest rates of delinquency.

Shaw and McKay concluded that delinquency could be explained through an examination of social disorganization. The zone of transition, where delinquency rates were high, also had the highest rates of social disorganization: mental illness, alcoholism, poverty, and a large percentage of foreign-born residents were all found in this area. While these pathologies did not directly cause crime, they did make social norms ineffective. In the absence of adequate social norms, crime and delinquency were free to flourish. The research of Shaw and McKay also led them to conclude that a delinquent tradition is transmitted from one generation to another. If a community has a delinquent tradition and an absence of social controls than delinquency is likely. Later researchers have referred to this criminogenic process as the theory of "cultural transmission." In *Delinquency Areas* Shaw and McKay (1929) discuss this criminogenic process, "Delinquency and criminal patterns arise and are transmitted socially just as any other cultural and social pattern is transmitted. In time these delinquent patterns may become dominant and shape the attitudes and behavior of persons living in the area. Thus the section becomes an area of delinquency" (p. 206). This notion of a delinquent tradition was influential in the subsequent "subcultural" hypotheses of Albert Cohen (1955) and Walter Miller (1958). In fact, although they did not define it as such, Shaw and McKay were describing what criminologists today would call a "delinquent subculture."

Social Factors in Juvenile Delinquency, published by Shaw and McKay in 1931, was originally in a report prepared for the Wickersham Crime Commission (1931). The publication is an elaboration of the data and findings in *Delinquency Areas*. The book includes such topics as the origins of criminal behavior, the geographical location of delinquency, the social world of the delinquent, the activities and traditions of delinquent boys, and the relationship between delinquency and broken homes (which appears to be the only new material).

The life history or personal document approach was favored by Shaw. Influenced by Thomas, that society must be studied from both the objective and subjective aspects of social life, Shaw believed that the subjective aspects of juvenile delinquency could best be uncovered through the life history method. "So far as we have been able to determine as yet, the best way to investigate the inner world of the person is through a study of himself, through a life-history" (Shaw 1929, p. 9). Shaw and McKay agreed with Thomas that all phenomena should be examined from both the individual and group aspects. Therefore, Thomas blended both sociology and social psychology in his work, as did Shaw and McKay. From the group or society level they examined the changes which were rapidly taking place around them; in particular they plotted their maps showing the geographical distribution of delinquency in Chicago. On the other hand, from a social psychological or individual perspective they collected life histories to understand how one becomes a delinquent.

Shaw collected a variety of life histories throughout his career and three were eventually published as books: *The Jack-Roller* (1930), *The Natural History of A*

Delinquent Career (1931), and *Brothers in Crime* (1938). Two of these books are briefly discussed here. The individual who specializes in jack-rolling robs drunken hobos on skid row (Burgess and Bogue 1964, p. 601). *The Jack-Roller* is a case study of a young male of Polish parentage whom Shaw called Stanley. The book tells of Stanley's life as a delinquent from age sixteen to twenty-two. *The Natural History of A Delinquent Career* is similar to *The Jack-Roller* in that it involved a young man also of Polish heritage. Again, the book details the crimes of the delinquent which escalated from shoplifting and truancy to rape. The book examines the realities of an offender's life and the public's outrage over a case of rape (Bennett 1981, p. 187).

Overall, the Chicago school criminologists made several contributions in the field of crime and deviance: Thrasher's early social disorganization theories, Shaw and McKay's social control and subcultural theories, and Sutherland's interactionist concepts of differential association and white-collar crime (Kurtz 1984, p. 72). The work of these criminologists, however, is not identified with the study of organized crime. In fact, the work of the Chicago school criminologists is primarily associated with the study of delinquency, not adult criminality.

The Chicago School of Urban Sociology: Some Concluding Remarks

This chronological documentation illustrates many of the distinguishing characteristics of Chicago sociology, including their theoretical, methodological, and ideological orientations. The monographs selected for illustration, with the exception of the published works of Sutherland, were all written by graduate students in the department of sociology during the 1920s and 1930s. Generally, both objective and subjective methods were employed. The monographs were more descriptive than analytical and reflected the intellectual thinking of Park and/or Burgess. Each monograph was directed at a particular audience and recommendations were suggested for the amelioration of the problem being addressed.

In 1892, the University of Chicago established the first graduate department of sociology. Subsequently the task fell upon the founders to define the scope and methods of an emerging discipline. The city of Chicago, during this period, was a shining example of industrial growth and capitalism. On the other hand, Chicago became a city of immigrants and a city besieged by social problems. Social problems were viewed as analogous to a disease, as a pathological condition affecting the social landscape. The condition could be improved if the appropriate treatment was administered. There was little disagreement as to what was "normal" and what was a "problem." Social problems were topics for the new science of sociology developing at the University of Chicago in the 1920s. These problems could be studied empirically and objectively. The social survey movement had been launched. It was a movement that emphasized the objective collection of facts (Burgess and Bogue 1964, p. 488). It was believed "that scientific sociological research could produce knowledge which could be put to practical use by welfare workers to arrive at, improve, or remedy the conditions regarded as pathological" (Burgess and Bogue 1964, p. 488).

A major contribution of the Chicago school during the 1920s and 1930s was its theory of social disorganization and its view of social change and social problems. When individuals are inadequately socialized by existing social institutions and the community, then social solidarity and social controls are weakened. The theory of social disorganization did an excellent job of explaining the social problems of the day. The communities in the city were filled with ethnic immigrants who left their old established customs behind and who, in America, had not yet adopted new ways of adjusting to the American social landscape. The city lacked social organization and disorganization was common. But disorganization could disappear when social reorganization took place, for example, accommodation and assimilation. Social problems were viewed as temporary consequences of social change (Burgess and Bogue 1964, p. 458). Immigrants, therefore, needed to adopt the social values of the larger American society. There was a tendency on the part of the Chicago school sociologists to support the status quo. Their social policy reflected this view. Disorganized communities and individuals could be reformed through proper human intervention. Effective social controls (church, family, schools) were seen as one way to improve a disorganized community. According to Robert Park social control was the pivotal problem of sociology, and the study of social control consisted of a "description and analysis of specific aspects of deviant or otherwise socially defined problem behavior" (Short 1971, p. xxxix). What was considered to be deviant or otherwise socially defined problem behavior? The answer for the Chicago school sociologists included ethnic immigrants, racial and religious minorities, hobos, patrons of hotels, taxi-dance halls, and vice resorts, victims of suicide and family disorganization, juvenile delinquents, and homeless men. This group of so-called deviants confirms Thio's (1973) argument that sociologists of deviance have, for the most part, concentrated their research efforts on powerless individuals and their surrounding habitats. In fact, the organized and highly public phenomenon of racketeering and gangsterism did not figure as paramount to either the study of the city or of crime. This is quite remarkable considering how visible mobsters and gangsters had become in the city of Chicago where United States sociology was born. Because organized crime was so much a part of the environment of Chicago, it was taken for granted by the Chicago school sociologists. It existed in response to a profitable illegal market and there was nothing that could be done about it. The Chicago school sociologists did not see the strange in the familiar. Organized crime was not identified as a social problem that could be eliminated by human intervention but as a political problem that was not correctable. In fact, it was easier for the Chicago school sociologists to view organized crime in this manner because they did not have access to the social world of organized crime and organized criminals. Apparently the theory and methods of the Chicagoans, while well suited for the description and analysis of urban social problems, were not adaptable for studying organized crime. Organized crime was not open to sociological scrutiny, to the case study method (Kobrin, personal communication, June 1, 1991).

Chronological comparison:
organized crime and studies of deviance and crime

Table 1 below illustrates the extent to which the critical public events in the history of Chicago's organized crime coincided with the studies of crime and deviance by the Chicago school sociologists. It is apparent from the chronologies

Table 1. Comparative chronology of critical public events in Chicago's organized crime and classic works in deviance and crime by the Chicago school sociologists

ORGANIZED CRIME		CLASSIC WORKS IN DEVIANCE AND CRIME	
1870	Syndicate of Mike McDonald		
1890	Murder of Chief Hennessey Black Hand Crimes Escalate		
1914	Syndicate of James Colosimo		
		1918	Thomas and Znaniecki, *The Polish Peasant*
1920	Passage of Prohibition Murder of Colosimo		
		1923	Anderson, *The Hobo*
1924	Sieben Brewery Raid Murder of Dion O' Banion Gang Wars Escalate		
		1925	Park and Burgess, *The City*
1926	Murder of Hymie Weiss		
1927	Murder of Vincent Drucci	1927	Thrasher, *The Gang* Mowrer, *Family Disorganization*
1928	Capone Moves into Large-Scale Racketeering. Murder of Spike O' Donnell	1928	Wirth, *The Ghetto* Cavan, *Suicide*
1929	St. Valentine's Day Massacre Gang Convention Held in Atlantic City, N.J. Ness and the Untouchables Move Against Capone Breweries	1929	Shaw and McKay, *Delinquency Areas* Zorbaugh, *The Gold Coast and the Slum*
		1930	Shaw, *The Jack-Roller*
1931	Conference Hosted by Capone at the Congress Hotel	1931	Shaw, *The Natural History of A Delinquent Career* Shaw, *Social Factors in Juvenile Delinquency*
1932	Capone Enters Federal Prison	1932	Young, *The Pilgrims of Russian-Town* Cressey, *The Taxi-Dance Hall* Frazier, *The Negro Family in Chicago*
1933	Repeal of Prohibition	1933	Reckless, *Vice in Chicago*
1934	National Crime Confederation Organized		
		1935	Sutherland, *Twenty Thousand Homeless Men*
		1936	Hayner, *Hotel Life*
		1937	Sutherland, *The Professional Thief*

presented here that organized crime and Chicago sociology were each developing simultaneously and in different directions. Organized crime was not, in itself, a topic of sociological inquiry for the Chicago school sociologists. As previously mentioned, when organized crime was discussed in Thrasher (1927), it was in terms of the evolutionary process of juvenile gangs into adult criminal gangs. Some of these adult criminal gangs, the master gangs, specialized in organized criminal activities. Thus Thrasher's focus was limited to the role of the gang in organized crime. Reckless (1933) discussed organized crime only in terms of its ecological and spatial dimensions, which were often identical to the areas of commercialized vice in the city.

Summarizing, the Chicago school sociologists produced case studies of lower-class deviants and delinquents. They explored the moral worlds of these groups. They had access to these groups and therefore were able to implement the case study method. On the other hand, there was a good deal of social and behavioral distance between Chicago sociologists and the gangsters and racketeers they read about in the newspapers or saw on the movie screens. However, the Chicago school sociologists knew a great deal about the environment of crime they were working in. For example, in the summary and recommendations of Landesco's (1968) *Organized Crime in Chicago*, Burgess remarks that "All intelligent readers of newspapers in Chicago know that for years there has been a succession of exposes of crime, of vice, of gambling, of bootlegging and of graft, and likewise a series of crusades against those evils, with little or no permanent effect" (p. 277). Moreover, others (Abadinsky 1981b; p. 10; Woodiwiss 1987) have noted that Al Capone loved publicity. Virtually immune from prosecution, Capone and his contemporaries often gave press interviews about their activities.

James Cary (1975) in conducting the research for his book *Sociology and Public Affairs* interviewed twenty-five sociologists who were part of the Chicago school during the 1920s. In a personal interview with Edgar Thompson, on March 27, 1972, Thompson commented:

> We talked sociology from morning till night . . . Those were the days of Big Bill Thompson, Big Bill the builder . . . We read the newspapers, we knew what was going on. There was a good deal of gangsterism, you know, and except insofar as Thrasher and Landesco were bringing back stuff about this, I don't recall much about this either. . . . It was brought back, but it was not brought back in the context of immediate action, immediate politics, or immediate political concerns. (p. 155)

This passage by Edgar Thompson implies that the Chicago school sociologists knew organized crime existed, and that existence was taken for granted; with that, attention turned to other matters. The variety of theoretical, ideological, methodological, and political explanations for the lack of academic attention organized crime received from the Chicago sociologists will be explored more fully in subsequent chapters.

NOTES

1. See John Landesco. 1968. "The Rule of the Underworld: Tennes as Vice Chief." Pp. 45-83 in *Organized Crime in Chicago*.
2. Between the period 1921 to 1933 the following monographs were published by the University of Chicago Press in its Sociological Series: Robert E. Park and Ernest W. Burgess, *Introduction to the Science of Sociology* (1921); Nels Anderson, *The Hobo* (1923); Robert Park and Ernest Burgess, *The City* (1925); E. W. Burgess, ed., *The Urban Community*, Charles William Margold, *Sex, Freedom and Social Control*, and the LCRC's *Social Base Map of Chicago* (all 1926); Lyford Edwards, *The History of the Revolution*, Ernest Mowrer, *Family Disorganiztion*, Frederic Thrasher, *The Gang*, and Harry Emerson Wildes, *Social Currents in Japan* (all 1927); Ruth Shonle Cavan, *Suicide*, Ernest J. Hiller, *The Strike*, Ernest Mowrer, *Domestic Discord*, and Louis Wirth, *The Ghetto* (all 1928); E. W. Burgess. ed., *Personality and the Social Group*, Frances Donovan, *The Saleslady*, and Harvey Zorbaugh, *The Gold Coast and the Slum* (all 1929); Albert B. Blumenthal, *Small Town Stuff, Paul G. Cressey,* The Taxi-Dance Hall, E. Franklin Frazier, *The Negro Family in Chicago*, Pauline V. Young, *The Pilgrims of Russian-Town*, (all 1932); and Walter Reckless, *Vice in Chicago* (1933) (see Bulmer 1984, p. 257).
3. Faris (1970, p. 32) lists Park, Burgess, Farris, and Small as the regular departmental faculty at Chicago in 1920. In addition he lists the following people as either instructors and/or students in the department during the 1920s: Scott Bedford, Louis Wirth, Herbert Blumer, Carl Dawson, E.T. Krueger, Frederic Thrasher, Eyler N. Simpson, Nels Anderson, Clifford Shaw, Walter Reckless, Andrew Lind, Ernest Mowrer, William Byron, Harry Sell, E. H. Shideler, John H. Mueller, Samuel Kincheloe, Erle Fisk Young, Norman Hayner, Ruth Shonle, George Vold, Willard Waller, Helen McGill, Harvey Zorbaugh, L. Guy Brown, Floyd House, Charles S. Johnson, Jesse F. Steiner, R. D. McKenzie, Earl Johnson, Robert Redfield, Everett Stonequist, Howard Paul Becker, James A. Quinn, E. Franklin Frazier, Carroll D. Clark, Edgar T. Thompson, Philip M. Hauser, Richard A. Lang, John Dollard, Paul G. Cressey, Paul F. Cressey, Ellen Black, and Clarence Glick.

4

John Landesco:
Chicago school sociologist

T HE FOCUS of this chapter is John Landesco, a graduate student in the
Department of Sociology at the University of Chicago from 1924 to 1929, and
his major work *Organized Crime in Chicago*. The study is the one notable
exception to the absence of any major studies of organized crime in American
sociology during the heyday of organized crime in the city of Chicago. However, the
principal importance of Landesco's study is not the fact that it was written. More
important is its "career" in American sociology. It was almost entirely overlooked
by the Chicago school sociologists and others working in sociology after them. In
fact it was not widely known at all until its separate publication by the University
of Chicago Press in 1968.

We must then raise the question why a study on such an important and timely
subject was not viewed as an important work by the Chicago school sociologists.
Among others, there are three possible explanations: (1) John Landesco was a
marginal member of the Department of Sociology at the University of Chicago and
his work was considered inconsequential; (2) the study was viewed as either an
inadequate or minor work of sociological research; and (3) the study was suppressed.

In order to explore these possible explanations it is first necessary to examine
Landesco's early history and academic career and his affiliation with three institutions, the Illinois Association for Criminal Justice, the Department of Sociology at
the University of Chicago, and the American Institute of Criminal Law and
Criminology. It will also be necessary to examine the public and professional impact
of the *Illinois Crime Survey* and Landesco's section of the *Survey*, including Landesco's
theoretical orientation and research methodology. Finally, we will return to our
possible explanations of why Landesco's research was overlooked by the Chicago
school sociologists. We will then draw some tentative conclusions by examining the
documentary evidence presented in this chapter.

Landesco's early history and academic career[1]

In the introduction to Landesco's *Organized Crime in Chicago*, historian Mark Haller (1968, pp. xiv-xvii) provides a biographical sketch of Landesco's early history and academic career. John Landesco, a Romanian Jew, was born in Piatra, Romania, on June 15, 1890. The family settled in an immigrant community on Chicago's West Side. They stayed there for a short time and then moved on to Milwaukee. Landesco studied in the public schools of Chicago and Milwaukee. He completed high school at the Milwaukee University School. His father was the owner and operator of a grocery store which also served as a gathering place.

Landesco attended the University of Wisconsin in the fall of 1907. He remained at the university for only one and one-half years. Subsequently he moved to Cincinnati, Ohio, to live with his brother. In Cincinnati he went to school to learn banking and took a job at the immigrant bank where his brother was director. After a few years of involvement with immigrant banks in Cincinnati and later Indianapolis, he returned to Milwaukee. During much of the period between 1915 and 1922, Landesco was an assistant to the director of vocational education in the Milwaukee school system. During World War I he served as a naval officer. After the war he became director of the Abraham Lincoln Settlement in Milwaukee, a post he held for one year.

Landesco's relationship with the University of Chicago began in 1922, when, at the age of thirty-two, he enrolled to complete his undergraduate education. In 1924, he earned his bachelor's degree with honors in sociology. Shortly thereafter, Landesco became a graduate student in the Department of Sociology at the University of Chicago. He remained a full-time or part-time student through the summer of 1929. At the time, the University of Chicago provided the best sociological training available.

It was also during this time that Landesco began his research into organized crime in the city of Chicago. Landesco held a grant from the Local Community Research Committee of the University of Chicago, from 1925 to 1927, to help fund his research. Simultaneously, he became the research director for the American Institute of Criminal Law and Criminology, which was founded in 1909 to stimulate both academic and scientific interest in crime (Sellin and England 1956, p. 120).

Landesco was well suited for his study of organized crime. As a Romanian Jew who grew up in an immigrant community, he was sympathetic to the needs and concerns of the immigrants in the city. Through his research efforts Landesco became acquainted with a number of prominent gangsters. Some of these men made newspaper headlines through their involvement in gang warfare. He was forthright with his research subjects and the police, and they cooperated by giving Landesco the help he needed (Faris 1970, p. 78).

Landesco interrupted his studies of organized crime when, in 1927 and 1928, he became a research associate in a study investigating the probation and parole system of Illinois. There was a request from the Parole Board of Illinois to the presidents of Illinois, Chicago, and Northwestern universities to take up a study on the workings of the indeterminate sentence law and of parole in the state of Illinois. A three-man committee was established consisting of Albert J. Harno, dean of the Law School at the University of Illinois, Andrew A. Bruce, former judge and president of the American Institute of Criminal Law and Criminology, and Ernest W. Burgess, sociologist at the University of Chicago. John Landesco and Clark Tibbits, two of Burgess's students, were employed by Burgess as research assistants. On the strength of this work, Landesco would become a member of the Illinois Parole Board in 1933. The use of graduate students as research assistants was critical to the development of the Department of Sociology at the University of Chicago. As documented in chapter 3, these graduate students/research assistants were responsible for a number of important monographs published by the Chicago school of sociology during the 1920s and early 1930s. It was hoped that students would be provided with the opportunity to gain a doctorate and to engage in research of considerable scientific interest (Bulmer 1984, p. 125, pp. 145-46).

Bulmer (1984, p. 125) writes that Burgess's chapter on parole prediction was the best recalled section of the committee's report. Burgess demonstrated how the social background and individual characteristics of parolees could be used to predict the likelihood of a parole violation. Burgess's effort was an early attempt to show how sociology could be used in an applied setting.

In early 1928, Landesco returned to his studies of organized crime (Haller 1968, p. xv). At this time the Illinois Association for Criminal Justice was already formed. As already noted, Landesco had been involved in organized crime research even before publication of his report on organized crime in the *Illinois Crime Survey* of 1929.

During the next several years, Landesco had many projects in varying stages of completion. One such project was a biography of Eddie Jackson, The Immune Pickpocket. Like Shaw's *The Jack-Roller* (1930) and Sutherland's *The Professional Thief* (1937), the biography of Eddie Jackson was intended to give, in detail, the life history of a single individual who had made a career of crime (Haller 1968, p. xvi). Landesco (1934, pp. 341-42) met Eddie Jackson through some mutual friends. Landesco (1934) states, in "The Criminal Underworld of Chicago in the '80's and '90's," that he was able to persuade Eddie Jackson "in the interests of science to give me an accurate history of his life and career" (p. 342).

A second project undertaken by Landesco was that of the Forty-Two Gang. The "42" gang was located in the West Side Italian district, an immigrant community with low rents and the constant movement of its more disadvantaged citizens. Landesco (1933) comments that "The '42' gang was chosen for intensive study because it is a typical neighborhood gang which had its beginnings in the play group of the little boys of this West Side neighborhood" (p. 965). The materials collected for the study included life histories of individual gangsters, personal documents, and observations of the boys in their neighborhood play groups. The study looks at the inception, formation, and growth of this gang.

Landesco also collected materials concerning criminal activity in Cicero (Al Capone's domain), racketeering in labor unions and business, and the internal structure of organized crime in such fields as bootlegging and gambling. The projects of Eddie Jackson and the Forty-Two Gang were not included in the *Illinois Crime Survey* of 1929. Instead they were to appear in book form, in two volumes, to be respectively titled *Eddie Jackson, the Immune Pickpocket* and *The Story of the Forty-Two Gang* (Bruce 1933, p. 964). In addition, Landesco also intended to complete his doctoral dissertation dealing with crime in Chicago. Landesco never did publish a book on Eddie Jackson or the Forty-Two Gang, nor did he complete his doctoral dissertation (Haller 1968, p. xvii).

In 1932, Henry Horner, a Democrat, was elected governor of Illinois. Horner was a reform governor and was sympathetic to the idea that the prison and parole system should be transformed to run in a professional manner. Many of Landesco's friends campaigned for him to be placed on the Illinois Parole Board. The appointment of Landesco would be an important victory for many reformers, including Burgess. In support of Landesco's appointment to the Illinois Parole Board, many prominent academics wrote directly to the governor. Others worked hard to gain the support of the Cook County Democratic Organization. As a result, Landesco was appointed to the Parole Board in 1933. He subsequently hired three sociologists and placed them in the state prisons to conduct research on parole prediction tables for the prisoners who came up for parole. Landesco was instrumental in making Illinois the first state to use parole prediction in reaching decisions (Haller 1968, p. xvi).

Landesco's appointment in 1933 to the Parole Board ended his involvement in the study of organized crime. He served on the Parole Board throughout governor Horner's two terms. During this time he also became the executive director of the Central States Probation and Parole Conference. Landesco resigned from the Parole Board in the early 1940s, when he became "dismayed by the policies of the new governor" (Haller 1968, p. xvii). Following his period of service with the UNESCO section of the United Nations, Landesco retired to Lemon Grove, California, a suburb of San Diego, in 1950. He had suffered a heart attack in 1946 from which he never fully recovered. Landesco died in Lemon Grove, California, in 1954, at the age of sixty-four (Haller 1968, p. xvii).

The formation and purpose of the Illinois Association for Criminal Justice

The Illinois Association for Criminal Justice was responsible for the completion and publication of the *Illinois Crime Survey* in 1929. In order to understand the role played by Landesco in the *Survey*, we must first understand the purpose of the Illinois Association for Criminal Justice and its subsequent *Survey*. The Illinois Association for Criminal Justice and its subsequent crime *Survey* was a response to the critical crime conditions of the time. The *Illinois Crime Survey* was conducted in 1927 and

1928 for "the purpose of ascertaining and making known the factors responsible for crime conditions, which were regarded as sufficiently grave to justify the investigation" (Lashley 1930, p. 588).

In the period between 1920 and 1927 gang murders were commonplace. Gangsters had a total disregard for the law. Rival gang members would fire machine guns at each other from speeding automobiles. Gangsters were killed by other gangsters and by the police. Police officers and an assistant's state attorney were also killed during this period. An investigation into the killing of Assistant State Attorney William H. McSwiggen in 1927 uncovered close alliances between gangsters and politicians. Yet the murderers were never brought to justice. The entrenchment of organized crime and politics was so strong that it was obvious that crusades against organized crime were not working. It was believed that through the survey method a thorough investigation of all phases of crime could be initiated. After all the facts were known there could be an intelligent understanding of the crime problem and suggested solutions (Lashley 1930, pp. 589-90).

The Illinois State Bar Association was instrumental in forming the Illinois Association for Criminal Justice. In the early summer of 1925, the Illinois State Bar Association and the elite businessmen and lawyers of Chicago "had established committees to make recommendations for combating the breakdown of law and order" (Haller 1968, p. viii). Subsequently, the two committees decided to join in establishing a single organization to study the problems of crime and to lead a campaign for reform. On February 6, 1926, after complex negotiations, the Illinois Association for Criminal Justice emerged as the organization to carry out the program.

The Illinois Association for Criminal Justice was a body of civic leaders, lawyers, and academics in the city and state in 1925. Organizations representing the city and state included the Illinois State and Chicago Bar Associations, the Chicago Association of Commerce, the Industrial Club, the Chicago Crime Commission, the University of Chicago, Northwestern University, and many other such organizations. A prominent lawyer, Rush C. Butler, became the president of the Illinois Association for Criminal Justice (Haller 1968, p. viii).

Two previous published surveys, in Cleveland and Missouri, served as models for the *Illinois Crime Survey*. Arthur V. Lashley was selected as the director of the *Illinois Crime Survey*. Lashley was a former prosecutor for St. Louis County and the director of the Missouri survey. Raymond Moley, a professor of public law at Columbia University, was selected as consultant to the Illinois survey. Moley had served as director of the Cleveland Foundation during the Cleveland survey and had acted as research director for the New York Commission. Finally, there was C. Gelhke, the statistician for the survey. Gelhke was a professor at Western Reserve University and the former statistician for the Cleveland and Missouri surveys. In April of 1927, the Illinois Association for Criminal Justice "opened its offices on the eighth floor of a building at 300 West Adams Street in Chicago—one floor below the Crime Commission" (Haller n.d.a, p. 14). Subsequently, various experts were recruited to supervise or prepare the various sections of the crime survey.[2]

Members of the Illinois Association for Criminal Justice were closely aligned with the academic world. Close ties existed between prominent lawyers and the best law schools. Six members of the association were also on the Board of Trustees at the University of Chicago. Professors, like Burgess, Harno, and Bruce were central figures within the association. Lashley (1930, pp. 593-95), for example, indicates that Burgess was in charge of the section on "Factors Determining Success or Failure on Parole," Shaw prepared the report on juvenile delinquency, and Landesco prepared the report on organized crime.

Figure 1 below diagrams the association between Landesco, Shaw, McKay, Burgess, and Bruce with four institutions: the Illinois Association for Criminal Justice, the Department of Sociology at the University of Chicago, the American Institute of Criminal Law and Criminology, and the Institute for Juvenile Research. First, all five of these men conducted studies for the Illinois Association for Criminal Justice. Second, Landesco, Shaw, and McKay were all graduate students in the Department of Sociology at the University of Chicago. In addition, Landesco was the research director of the American Institute of Criminal Law and Criminology, where Bruce was the president.

Shaw was the research director at the Institute for Juvenile Research, a position which he secured with the help of Burgess. McKay was an associate of Shaw's at the Institute for Juvenile Research. Burgess, a professor of sociology at the University of Chicago, was friend and mentor to both Shaw and Landesco (cf. Haller 1968, p. xi; Bulmer 1984, p. 106, pp. 124-25). It can be said then, that the men constituted a close-knit group, who shared ideas and research interests. They moved in the same circles and had a great deal of influence on each other.

Many of the experts completed their reports in the summer of 1928. The completed reports were then edited and the chapters approved. The *Illinois Crime Survey* appeared in print in 1929. The public impact of this survey will be considered later in this chapter. For now, we will turn to an examination of the influence of the Chicago school upon Landesco. Landesco's study of organized crime in Chicago, was, in many ways, a product of his association with the Chicago school of urban sociology.

Landesco's association with the Chicago school of urban sociology

As documented in chapter 3, the Department of Sociology at the University of Chicago published a series of monographs on urban social life during the 1920s and 1930s for which it became well-known. Burgess was both friend and mentor to Landesco. The men shared an interest in urban crime and delinquency and both sought to continually improve the criminal justice system. It can be said that "Landesco was a product of the Chicago school and of Burgess's supervision" (Bulmer 1984, p. 125). Landesco's approach toward studying organized crime in Chicago followed in the tradition of the Chicago school.

Figure 1. The Institutional Affiliations of John Landesco in Chicago, Illinois:
1924-33

ILLINOIS ASSOCIATION FOR CRIMINAL JUSTICE
Produced the *Illinois Crime Survey* of 1929
The Illinois Association for Criminal Justice Initiates
Areas of Crime Research to be Conducted.
Members: Landesco, Shaw, McKay, Burgess, and Bruce

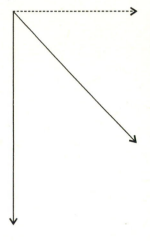

INSTITUTE FOR JUVENILE RESEARCH
Study of Juvenile Delinquency
Research Director: Shaw
Research Assistant: McKay
(Landesco has only an indirect link to the Institute through Shaw and Mckay)

AMERICAN INSTITUTE OF CRIMINAL LAW AND CRIMINOLOGY
Study of Probation and Parole
Study of Organized Crime
President: Bruce
Research Director: Landesco

UNIVERSITY OF CHICAGO
Study of Probation and Parole
Professor of Sociology: Burgess
Graduate Students: Landesco, Shaw, and McKay

In actuality, the *Illinois Crime Survey* was represented by two divergent traditions. The Illinois Association for Criminal Justice believed that the increase in Chicago's crime was due to an indifferent criminal justice system, which was corrupt and inept. The system would be improved through a study and analysis of its problems. According to the philosophy of the association, criminals could be deterred if the police, courts, and prisons operated more efficiently. The ultimate goal was to reform these agencies of justice. A dissimilar tradition in the *Survey* was that urban crime was the result of the disorganized urban social structure. This view was represented by the Chicago school theorists in their reports on organized crime and juvenile delinquency. The processes and procedures of criminal justice were given minimal importance in explaining the nature and extent of urban crime.

It can be said that the Chicago school sociologists were adherents of "cultural relativism," the view that a culture should be studied from that culture's point of view, that culture's value system, and not by the terms and standards of the researcher's culture. It can also be said that they supported cultural pluralism, the view that immigrants, while adopting the traditions, customs, values, dress, and behaviors of the larger society, should at the same time continue to preserve their own values, traditions, customs, and behaviors. The eugenics movement was gaining in momentum at this time and the Chicago school sociologists did not support this philosophy.

The shared beliefs of the Chicago school theorists influenced their decision to describe the social world of the criminal from the criminal's point of view. From the criminal's point of view, then, their life-style was not deviant but was part of the normal pattern of urban living. It was in this way that Landesco (1968) perceived the meaning of organized crime; organized crime was a product of urban living. Landesco (1968) never gave a specific definition of organized crime but he apparently took it to mean "that the gangster is a product of his surroundings in the same way in which the good citizen is a product of his environment" (p. 221). The good citizen has been reared in an environment which teaches conformity to the law. The gangster has been reared in an environment where a criminal code prevails. How can the good citizen and the criminal understand each other when they have grown up in two different worlds (Landesco 1968, p. 221)? With this interpretation of organized crime Landesco was drawing a comparison between criminal and noncriminal behavior. The implication is that the organized criminal is not different from the noncriminal, that he is not an outsider. This interpretation of organized crime by Landesco was in contrast to later law enforcement efforts to identify the organized criminal as an outsider; therefore, Landesco's "Original meaning for organized crime has been abandoned in today's conventional theory" (Smith 1975, p. 17). Organized crime, either rightly or wrongly, has been understood by most Americans as an "alien ethnic conspiracy"; this view was not shared by Thrasher (1927) nor Landesco (1968). Once again the very problem of defining organized crime arises. As previously suggested, one's definition of organized crime is based on the researcher's beliefs about the phenomenon. Apparently these beliefs also shape the researcher's policy for eliminating the problem.

The scholarship of organized crime has often taken one of two directions. The first views organized crime and the organized criminal as deviant to American soil, the belief that organized crime has nothing in common with the social, economic, and political aspects of American life. Organized criminals are viewed as secretive and dangerous; they are mercenaries. An opposing view sees organized crime as products of American social, political, and economic experiences. Organized crime can be explained by the same conditions that explain any legitimate American enterprise, namely, status and wealth. It is this latter view that Thrasher (1927) and Landesco (1968) came to share. For, as Landesco (1968) has suggested, "Where the choice of a young man is between a low paid job as an unskilled laborer and good wages for driving a beer truck, a stigma is soon attached to legitimate employment" (p. 210).

Landesco's research was simultaneous with the delinquency research of Shaw and McKay and he was strongly influenced by them. The view was purely sociological (and a liberal theory at that!) rather than psychological. The adult criminal was not psychologically abnormal. The criminal was a "natural product" of his immediate environment. It was just this view of the criminal as a "natural product" of his environment that precluded Landesco, and other Chicago school sociologists, from examining the fact that a good deal of mobsterism was ethnically based and may have been transported from the immigrant's native countries. Sociologists are often hesitant to portray ethnic groups in a negative light for fear of charges of bigotry. Their commitment to egalitarianism and democracy often prohibit sociologists from accepting any evidence which might cast an unfavorable light on any ethnic group (see Foster 1977, p. 17). More important, for the Chicago school sociologists, crime was somehow a normal response to the socially disorganized urban environment. Criminals were not inherently evil. It was those who did not turn to crime in such a disorganizing environment who were deviant. If crime was caused by social disorganization, then it could not be caused by old world traits transplanted. As criminologist Jon Snodgrass (1972) stated in his analysis of "The American Criminological Tradition," "the causes of crime were always understood in terms of what were not the causes" (p. 20).

Landesco's views on adult criminality were influenced by the previous research of Thrasher (1927) and Shaw (1929). Like Thrasher and Shaw before him, Landesco believed that organized crime was a consequence of the social disorganization found in urban slums. Based on this view two themes prevail in his book: (1) the relationship between organized crime and other institutions in the community; and (2) the rooting of organized crime in the culture and social relationships of the neighborhood.

As already indicated, Thrasher, Shaw, McKay, and Landesco all rejected the common view of the day that criminality could be explained by ethnic traits of immigrants which they brought with them to the new world. It was not ethnic or racial groups which were criminal, it was the disorganized urban slum neighborhoods which caused crime. Criminals were not products of Sicily, Ireland, or Poland, they were products of the urban slums of Chicago. It was urban life and not race or ethnicity that was criminogenic. The focus of Thrasher, Shaw, and McKay on the social organization and disorganization of urban slum neighborhoods drew attention away from race or ethnicity as a causative factor of criminality. Thrasher, Shaw, and McKay were more readily concerned with the "natural" areas of the city which were criminogenic. The same may be said of Landesco. When describing the culture and social relationships of urban criminals, Landesco looked at the patterns of urban living and not at racial or ethnic traits (see Haller 1968; Smith 1975). In fact, the image of the Italian and Irish gangsters and bootleggers that prevailed in popular culture, journalism, and film was somehow entirely ignored. In its place was a liberal vision of the criminal created anew from the ghettos and backstreets of American cities and slums. Perhaps this liberal vision also explains, in part, why the principal crime breakers were youths, the boys, and not the men. The youths revealed to the sociologists criminals in the making; the adult mobsters and thugs raised questions of origin. These liberal academics could explain the origins of the crimes of youth but they did not have the wherewithal to confront the origins of the criminality of adults.

For example, although Landesco believed most gangs to be an outgrowth of the neighborhood play group, he knew this was not true of the Capone gang. The Capone gang was "an organization of professional gangsters. It differs from the Ragen Colts in that it is not an outgrowth of a neighborhood play group. The Capone gang was formed for the business administration of vice, gambling, and booze" (Landesco 1968, p. 180).

The methods, impact, and findings of Landesco's study

Landesco's study was, in several respects, very much like the kind of sociology of the city neighborhood produced by the Chicago sociologists. However, in other respects it was remarkably different, especially in regard to its principal focus on organized crime.

The *Illinois Crime Survey* was published in 1929 and contained over one thousand pages of text. Reports included in the *Survey* were grouped under three principal headings: "The Machinery of Justice," "Specific Types of Offenses," and "Organized Crime." Except for the final grouping , which was devoted to organized crime, each grouping had a number of sections on topics written by different people. For example, under "Specific Types of Offenses" were sections on juvenile delinquency, homicide, and the defective and deranged delinquent. Only the section on organized crime was prepared by one individual, John Landesco. Landesco's report included several sections: exploitation of prostitution; the rule of the underworld (gambling, beer wars, and gang feuds); terrorization by bombs; racketeering; the gangster and the politician; funerals of gangsters, the gangsters apologia for his criminal career; and finally a Who's Who of Organized Crime in Chicago. As is apparent from the numerous subject headings, this was an in-depth study of the organization and operation of organized crime in Chicago. The summary of findings, conclusions, and recommendations was prepared by Burgess in 1928.

The theoretical orientation and research methodology of Landesco's study has much in common with the monographs published by the Chicago school of sociology in the 1920s and early 1930s. The theoretical framework was the ecological approach to urban social structure and the theory of social disorganization (see chap. 2). Similar to the research techniques of other Chicago school theorists Landesco's methods of data collection included personal documents, public documents, interviewing, life histories, and direct observation.

Given the fact that Landesco's theoretical approach and methodological approach were representative of the Chicago school, it is difficult to understand why this study was overlooked by the Chicago school theorists. If Landesco's study, among others, provided substance for a Chicago school, then why did Burgess ignore such an important work? It is this question, and others like it, that will be considered in the concluding section of this chapter. For now, let us turn to the reception of the study by public officials and by academics.

First, it is quite accurate to state that the recommendations of the *Illinois Crime Survey* went unacknowledged by public officials and agencies. Landesco's section had almost no public impact at all. This includes the study's recommendations by Burgess (1968, pp. 282-86). Burgess (1968) states that his recommendations are "based upon the conclusion that the crux of the crime problem lies in its relation to public opinion" (p. 282). Burgess recommended several ways to control crime and organized crime in particular: (1) the public needed to be informed about the work and progress of law enforcement agencies in combating crime; (2) the newspapers were not sufficient for this purpose, and existing agencies (Bureau of Identification, Chicago Crime Commission, Committee of Fifteeen, Juvenile Protection Associa-tion, Research Institutions) needed to extend their activities of field investigation and reporting; (3) immigrant communities and the outside American public needed to develop understanding and friendly relations (immigrants could be better represented in community organizations); (4) boys' gangs needed to be controlled by various community and welfare agencies because criminals and gangsters often originate from the boys' gang; (5) the police department needs to be reorganized so that it operates more efficiently; (6) election fraud needs to be curbed; (7) because organized crime has become nationalized the control of organized crime must also expand; (8) concentrate prohibition enforcement efforts on organized gangs, thus breaking the foundation of organized crime; (9) the Illinois Association for Criminal Justice should become an agency which will specialize in fact finding, crime reporting, and preparing special studies as required to develop intelligent public opinion in the field of crime; and (10) business and industrial violence should be handled by an arbitration board. Burgess attempted to combine the two divergent traditions represented in the *Survey*. As already noted, one tradition believed that crime could be prevented if the machinery of justice operated more efficiently and the other that crime could be prevented by altering the neighborhood environment.

The reasons for the lack of impact of the *Illinois Crime Survey* were many. While the leadership behind the survey centered in Chicago, it was far from representative of Chicago. The influential members of the Illinois Association for Criminal Justice were the elite of business and industry, who met at exclusive clubs, and dominated the leading civic organizations of the city. These men were far removed, in values and life experiences, from those who committed crimes and those who handled criminal justice procedures. The members of the Illinois Association "were separated from the criminal processes they hoped to change and from the political organizations through which these changes would have to take place" (Haller n.d.a, p. 22).

The city of Chicago at this time was heavily Catholic and heavily immigrant in origins. The elite of the Illinois Association were American born, had some college education, and were not Catholic. The elite members of the Illinois Association lived in the prestigious areas of the city, the Hyde Park and Woodlawn areas around the University of Chicago, the Gold Coast along the lake on the near North Side, and the elite northern suburbs such as Evanstan and Winnetka. Only one member of the Illinois Association lived in an "ethnic" neighborhood. This was Jessie Binford, director of the Juvenile Protective Association and a resident of Hull House. Members of the association with little power and influence were Catholic, foreign born, or lacked higher education (Haller n.d.a, p. 21). Perhaps, then, it was Landesco's foreign-born status and his failure to obtain his doctorate which contributed to his lack of recognition within the association.

Members of the association, who were also members of the Chicago school, knew the city housed a variety of different cultures, each maintaining its social distance from the other. The association could not change those groups that they did not understand. The social and behavioral distance between the elite members of the association and the very groups they wished to change was too much to overcome.

As already stated, the recommendations of the *Illinois Crime Survey* went unnoticed. The *Survey* had no particular audience to which it was addressed. Because no public official had the responsibility for implementing the recommendations of the *Survey*, public officials were able to ignore the recommendations (Haller n.d.a, p. 24).

Time worked against it. Four years passed between the time the plans for the *Survey* began in 1925, and the time the *Survey* was published in 1929. It was three years, 1928, before the first sections of the *Survey* appeared, and then only little by little. Many of the elite reformers found other avenues for their civic responsibilities. The *Survey* seemed to lose its significance as time went on (Haller n.d.a, pp. 24-25). "When the Illinois Association for Criminal Justice passed out of existence, there was no prospect that the *Survey* might become the platform for change. It was published stillborn" (Haller n.d.b, p. 33).

The *Survey*, and in particular Landesco's section of the *Survey*, had almost no public impact at all. "Because of its original publication in 1929 as part of a massive, 1,000 page *Illinois Crime Survey*, his study has unfortunately not been widely known or easily available, even though his chapters on organized crime were clearly the most important part of the *Survey*" (Haller 1968, p. vii).

For reasons unknown, the University of Chicago Press published Landesco's study of organized crime in Chicago as a separate publication in 1968. However, it is reasonable to conclude that the publication of this study at this time was a response to an interest in crime and in organized crime, in particular, by American sociologists. The science of sociology, first outlined by the Chicago school, and subsequently by sociologists at other predominant universities, did not particularly attend to organized crime. Until 1967, general sociological interests focused on the types of crimes committed by individuals, who were primarily youthful offenders. The publication of Landesco's study coincided with the work of the President's Crime Commission of 1967 and the publication of Donald Cressey's (1969) *Theft of the Nation.* Prior to Cressey's *Theft of the Nation*, few books were written by American sociologists concerning organized crime. However, due to reasons which will be discussed in chapter 8, the late 1960s and afterwards saw an increase in books and articles about organized crime published by American sociologists. As Ruth (1969) stated in his review of the 1968 printing of Landesco's study, "The combination of this book and professor Cressey's recently published *Theft of the Nation* should impel more sociological research into organized crime. The current research void should be embarrassing to all sociologists" (p. 805). Likewise, Cohen (1970) states, "very little like Landesco's analysis has been carried out on organized crime until the current work of the President's Commission" (p. 92). Therefore, chapter 8 will provide insight as to why there was such a research void until the publication of Cressey's *Theft of the Nation.*

Landesco's study has been faulted for being merely a historical and descriptive account of organized crime (cf. Ruth 1969; Faris 1970; Cohen 1970). Generally speaking this assessment is accurate. Yet this was the typical research style of the Chicago school sociologists, and (see chap. 5 below) the significance of Landesco's work goes beyond a mere description and historical account of organized crime in Chicago. The historical, and more important, sociological significance of Landesco's study is that he is one of the first academics (the other being Thrasher) to present a view of organized crime that does not fit the stereotype of the "alien conspiracy model." Landesco, as early as 1929, provided a model of organized crime as a network of temporary relationships and alliances, that future researchers would expand upon. It is unfortunate that it took a later generation of scholars to see just what it was that Landesco contributed to the sociology of organized crime. Furthermore, Landesco does provide the reader with a firsthand account of the nature, size, and scope of organized crime during the 1920s and 1930s, especially with regard to the intimate alliances of gangsters and politicians—and what the social consequences of this alliance meant for society.

When Landesco's study was published as a separate publication in 1968, it received more praise than criticism. Cohen (1970) comments, "We are again indebted to the University of Chicago for reprinting one of the classic works of the Chicago school in the 1920's. Landesco's study of organized crime in Chicago . . . deserves a much wider audience than it previously had" (p. 92). Milne (1969) states, "this book is unquestionably a classic in sociological investigation, and the University of Chicago Press is to be congratulated for publishing it again at a this time of tremendous concern about crime in our society" (p. 407). Milne (1969) continues "Landesco's study should be ranked with William F. Whyte's famous *Street Corner Society* as a classical demonstration of participant observation. In fact, it should probably be ranked above Whyte's work, because it preceded Whyte in time, and was accompanied by some elements of real physical danger" (pp. 407-08). Reynolds (1969) comments, the "Illinois report is a remarkable piece of sociology, written with such easy drama that it is as readable as a novel while still crammed with facts about crime and political bribery and theories about the seemingly irresistible rise of gangsterdom in Chicago" (p. 14). Lastly, a review in the *Times Literary*

Supplement (1969) states, "this reprint of a minor classic is welcome" (p. 386).

The study, since its publication in 1968, has been cited by some scholars of the Chicago school. Most notably by Carey (1975) and Bulmer (1984). There is brief mention of Landesco in Kurtz (1984) and Smith (1988). Faris (1970, pp. 78-79) discusses the work of Landesco in his chapter "Urban Behavior Research." Yet, just as significant is the neglect of Landesco's work in two biographies on Robert Park by Matthews (1977) and Raushenbush (1979).

Equally important is the inability of Julia and Herman Schwendinger, critics of the Chicago school, to provide the present author with any information on John Landesco. In a correspondence dated July 26, 1989, the Schwendingers' reply, "Just received your request for information on John Landesco, etc. and regret to say that we are not familiar with him." This is surprising considering they critique the work of the Chicago school, in particular, the work of Thrasher (1927) and Zorbaugh (1929), in their 1974 text, *The Sociologists of the Chair: A Radical Analysis of the Formative Years of North American Sociology (1883-1922)*. Based on this limited information it seems reasonable to suggest that Landesco was a relatively marginal member of the Department of Sociology at the University of Chicago, a point which will be examined more closely in the final section of this chapter.

In addition to some scholars of the Chicago school, Landesco's study, since its 1968 publication, has been cited by numerous historians and researchers of organized crime. Most notably, historians Mark Haller and Humbert Nelli have cited Landesco in their own research on the history of organized urban crime. Dwight C. Smith (1975) cites Landesco's work throughout his book *The Mafia Mystique*. In short, while the study was little known and virtually inaccessible prior to 1968, it has since become one of the representative works of the Chicago school. It has received acknowledgment from scholars of the Chicago school and from scholars of organized crime. Therefore, we return to the question raised at the beginning of this chapter. Why did the Chicago school sociologists and other social scientists, until recently, ignore such an important work? This question, and others will be considered in the following section.

Some reasons why Landesco's study was not given academic attention

In this chapter we have documented Landesco's early history and academic career, his affiliation with the Illinois Association for Criminal Justice, the Department of Sociology at the University of Chicago, and the American Institute of Criminal Law and Criminology. We have also examined the public and professional impact of the *Illinois Crime Survey* and the theoretical and methodological approaches utilized in Landesco's study. Therefore, we can now return to our three possible explanations for the lack of scholarly attention Landesco's work received: (1) John Landesco was a marginal member of the Department of Sociology at the University of Chicago and his work was considered inconsequential; (2) the study was viewed as either inadequate or minor; and (3) the study was suppressed.

While it may be impossible to prove or disprove our possible explanations, it will be possible to draw some tentative conclusions based on the documentary evidence presented in this chapter.

Was John Landesco a marginal person in the Department of Sociology at the University of Chicago? To that question, however tentatively, we can answer yes—in a relative sense. There is reason to believe that Landesco's work could have been given more scholarly attention within the Chicago school. First, Landesco was a graduate student in the Department of Sociology at the University of Chicago until 1929. Second, he was closely associated with Burgess, Shaw, and McKay through the University of Chicago, the Illinois Association for Criminal Justice, and the Institute for Juvenile Research. The intellectual influence of these three men on Landesco's thinking was strong.

Burgess was one of three members of the editorial committee for the University of Chicago *Sociological Series*. He was influential within the University of Chicago and within the Illinois Association for Criminal Justice. As documented in chapter 3, Park and Burgess were instrumental for numerous publications by their graduate students during the 1920s and early 1930s. A considerable number of these students published little or nothing subsequently (Matthews 1977, p. 109). Cavan (1983) states, "It has been noted that only a few of the students who produced publishable dissertations continued to carry out research or to publish after they left the university" (p. 417). So why were these other studies published and Landesco's work overlooked? Landesco was not marginal more than any other graduate student who was at the same time professionally active. Burgess was fully supportive and knowledgeable of Landesco's work. Yet Landesco was relatively marginal in that he was institutionally separated from the University of Chicago, while other graduate students in sociology were not.

Landesco was institutionally separated from the department by his role as research director at the American Institute of Criminal Law and Criminology. His publication of various articles on Eddie Jackson and the Forty-Two Gang, in the late 1920s and early 1930s were credited to John Landesco, research director at the American Institute of Criminal Law and Criminology. They were not credited to John Landesco, graduate student at the University of Chicago. Further, Landesco did not complete his studies for the Ph.D. and therefore did not qualify to receive the title of sociologist. He also became institutionally separated when he became a member of the Illinois Parole Board in 1933. The year 1933 marks the last year when funds were available through the Local Community Research Committee to publish students' dissertations (Cavan 1983). This fact may also help to explain why his study was never published by the Chicago school. In any event, it appears that since he was institutionally separated, he was also institutionally overlooked.

The Chicago school is well-known for the delinquency research of Shaw and McKay. Delinquency research in the United States commenced with the Chicago school of criminological sociologists (cf. Kornhauser 1978, p. 21; Gaylord 1984, p. 125). Yet Shaw and McKay did not complete their studies for the Ph.D. because they failed to master the language requirement (Snodgrass 1972, pp. 132-33). However, when one thinks of the Chicago school, the research of Shaw and McKay immediately comes to mind. As sociological criminologists of the Chicago school Thrasher, Shaw, and McKay are familiar names to academic sociologists; Landesco is not.

It can be suggested that a possible explanation for Landesco's lack of reputation among academic sociologists has to do with the fact that he never taught sociology or criminology courses. This is not true of Shaw, McKay, and Thrasher, all of whom remained in academia. Perhaps, then, Landesco's not remaining in the academic community at Chicago, or elsewhere, contributed to his marginality. In other words, Landesco's work on the *Illinois Crime Survey* and with the American Institute of Criminal Law and Criminology, and later with the Illinois Parole Board took him outside the work of the department of sociology. His only involvement with the department included the graduate work he began on organized crime under Burgess's supervision and which he never completed (refer to figure 1 above and the earlier discussion of Landesco's institutional affiliations).

The second possible explanation raised in this chapter for the neglect of Landesco's work was that his study was not an outstanding piece of sociological research. This can be countered in several ways: first, Landesco was a product of the Chicago school and his theoretical orientation and research methodology were entirely consistent with the quality and type of work done by faculty and students. It was not inferior. In fact, the few written commentaries of the *Illinois Crime Survey* praised the work (Haller n.d.a, n.d.b, 1968). Furthermore, book reviews (Ruth 1969; Milne 1969; Reynolds 1969; Cohen 1970), and commentaries in texts by scholars of the Chicago school, written when the book was reissued (Faris 1970; Carey 1975; Bulmer 1984), all indicate that the work was an outstanding piece of sociological research. Landesco's work has been praised particularly for its research methods (Milne 1969; Bulmer 1984) and called a classic in sociological investigation (Milne 1969; Cohen 1970). Therefore, we can safely conclude that one reason the Chicago school did not publish Landesco's study at the time it was written was not because it was an inferior piece of sociological research below the standards of the Chicago school.

Finally, our third possible explanation for the neglect of Landesco's work was that the study was suppressed. By this we mean that the work was consciously and systematically kept out of print by one or more figures of the department. While this thesis may seem extreme, it should certainly be entertained and examined with some seriousness. Based on the documentary evidence presented in this chapter, it does not appear that Landesco's study was actively and intentionally suppressed. However, it is more likely that the work was overlooked and, even possibly, considered by some members of the department to raise issues with which they were unwilling to engage.

As already documented, the *Illinois Crime Survey* had almost no public impact and no public official was responsible for the implementation of recommendations made in the *Survey*. Once the *Survey* was completed the members of the Illinois

Association for Criminal Justice disbanded believing their work had been completed. Individuals completing the various sections of the report returned to their normal work activities (Haller n.d.a, p. 18). Haller (n.d.a) comments that "The dissolution of the Illinois Association for Criminal Justice was important, for it meant that no organization existed with any commitment to secure the reforms advocated by the *Illinois Crime Survey*. The dissolution was also ironic, for the major recommendation of the *Survey* had been that the Illinois Association take on the crucial task of mobilizing public opinion and of coordinating the many private activities in the realm of crime fighting. By disbanding, the Illinois Association failed to carry out its own major recommendation" (pp. 18-19).

Based on these facts it is likely that the *Illinois Crime Survey* and Landesco's section of the *Survey* was neglected, brushed to the side, or conveniently, for some, kept out of the public's attention. There was no one person, or several persons, either as members of the *Illinois Crime Survey* or as members of the sociology department, with sufficient interest and influence to press for its publication and to press its findings into public view. It would even seem that Landesco and the members of the *Illinois Crime Survey* did not themselves really understand the extent to which they had identified an issue that others had previously ignored. Only later generations would find the *Survey* significant.

In understanding the neglect of Landesco's study we should also distinguish between the views of the members of the *Illinois Crime Survey* and the members of the Department of Sociology at the University of Chicago. For the latter, especially, Landesco's work was too political, too controversial. As Landesco (1968) comments on the funerals of gangsters: "These ceremonies are . . . a revelation of the intimate relations between politics and crime" (p. 191). As we will discuss in chapter 5, an entire chapter of his book is titled, "The Gangster and the Politician." Landesco's work was an indictment of politicians as much as gangsters. It raised issues and concerns that were patently public ones. To put it in terms of interests (political and ideological), it was not in the best interests of the Chicago school to make the study public knowledge. Organized crime and Prohibition, in particular, were highly charged political problems, not merely social ones. To take a stand against Prohibition would have subjected the *Survey* to attack. This is probably why Burgess in writing his conclusion to the *Illinois Crime Survey* did not take a stand on this issue (Haller 1968, p. xviii).

As we will see in chapter 5 Landesco's research findings point to the alliances between organized criminals, police, politicians, state attorneys, and other law enforcement personnel. If such alliances were made public there could be serious repercussions, The Chicago sociologists viewed Prohibition as a political problem, one of public opinion and competing ideologies. It was not a social problem that was "naturally" caused, ecologically based, and technically correctable. Therefore, it was not viewed as an area of sociological interest. Only a later generation of scholars would come to view organized crime as a social problem, for example, by scholars of the 1960s and 1970s who upheld the radical theories that were gaining momentum in the field of sociology (see chap. 8 below).

As a Marxist might argue, Landesco's views on immigrants and ethnic gangs were different from those of the academic and business elite who hired him to do his study. Furthermore, Landesco, as an immigrant himself, was sympathetic to the concerns of the ethnic gangs. The bulk of the criminological literature from 1915 to 1950 was focused on the immigrant youth residing in the urban slums. Landesco did not see ethnic minorities as the bad guys. Sociologists often have a commitment to democracy and egalitarianism. It is this commitment that dissuades them from suggesting the possibility that lower-class racial or ethnic minorities might, in any way, be responsible for the crime in their midst. The fact that many ethnic immigrant groups were and are involved in organized crime might help explain the reluctance of the Chicago school in publishing the study. Today we would say that it is politically incorrect to make such a suggestion. Social scientists often shy away from research which might portray certain identifiable groups as criminally inclined for fear of charges of bigotry (see Foster 1977, p. 17).

Finally, the concerns of the Chicago sociologists were remarkably similar to those who agreed to fund their research. Therefore, it is not unusual that the Chicago school might have ignored Landesco's work, since it contrasted strongly with what many well-positioned persons of the Illinois Association for Criminal Justice wanted him to find in his study of organized crime. As previously stated, Landesco did not believe that the inefficiency of the machinery of justice was responsible for the crime problem in the city. Instead, Landesco believed that by altering the neighborhood environment crime could be prevented. Perhaps if Landesco's conclusions and findings were more agreeable to the elite members of the Illinois Association for Criminal Justice, his study would have received more attention. The power elite often define the types of studies the sociologist will engage in and often dictate what those research results will say. Every profession, including sociology, has "a vested interest in . . . promoting itself" (Thio 1973, p. 9). It is this self interest in its own promotion and survival that makes the sociologist turn to the power elite for support (Thio 1973).

While it has been demonstrated that Landesco's study was overlooked by the Chicago school, it is difficult to verify exactly why. We have provided a number of sound reasons based on the many circumstances known to us about Landesco, the *Illinois Crime Survey*, the philosophical, political, and methodological interests and viewpoints of everyone concerned. We have tried to offer some plausible explanations. In short, we can conclude that a number of factors together had a role to play. Landesco was a marginal member of the Department of Sociology at the University of Chicago. It would also seem that it is safe to conclude that Ernest Burgess must have been a critical figure in the outcome of Landesco's study, and Burgess was probably disposed to let Landesco's report go by the wayside. Either he neglected to see the importance of organized crime as a topic for sociological research, the importance of the study's findings, or the fact that Landesco never completed the work that Burgess had set out for him, helps to account for Burgess's failure to press for the book's publication. In the final analysis, the fact that the controversial nature of Landesco's book, with its explicit criticisms of politicians and the public scandal of election frauds, must have also played a role in keeping Landesco's book out of public view.

NOTES

1. The research of Mark Haller, Professor of History, at Temple University, Philadelphia, Pennsylvania has been extremely helpful in the writing of this chapter. Professor Haller's area of interest is the history of American urban crime and criminal justice. Professor Haller has written extensively on the history of the police, gambling, bootlegging, loansharking, and other aspects of urban crime and vice. Much of Professor Haller's historical research on urban crime has centered on the city of Chicago. Three principal sources written by Mark Haller are utilized in this chapter. These sources include Haller's (1968, pp. vii–xviii) introduction to Landesco's (1968) *Organized Crime in Chicago*, and two unpublished manuscripts, one on the formation of the Illinois Association for Criminal Justice and the other on the principal work of the Illinois Association for Criminal Justice, the *Illinois Crime Survey*.

   This writer has made several attempts to obtain information on John Landesco which might provide insight into his relationship with the Department of Sociology at the University of Chicago and provide an explanation for why his study was almost entirely overlooked until its separate publication in 1968. In addition to Mark Haller, written correspondence was sent to the following social scientists: Howard Abadinsky, Mary Jo Deegan, Virginia Fish, Daniel Glaser, Solomon Kobrin, Lester Kurtz, and Herman and Julia Schwendinger. All of these social scientists are either scholars of organized crime or scholars of the Chicago school. Of those who responded to my inquiries (Howard Abadinsky, Mary Jo Deegan, Virginia Fish, Daniel Glaser, Solomon Kobrin, and Herman and Julia Schwendinger), none could provide any information on John Landesco's status within the Department of Sociology at the University of Chicago nor could they provide any explanation for the neglect of Landesco's study on organized crime. However, Mary Jo Deegan does state that there are many "marvelous sociology studies that are unreported/not discussed today" and there are usually "political/class network/hegemonic reasons that are embedded in this process of obscurity" (M. Deegan, personal communication, May 11, 1991). Also, both Daniel Glaser and Solomon Kobrin offer some partial answers why the Chicago school did not publish any monographs on organized crime or organized criminals and their commentaries are part of the subject matter of chapter 8.

   In addition to written correspondence to the above named scholars, a personal interview was conducted with Dr. John Martin of Fordham University on April 23, 1991. Dr. Martin is a member of the Department of Sociology and Anthropology at Fordham University and a scholar of international crime. Dr. Martin is the coauthor of *Multinational Crime: The Challenge of Terrorism, Espionage, Drugs, and Arms Trafficking* (1992). I regret to say that Dr. Martin was not familiar with John Landesco nor with his study of organized crime.

   It should also be noted that this writer has consulted several books written about the Chicago school and about specific scholars of the Chicago school (Faris 1970; Carey 1975; Matthews 1977; Raushenbush 1979; Lewis and Smith 1980; Bulmer 1984;

Kurtz 1984; Smith 1988). Some of these books make no mention of John Landesco at all. Others discuss Landesco's work but do not provide any personal information on Landesco which would provide insight into his status within the Department of Sociology at the University of Chicago.

An additional effort to obtain information on John Landesco included personal communication with the archivist at the Regenstein Library at the University of Chicago, where Landesco's papers are deposited. The materials received provided no insight into Landesco's status within the Department of Sociology at the University of Chicago nor did they provide any explanation for the neglect of Landesco's study of organized crime until 1968. Finally, a classified advertisement was placed in the May, 1991, issue of *Footnotes*, the official newsletter of the American Sociological Association, requesting information on the sociologist John Landesco that would be useful for a dissertation on studies of organized crime in American sociology (this book was originally the author's Ph.D. dissertation). No useful information was ever received in response to the classified advertisement.

2. For a complete review of the major sections of the *Survey* and the experts who wrote them, see Arthur V. Lashley. 1930. "The Illinois Crime Survey." *Journal of Criminal Law, Criminology and Police Science* 20:588-605.

5

The Landesco study:
Its historical and sociological
significance

Introduction

THIS CHAPTER takes a closer look at Landesco's study of organized crime in Chicago. The principal purpose of the chapter is to assess the historical and sociological significance of the study through a description, analysis, and interpretation of it, focusing primarily on certain selected topics and findings of the study, as well as, the explanations it offers for organized crime.

Originally Landesco's study appeared as pages 865 to 1087 of the *Illinois Crime Survey*. It was the concluding section of the *Survey*, covering chapters 19 through 27. The introduction to the study was prepared by Andrew Bruce, president of the American Institute of Criminology, and the summary of findings, conclusions, and recommendations were prepared by Ernest Burgess. The study tells the history of organized crime in Chicago and its surrounding communities for a period of twenty-five years. More descriptive than analytical, the study details important names, dates, places, and events in Chicago's history of organized crime. Landesco used the many aspects of organized crime as subject headings for the study, (e.g., the exploitation of prostitution, the rule of the underworld, terrorization by bombs, racketeering, the gangster and the politician, funerals of gangsters, the gangster's apology for his criminal career, and a Who's Who of organized crime in Chicago). In fact, the study is so comprehensive that the book is now a principle reference source on the early history of organized crime in Chicago. Along with Virgil Peterson's *Barbarians in Our Midst* (1952) and Herbert Asbury's *Gem of the Prairies: An Informal History of Chicago's Underworld* (1942), it is probably the most complete source of Chicago's early history of organized crime that we have. Landesco's study is even more significant than either

Peterson's or Asbury's because he was writing a firsthand account of organized crime during the 1920s, and was exposed to the dangers and consequences of organized crime as both a researcher and as an ordinary citizen. Historical accuracy is important for organized crime research. Organized crime is not static, it is always changing. "Because organized crime is an ongoing and continually developing process, histories can have great explanatory power in tracing that process and demonstrating the means of adaptation and change used by the mob" (Potter 1994, pp. 41-42). Of course, when Landesco was writing his study during the 1920s, no one individual had the foresight to see its historical, or sociological for that matter, value; this was left for a later generation of scholars to uncover.

In 1968, when American sociologists seriously turned their attention to the study of organized crime, Landesco's study was published by the University of Chicago Press as *Organized Crime in Chicago*. Essentially the same as the 1929 study with changes in page and chapter numbers, the book adds an introduction by Mark Haller, professor of history at Temple University, and a scholar of urban crime and vice. The introduction details Landesco's background, academic career, and affiliation with the Chicago school. The book also contains a section on the juvenile delinquent originally prepared by Shaw and McKay for the *Illinois Crime Survey*. The section on juvenile delinquency is a glance at the views of Shaw and McKay concerning delinquency, which would later make the two men famous. It was probably included in the 1968 edition because it lends understanding and support to Landesco's own views and analysis of adult criminality in Chicago. As previously indicated, Landesco was strongly influenced by the research and views of Shaw, McKay, and Burgess. Landesco believed, as did Thrasher before him, that adult criminals were often juvenile gang members who grew up in an environment conducive to criminality; an environment where the gang tradition was firmly established. The 1968 edition contains eleven chapters: "The McSwiggen Assassination as a Typical Incident,"; "The Exploitation of Prostitution,"; "The Rule of the Underworld: Tennes as a Vice Chief,"; "The Rule of the Underworld: Torrio as Overlord,"; "The Beer Wars,"; "Terrorization by Bombs,"; "Racketeering,"; "The Gangster and the Politician,"; "Funerals of Gangsters,"; "The Gangster's Apologia Pro Vita Sua,"; and "A Who's Who of Organized Crime in Chicago."

Landesco begins by outlining the history of vice in Chicago prior to Prohibition. This meant primarily the activities of gambling and prostitution. He then proceeds to the Prohibition era and concludes with a discussion of the growth of large-scale racketeering in Chicago. Throughout the study Landesco was cognizant of the continuity and change in leadership from the vice and gambling lords of the late 1800s to the bootlegging racketeers of the 1920s. Landesco also had the foresight to notice the business aspects of organized crime which were typical of the O'Bannion and Capone gangs. "The old basis in friendly relations is being superseded by a cash nexus. Political protection for the powerful financial interests of organized crime is coming to rest less and less upon friendship and more and more upon pecuniary considerations" (Landesco 1968, p. 205). He viewed the Capone and

O'Bannion gangs as evidence of what the future of organized crime would be like. Landesco noted that both the Capone and O'Bannion gangs were formed to exploit the business of crime. In both cases the members were first involved in criminal activities in their neighborhoods and gained reputations for themselves. The relationship between the politician and the gangster is different in these types of gangs. "Neighborliness and friendly relations recede to the background. Operations in crime and political protection from its consequences are no longer local but city-wide. Immunity is no longer obtained by friendship, but from graft. Organized crime and organized political corruption have formed a partnership to exploit for profit the enormous revenues to be derived from law-breaking" (Landesco 1968, p. 189). Landesco saw that the strongest criminal gangs, like the Capone gang, were losing their neighborhood character and becoming mercenaries. Unlike the neighborhood criminal gang that relies on the local politician, mercenary criminal gangs have contacts with the highest levels of government in the county, the city, and nearby towns and villages (Burgess 1968, p. 281).

Landesco (1968) poses the following set of eight questions which his study attempts to answer:

1. Why have grand jury investigations and police drives failed time after time to crush organized crime? What is the reason why gang rule has successfully defied every attempt to suppress it?

2. Why has gang warfare over the profits of beer running and whiskey distribution, with its startling toll of the lives of gunmen, not resulted in the extermination of gangsters?

3. What is the role of bombing as a method of intimidation and control in Black Hand, labor, racial, and political conflicts?

4. Just what is the basis of relation, if any, between gangster and politician? Does the immunity of the gangster and the gunmen from punishment rest upon graft, corruption and intimidation, or upon neighborhood influence?

5. What are the different types of organized gangs in Chicago, and what place and power do they possess in their own neighborhoods?

6. What does a "Who's Who of the Gang in Chicago" disclose about the career of gangsters and the fortunes of criminal gangs?

7. How does the gangster look at his own life and what apology for it has he to make to society?

8. If previous methods of crushing organized crime have failed, are there any feasible methods of control? (p. 9)

Keeping in mind that Landesco's study was limited to the 1920s and the city of

Chicago, some of the questions he asked still have relevance to the study of organized crime today. It might be said that Landesco was before his time in his critical analysis of organized crime in Chicago. He asked most of the right questions, unlike many researchers of organized crime who have focused their attention on the organization of organized crime (its hierarchical structure), in detriment to its social, economic, and political aspects. They rarely raise questions about illicit markets, power relationships, corruption, and graft as Landesco did (see Potter 1994, pp. 38-42).

Furthermore, researchers of organized crime spend too much time studying the criminal instead of the crime. The literature is filled with accounts of the lives of well-known organized crime figures. Most of these accounts are written by nonacademics for the curiosity of the general public. Books about Al Capone, Bugsy Siegel, Dutch Schultz, Meyer Lansky, Lucky Luciano, John Gotti, and others abound. Unfortunately, one gets the impression that individual actors in organized crime have a more important role than they do. Yet the very term organized crime infers cooperation and coordination with others (Potter 1994, pp. 38-42). Landesco did not focus on any one gangster in particular; his purpose was not to make ordinary gangsters into notorious figures. His purpose was strictly academic: to understand the nature and extent of organized crime in Chicago during the 1920s. Even the infamous Al Capone and his gang did not get any special attention in Landesco's study, except as an example of how organized crime was changing. The Capone gang was treated as an example of one type of gang.

Burgess showed tremendous insight when he wrote in the "Summary and Recommendations," section of Landesco's study that there was need for studies and publications on the conditions and causes of organized crime by research institutions. Furthermore, Burgess (1968) wrote, "Most of the research in the past has been based upon studies of men in prisons, but little study has been made of the behavior of the criminal in his own environment in the gang and in the neighborhood. In fact, more studies have been made of the criminal than of crime. Further research in this field is imperative" (p. 283). The fact that this recommendation was written in 1929 is quite astonishing since it is still being said by scholars today. Many have said that those who wish to study organized crime must go into the field to carry out their research (see Polsky 1967; Albini 1971; Chambliss 1971; Ianni and Ianni 1972; Potter 1994).

Empirical studies that have used participant observation as a primary research method (Albini 1971; Chambliss 1971; Ianni and Ianni 1972; Potter 1994) have provided some of the most valid and reliable data ever collected about organized crime. Participant observation was the primary method of investigation for Landesco. Landesco also utilized life histories "not only to check the materials obtained from other sources, but also to find out how the *gangster* looks at his own life" (p. 280). Field research has its limitations but the combining of methodologies, as Landesco did , helps to overcome some of these limitations. As previously indicated, Landesco used observation, interviews, public documents, and life histories in his research.

Before proceeding with a discussion of selected topics found in *Organized Crime in Chicago,* it is necessary to mention two points about the Landesco study. The first is that a significant finding of the Landesco research was that organized crime was not viewed as a formal structure. It was not seen as a monolithic criminal organization but as a network of fluid relationships. "This extra-legal government has no formal organization, but is best described as a *feudal system,* held together by powerful leaders, by intense personal loyalties, by the gangster's code of morals, by alliances with rival gangster Chiefs, and by their common warfare against the forms of organized society" (Burgess 1968, p. 278). Furthermore, writing about the O'Bannion gang Landesco (1968) states, "They probably operated more frequently together than the records show, but these occasional, changing partnerships for single projects are characteristic in this type of crime. Of course, connections with powerful fences, who take in and dispose of the loot, and with politicians and 'fixers' are as necessary here as in any field of crime" (p. 182). This conclusion by Landesco about the structure of organized crime is similar to that of many contemporary scholars (Albini 1971; Chambliss 1971; Ianni and Ianni 1972). It is a conclusion that challenges the view of organized crime as a hierarchical formal structure and as an "alien ethnic conspiracy." The second point the author wishes to make is that Landesco never defines organized crime for the reader. Today this would be a serious omission on the part of any researcher. As already indicated (chapt. 1), the very problem of defining organized crime is well documented in the criminological literature. Landesco was the first social scientist to give full-scale attention to organized crime, and it may be that he believed that what organized crime was would be obvious to any one reading his study; there were no scholarly definitions of organized crime at the time he was conducting his research. As stated repeatedly throughout this book, organized crime, for Landesco, was the environment of the gangster; that is, the gangster's social world. For Landesco, organized crime was part of the normal activities of urban centers.

The Landesco study: selected topics and findings

The opening chapter of *Organized Crime in Chicago* is titled "The McSwiggen Assassination as A Typical Incident." William McSwiggen was a young assistant state's attorney who was murdered in 1926. McSwiggen was killed by machine gun bullets in the front of a saloon. The incident was significant because it marked "the beginning of intense public interest in organized crime" (Landesco 1968, p. 22). The case demonstrated to the public the alliance between criminal gangs and the political machine. Theories about the murder abounded but a conspiracy of silence made it impossible for the coroner's jury and six grand juries to solve the murder. The findings did however convince the public that organized crime had a powerful existence in Chicago, "a power due in large part to its unholy alliance with politics" (Landesco 1968, p. 23).

Landesco's chapters on prostitution, Mont Tennes and Johnny Torrio describe and explain the "royal succession" in Chicago's organized crime, a succession which began with Colosimo and continued with Torrio (1920-24) and Capone (1924-32). Landesco especially notes the continuity and persistency of personalities in organized crime: "with the coming of prohibition, the personnel of organized vice took the lead in the systematic organization of this new and profitable field of exploitation. All the experience gained by years of struggle against reformers and concealed agreements with politicians was brought into service in organizing the production and distribution of beer and whiskey" (Landesco 1968, p. 43). Landesco's historical analysis of this so-called royal succession documents the existence of organized crime in Chicago prior to the great wave of Sicilian immigration to America in the late nineteenth century. "Organized crime is not, as many think, a recent phenomenon in Chicago. A study of vice, crime and gambling during the last twenty-five years shows the existence of crime and vice gangs during that period and how they have become more and more highly organized and powerful" (Landesco 1968, p. 25). This conclusion by Landesco challenges the normally held perception of many academics and nonacademics that organized crime was transported to America by foreigners, specifically Italians. In short, although Landesco was not aware of it at the time, he was the first sociologist to discredit the alien conspiracy theory!

Perhaps what stands out the most about Landesco's study of organized crime is the candor with which he talks about the power, influence, and immunity of gangsters, all of which he attributed to the alliance of organized crime and politics. Two chapters, "The Gangster and the Politician," and the "Funerals of Gangsters," document just how closely aligned organized crime and politics were during the late 1800s and 1920s. Landesco (1968) remarks that "The relation of the gangster and the politician becomes most obvious to the public on election day. Post-election contests and recounts expose the election frauds committed by the gangsters in behalf of the politicians" (p. 169).

Landesco (1968, pp. 185-89) describes vote frauds under three headings: (1) irregular practices of election officials; (2) irregular activities of party workers; and (3) proceedings subsequent to the announcement of the election returns. He then makes an outline of the practices and activities which fall under each heading. Landesco (1968, p. 184) draws the following conclusions about vote fraud based on investigations since 1900: (1) vote frauds occur in geographically limited areas; (2) investigations of election frauds are opposed and impeded by the incumbent state's attorney; (3) when the dominant party splits into factions, vote fraud investigations are carried out with great intensity with each faction trying to gain the political advantage; (4) election vote frauds that are legally proved are against the underlings who refuse to testify against their superiors; (5) centers of vote fraud have moved from the deteriorated areas of the city to territories controlled by the ethnic political machine; (6) conflict between young immigrant groups has resulted in political clubs aligned to a politician; (7) police witness and tolerate vote frauds because of the politician's power over their jobs; and (8) slugging and intimidation of voters is commonplace. Because the practice of vote fraud on the river wards was so common, nicknames were given to persons who engaged in certain activities. For example, a floater was "an amateur but usually homeless purchased voter, who votes many times during the day, going from precinct to precinct" (Landesco 1968, p. 189). Landesco concluded that it would not be easy to break up the amiable relationship between the gangster and the politician. The gangster and the politician came from neighborhoods in which the standards of morality accepted vote fraud; such was not the case in the lakefront districts. "The gangster depends upon political protection for his criminal and illicit activities. He, therefore, has a vital business interest in the success of certain candidates whom he believes will be favorably disposed to him" (Landesco 1968, p. 183).

The "friendliness" of the gangster and the politician is featured in Landesco's the "Funerals of Gangsters." Some of the funerals and their attendees that Landesco describes in this chapter are those of Big Jim Colosimo, Dion O'Bannion, Hymie Weiss, Vincent Drucci, and Frank Yale (the New York gunman of Colosimo and O'Bannion). Landesco comments that these ceremonies have attracted a great deal of public attention because of their ostentatiousness and because of the unusual membership of the attendees (gunmen, politicians, and other prominent citizens). Landesco (1968) writes:

> *Political power in a democracy rests upon friendship.* . . . Politics in the river wards, and among common people elsewhere as well, is a feudal relationship. The feudal system was one that was based not on law but upon personal loyalties. Politics tends, therefore, to become a *feudal system.* Gangs, also, are organized on a feudal basis—that is, upon loyalties, friendships, and above all dependability. (p. 193)

Therefore, the gangster and the politician understand one another and that is why they so readily enter into "friendships" against the established society. The idealists and reformers of the lakefront hold lofty values like justice, humanity, and righteousness, and do not make good friends. On the other hand, the inhabitants of the river wards are concerned with life's immediate goals and make good friends. The public has failed to destroy the relationship between the politician and the gangster because in this intimate world of ward politics there is no line between right and wrong as defined by the law (Landesco 1968, pp. 193-94).

Ward politics is carried on in a smaller, more intimate world, than is the larger, formal government. Ward bosses know the importance of participating in ceremonies which mark life events like birth, death, and marriage. The ward boss who attends the funeral of a gangster is linked in both life and death. As time went on, however, the flamboyance and number of prominent attendees at wakes and funerals declined. According to Landesco, there were a number of factors which accounted for this, notably: the disapproval by both the church and newspaper editorials of the gangster's life and career; and the growing sentiment by the public against the relationship between crime and politics. Landesco (1968) believed that the most powerful factor in explaining the decline of participants in gangster funerals was due to the changes "taking place in the nature of the relations of organized crime and machine politics" (p. 205). That is, that monetary considerations have superseded friendships in importance. Although Landesco discusses the alliance between organized crime and politics throughout his study, it is in the chapter on the funerals of gangsters that the more intimate picture of the friendly relations between gangster and politician clearly emerges. As Landesco (1968) writes, "In the hour of death personal ties are disclosed, which in life were concealed" (p. 205).

While the relationship between organized crime and politics has changed since Landesco's era it certainly emerges in new forms today. The fact that organized crime could not exist without the collusion and corruption of public officials is axiomatic. Yet contemporary researchers of organized crime have been faulted for not exposing these types of relationships. As Potter (1994) argues, "we need to raise the issue of corruption in a comprehensive manner.... We need to turn our attention away from the bad actors of the mob and look to the gatekeepers for the mob in the political system, in law enforcement, and in business. . . . writing books about money laundering, the subtle influences of organized crime on political leaders, and the accommodations between organized crime and law enforcement will make for important breakthroughs in our understanding of this phenomenon" (p. 44). In disclosing the alliances between politics and crime Landesco contributed much to our understanding of the complex nature of the interactions and processes of organized crime. Landesco knew that organized crime was a success because of the social, political, and economic environment in which it takes place. Yet at the time Landesco was writing, the public was probably not ready to hear such things. Beginning in the 1960s and afterwards, due to a number of historical events, there was a growing distrust of government and a greater willingness to believe that organized crime and politics were linked through corruption and collusion.

Landesco's chapter "The Beer Wars" has historical significance because it describes the primary characters and events during the Prohibition period in America. Landesco describes the South Side and West Side beer wars in some detail. His investigation (1968, pp. 104-5) led to the following conclusions: (1) the beer wars broke out when Torrio's organization no longer had political protection because of the Prohibition enforcement policy of the Dever administration; (2) few arrests and no convictions occurred during the period because of the gangster's refusal to speak; (3) the heavy casualties of the beer wars influenced leaders to call truces and divide territories; (4) the profits of beer running were well worth the risks involved; and (5) gangsters traffic in liquor despite a strong federal policy against it.

During the period in which Landesco was writing, racketeering, as a form of organized crime, was becoming visible. Landesco (1968) defines racketeering as "the exploitation for personal profit, by means of violence, of a business association or employees' organization" (p. 149). Landesco was interested in answering the question, "What conditions in Chicago have favored the rise, spread and persistence of extortion by violence as an aspect of organized crime" (p. 120)? In 1927, there were at least twenty-three separate businesses in Chicago in which racketeers were in control or were attempting to be in control. Landesco presents four cases in his chapter "Racketeering" which demonstrate how racketeering operates in business: (1) the laundry associations of Chicago, (2) cleaners and dyers; (3) the food dealers; and (4) the bootblacks. In each of these cases racketeering was a response to "an economic condition in which business is seeking agreements to end ruinous competition but where the Sherman Anti-Trust Act and similar legislation prohibit such agreements" (Landesco 1968, p. 279). Landesco concludes that the entrance of the "racketeer" into the field of business and industry in Chicago was due to the ruthless competition among small business enterprises and a tradition of lawlessness and violence in Chicago. Agreements to control competition in business or industry are illegal under the law. When an activity is illegal, be it the manufacturing of alcohol, gambling, or trade and price agreements, a situation is created wherein the gangster, on invitation or on his own, can gain entry. Equally important, law enforcement agencies in Chicago were unable to stop the strongmen tactics of the gangster and the gunmen (Landesco 1968, p. 167). In sum, Landesco felt that the machinery of justice had broken down. Just as the police and the courts failed in apprehending bootleggers and vice lords they also failed to maintain the law in labor and industry. Many necessary economic activities in Chicago were now controlled by the gunmen and the gangster. Landesco was writing during a time when gangsters were introducing the capitalist system into their operations, and he uncovered a form of organized crime that remains a problem of capitalistic economic systems today.

Before closing our discussion of selected topics and findings of the Landesco study, it is important to mention one last chapter, "A Who's Who of Organized Crime in Chicago." Landesco compiled a list of the four hundred most prominent men in Chicago's various fields of organized crime. How the list was compiled is explained in the chapter. However, more important than the method of compilation, are the conclusions Landesco reached about the men on the list. Landesco found that the hierarchs of organized crime were primarily engaged in four activities: bootlegging, gambling, vice, and racketeering. For these crimes the chieftains received enormous profits and are immune from punishment and prosecution because of political alliances and their strong financial positions. The associates of the chieftains were more likely to receive punishment for their crimes, yet even this punishment was petty. Many of the former vice lords moved from other forms of crime and vice to bootlegging, with the commencement of Prohibition. This does not mean however that they have given up their earlier criminal operations, but continue in these operations. Protected because of their political alliances and financial backing, these men were able to murder, rob, and burglarize without consequence. Landesco believed that identifying these organized criminals would help in the control and prevention of organized crime. Landesco (1968) writes, "Further research and continuous and complete records are necessary if any large sized urban community is to protect itself against the forces of organized crime and political corruption" (p. 249). One thing Landesco has done, without spelling it out for the reader, is to show how organized crime is quite capable of adapting to new and emerging markets. Furthermore, only with the increasing use of the Racketeer

Influenced and Corrupt Organizations (RICO) statute in the 1980s has the government been able to prosecute organized criminals. RICO is a provision in the Organized Crime Control Act of 1970 that makes it illegal for any individual or group to conduct or participate in any illegal enterprise through a pattern of racketeering activity. The federal government defines a pattern of racketeering activity as committing two or more "racketeering" offenses within a ten year period. The penalties for violating the RICO statute include, but are not limited to, up to twenty years of imprisonment and fines up to $25,000. Still, many top organized crime figures, even today, are able to escape prosecution for many years (e.g., witness the recent case of John Gotti). Furthermore, today we know that prosecuting and convicting the hierarchs of organized crime has not diminished the pool of organized crime figures (see Albanese 1985; Potter 1994). Therefore, Landesco was naïve in thinking that identifying organized criminals would greatly reduce the number of organized criminals.

Theorizing about the participation of individuals in organized crime

There has been little attempt on the part of social scientists to explain why people engage in organized criminal activities. Sociologists and criminologists have offered a variety of explanations to explain street crime, especially crimes committed by juveniles, but rarely have these explanations been directed solely at organized crime. Yet existing criminological theories can be applied to organized crime (see Abadinsky 1990a, pp. 45-59). In fact, although Landesco did not recognize his efforts as such, in "The Gangster's Apologia" Landesco makes several attempts to explain organized crime, stopping short of developing any full-blown theory of organized crime. If we look closely at this chapter, we can see the earliest efforts on the part of a sociologist to explain why individuals engage in organized crime. In the work of Landesco are found the core ideas of comprehensive theories developed by a later generation of scholars. These comprehensive theories are ethnic succession, anomie, differential opportunity, cultural transmission, and differential association. Only one, ethnic succession theory, was originally focused on adult criminality and the participants of organized crime.

Influenced by the previous work of the Chicago school criminologists, Thrasher, Shaw, and McKay, Landesco (1968) agreed that certain neighborhoods, "where the gang tradition is old" (p. 207), are criminogenic. In these neighborhoods delinquent attitudes and values are transmitted from one generation to the next (hence the theory of cultural transmission). In these neighborhoods adolescents form close relationships with adult criminals and learn from them a criminal way of life. Landesco (1968) notes that the life histories of gangsters "corroborate the conclusion arrived at by the famous French criminologist, Gabriel Tarde, that certain individuals become criminals in much the same way that other persons become police officers" (p. 210). This statement by Landesco is remarkably similar to Sutherland's notion of differential association. The theory of differential association states that one learns to become a criminal in much the same way that one learns any conventional activity, through social interaction and interpersonal communication. In the process of social interaction one acquires "an excess of definitions favorable to violation of laws over definitions unfavorable to violation of the law." The Chicago school theorists were convinced that criminality was not inherited. Race or ethnicity had nothing to do with why one turned to organized crime. Therefore, adolescents, through cultural transmission and differential association, would acquire the necessary skills and attitudes to gain entry into the world of organized crime.

Sociologist Robert Merton developed the theory of "social structure and anomie" in 1938. According to Merton all Americans desire economic success. However, not all Americans have the legitimate opportunities available to them to reach the culturally prescribed goal of economic success. Opportunities for success are not evenly distributed throughout the social structure. Merton referred to this disjuncture between the available legitimate means and the culturally prescribed goals as anomie. When individuals cannot obtain success through legitimate channels they will turn to illegitimate means, including organized crime. Differential opportunity theory, introduced by Richard Cloward and Lloyd Ohlin in 1960, is a blending of the principles found in cultural transmission, differential association, and anomie. Differential opportunity theory argues that just because legitimate opportunities are unavailable to adolescents does not necessarily mean that illegitimate opportunities will be available. In order for adolescents to be recruited into organized crime, a criminal subculture must exist in the neighborhood, characterized by organized and successful criminals, who act as role models to the younger boys. According to Landesco (1968, pp. 210-12) the role models for the young boys in the neighborhood are the gangsters who have achieved success. Furthermore, these young adolescents weigh the opportunities for success in a legitimate versus an illegitimate career, and are lured into organized crime by its economic advantages. Unlike most of the state crime surveys of the 1920s, Landesco was aware of the socioeconomic causes of organized crime. Landesco demonstrated another approach to our understanding of organized crime, one in contrast to the law enforcement approach of the early crime surveys.

Finally, Landesco's explanation of organized crime is strikingly similar to Bell's (1953) ethnic succession thesis. Ethnic succession argues that each new wave of immigrants into the country tries to succeed economically. Sometimes legitimate avenues to success are blocked and these immigrants turn to illegal means to achieve success. When illegal opportunities through crime result in economic success then legitimate opportunities for success become available too. The immigrant group then moves out of organized crime, a new immigrant group takes its place, and the ethnic succession process continues. Not all scholars agree with the ethnic succession thesis. Lupsha (1981), for example, argues that as an ethnic group becomes successful in organized crime, its members do not leave the business but are joined in their criminal pursuits by their offspring and other ethnic immigrants.

Perhaps the principal criticism of Landesco's explanations of organized crime are that they are overly deterministic. The gangster is a natural product of his environment and therefore destined to a life of crime. Landesco fails to recognize that individuals do make choices. Furthermore, some individuals who participate in organized criminal activities do so for easy money and excitement. Given an equally legitimate career choice these individuals would still engage in organized criminal activities; blocked opportunities have little to do with the career choice. Nevertheless, in Landesco's writing are found the very first efforts to explain organized crime. Although his ideas were not fully developed, they did provide the groundwork for later theories.

In sum, Landesco has presented us with a comprehensive description of organized crime in Chicago during the early part the twentieth century, complete with important names, dates, events, and places. If nothing else, it is an invaluable reference source. While it is true that Landesco's work is essentially descriptive, written in a journalistic style, it still has historical and sociological significance. Landesco deserves credit for being the first academic sociologist to study organized crime in its entirety, to present an alternative model to the alien conspiracy theory, and to theorize about the participation of individuals in organized crime. In fact, it is unfortunate that Cressey (1969) ignored this work. Perhaps Cressey's conclusions about the structure of organized crime would have been significantly different if he had consulted the Landesco study. Landesco's candidness about the social, economic, and political aspects of organized crime during the 1920s probably has much to do with why his study was brushed aside until a new generation of scholars uncovered it during the late 1960s and early 1970s. Landesco was the first academic to enlighten the American public about the true nature and extent of organized crime in a specific locality. He exposed organized crime and stripped it of its mystery and secrecy. The exposure of organized crime alerts the public about the true nature of organized crime and, therefore, to the need for prevention and control.

6

Organized crime: What the public knew and what sociologists studied, 1890-1994

A S STATED in chapter 1, an important aspect of the topic of this book concerns the extent to which organized crime was a vital part of public interest and opinion at the time that American sociology seemed to be ignoring it. If the American public, including its practitioners of social science and criminology, were unaware of organized crime, then it would not be interesting or surprising that the Chicago school sociologists ignored such a remarkable phenomenon as an object of professional scrutiny. However, as this chapter will document, the American public, including its practitioners of social science and criminology, were offered a portrait of the gangster as a familiar cultural object, primarily through the newspapers and movies of the day.

This chapter concentrates on how organized crime was presented to the American public, from 1890 to 1994, through journalistic accounts, governmental studies and reports, media portrayals, and, less frequently, social scientific studies. Through an examination of newspapers[1] and movies of the day, and classical and contemporary books and articles, we will come to see how organized crime was presented to the American public and what, if anything, American sociologists were contributing to the public's perception of organized crime through their social scientific studies. This chapter is divided into three major parts. Parts one and two consider public perceptions of organized crime in two historical periods: 1890 to 1949 and 1950 to 1994. In part three, an important source of public opinion which helped to shape the general public's perception of organized crime in the United States, the gangster film, is reviewed. In short, this chapter will document the extent of public knowledge of and interest in organized crime by the general public and American sociologists. Before we begin it would be useful to briefly examine why there is and has been such a public interest in and fascination with organized crime.

Public interest in and fascination with organized crime

Today the public is highly conscious of the phenomenon of organized crime. This is evident by the numerous government reports, newspaper articles, books, television programs, and movies involving American organized crime. The actual and mythical deeds of criminal societies such as the Black Hand, Mafia, Murder Incorporated, and La Cosa Nostra have captured the imaginations of Americans for generations. Homer (1974) notes that each new generation of Americans is introduced to a new criminal organization and to new law enforcement combatants "in the never ending battle between organized crime and law enforcement" (p. 1). Homer (1974, p. 1; cf. Ianni and Ianni, pp. 3-4) has traced the developments between organized crime and law enforcement combatants from the 1920s to the 1970s. During the 1920s, an era identified by organized crime, the gangsters of New York and Chicago fought Ness and his men. Men like James Cagney, Edward G. Robinson, Robert Stack, and David Jansen acted out these conflicts on the TV and movie screens. The late 1930s and early 1940s focused on a gang named Murder Incorporated by the press. In 1951 there were the televised Kefauver hearings, followed by the Apalachin meeting in 1957, and the testimony of Joe Valachi before the McClellan committee in 1963. According to Ianni and Ianni (1972; cf. Albini 1971; Albanese 1989), "After Valachi testified, *Mafia and Cosa Nostra* began to be used interchangeably as generic terms for organized crime" (p. 4). Subsequently, in 1969, the public disclosure of the "DeCavalcante Tapes" suggested that there was an Italian-American criminal organization in the New York-New Jersey-Pennsylvania region and that it was under the directorship of a commission.

In the 1970s, attention was focused on Meyer Lansky, a so-called gang leader, who refused to return to the United States from Israel to face charges resulting from his involvement in Las Vegas gambling casinos. Also in the 1970s Joseph Columbo, reputed Cosa Nostra leader, was shot at a rally he organized in New York City to protest the harassment of Italian Americans by the FBI and other enforcement agencies. In the 1980s, the battle between organized crime and law enforcement took on a new fervor. Rudolph Giuliani became "the most celebrated racketbuster in New York since Thomas E. Dewey" (Fox 1989, p. 399). The mob trials of the 1980s saw the alleged heads of the five New York crime families (Bonanno, Colombo, Gambino, Genovese, and Lushes) under indictment for racketeering and various other crimes (see Albanese 1989, pp. 62-69). In 1992, John Gotti, alleged head of the Gambino crime family, was finally imprisoned after several failed attempts by the American government.

Several writers (Ianni and Ianni 1972; Galliher and Cain 1974; Homer 1974; Smith 1975; Cashman 1981; Martens and Cunningham-Niederer 1985, and others) have commented on the role of the media in stimulating public interest about organized crime. The prominence of Italian Americans in organized crime has been trumpeted in the press. This interest in Italian Americans involvement in organized crime has been constant since the Kefauver committee hearings. Ianni and Ianni

(1972) write that "Each new government disclosure . . . is followed by books, articles and films presenting fictional or 'documentary' accounts based upon the data supplied by government sources" (p. 6). Journalists whose books are based on government data have been the biggest benefactors.

According to sociologist John E. Conklin (1973, p. 1; cf. Kooistra, 1989), public interest in the activities of gangsters may lie in certain social and psychological factors. The American public is fascinated with violence. Organized criminals often use violence and intimidation to gain power. People may like to see others act violently because they themselves would like to act violently but are unable to "due to lack of opportunities, fear of consequences, or repressed impulses" (Conklin 1973, p. 1). Furthermore, violence is often portrayed in the media as a battle between two competitors. This element of competition may also make violence fascinating even though it is at the same time loathed. "Public fascination with organized crime stems in part from the misperception that only 'deserving' victims suffer from the violence of organized crime" (Conklin 1973, p. 2). The mistaken belief is that gangsters only kill each other. In truth, witnesses, informants, and innocent bystanders have been the victims of gangland violence.

It has also been argued that the general public is interested in the activities of gangsters because they "reflect and distort dominant American values" (Conklin 1973, p. 2; cf. Lerner 1957; Landesco 1968; Allsop 1968; Haller 1971-72; Kooistra 1989). Gangsters have become "innovators" (to borrow a phrase from Robert Merton). They have turned to illegal means to achieve the American success goal of economic wealth. Daniel Bell (1953) has acknowledged that this "queer ladder of social mobility" has helped many ethnic minorities obtain upper- and middle-class respectability.

Allsop (1968) comments that the immigrant youth in American cities were taught the "New World credo of private enterprise, competition and material success" (p. 250). It was a lesson they learned well. They became wealthy and powerful bootlegging leaders. They were admired for going after what they wanted and for the authority they openly expressed. "To achieve self-advancement the bootlegger used methods—murder and violence—which the ordinary citizen stopped a long way short of, yet his attitude to life, his beat-your-neighbor tactics, his triumph in the competitive system at its most ferocious extreme, had a kind of romantic righteousness" (Allsop 1968, p. 250). This was capitalism operating at its best.

Social historian Max Lerner (1957) asks the question: Why are Americans drawn to gangster films which they know are "distortions of their urban life" (p. 603)? Lerner (1957) answers that "a gangster is an American 'cultural hero' in whom Americans recognize a symbol of the energy of their culture" (p. 603). For, the delinquent and the criminal value property so much that they will do anything to make it theirs. The adult racketeer is often an immigrant youth who came up from the slums and aims to be successful. While attempting to assimilate they absorb only the unrefined aspects of the culture. The slum youngster just wants to get ahead, even if violence has to be used. This drive to succeed points not to the destruction of

American life but to its forcefulness (Lerner 1957, pp. 604-05, 665).

Lerner has not been the only observer to comment on the gangster as a "cultural hero" Conklin (1973, p. 3) and others (Landesco 1968; Allsop 1968; Haller 1971-72; Shadoian 1977; Earley 1978; Cashman 1981; Kooistra 1989; Powers 1983) have also noted that we often consider the gangster a hero, though an asocial one. Sociologist Paul Kooistra (1989), writing about Capone, states that "He was a curious blend of American virtue and noble outlaw" (p. 138). Kooistra (1989, pp. 138-39; cf. Powers 1983, p. 6) explains that while Capone was a vicious outlaw he was also considered an "American Robinhood." He targeted the rich and aided the poor, he provided a service to the public during Prohibition, he interacted freely and frequently with luminaries and politicians which allowed him a sense of dignity, and he had warm friendly relations with the press so he could tell his side of the story before reformers could turn the citizens against him. Even when Capone was convicted of income tax evasion the American public sympathized with him as a victim of an overzealous government. Capone was a "political embarrassment" to the city government and therefore was made an example of by justice officials (Kooistra 1989, p. 138; cf. Powers 1983; Woodiwiss 1987). Kooistra (1989) comments that "Of all the noted Godfathers of American history, Capone comes closest to being an American Robinhood primarily because of the social context in which he emerged—the depression—and because he and his influential supporters attempted to create such an image" (p. 140).

Finally, the current interest in organized crime is due to its secrecy and mystery. Because of this secrecy we yearn to know more. We read all that we can and see all that we can. When we read or view *The Godfather* we feel as though we just took a peek at something illegal (Conklin 1973, p. 4).

Public perceptions of organized crime: 1890-1949

Public perceptions of organized crime have passed through several stages. These stages are often a direct result of the dissemination of public knowledge about organized crime. Dissemination often comes from governmental studies and commissions, journalistic accounts, media portrayals, and less frequently, social scientific studies. As Smith (1975, p. 168) acknowledges, our present imagery of organized crime has come primarily from three sources: government accounts of identifiable members of the Mafia, scholarly accounts based on a sociological concept called "organized crime," and fictional accounts of the gangster or racketeer. Smith suggests that the Mafia label came first. The label then disappeared during the interwar period. There was a search for new labels and "gangster," "racketeer," and "organized crime" appeared on the scene. Simultaneously, novelists created and moving pictures portrayed "a popular and widely understood fictional gangster hero" (Smith 1975, p. 22). These terms had little connection before 1950. After 1950 however this all changed with the Kefauver hearings (cf. Smith 1975, p. 22; Moore 1974).

As we have seen earlier (chap. 3), the Mafia label first appeared in New Orleans in 1890, after the death of superintendent of police, David Hennessy. The mayor of

New Orleans gave the following account of the murder in the *New York Times* (October 19, 1890):

> The circumstances of the cowardly deed, the arrests made and the evidence collected by the Police Department show beyond doubt that he was the victim of Sicilian vengeance, ... because he was seeking by the power of our American law to break up the foreign vendettas that have so often filled our streets with blood. Heretofore, these scoundrels have confined their murdering among themselves. . . . Bold indeed was the stroke aimed at their first American victim. (p. 1)

It seems that while Hennessy was conscious in his hospital room he had a visit from a Captain Beanham, a member of the Police Board. It has been suggested that Hennessy commented to Beanham that "the dagoes shot me" or "Sicilians have done for me" (Smith 1975, p. 22; Albanese 1989, p. 17). Albanese (1989) comments that these dying words were "interpreted as indicating an Italian connection with his death" (p. 17). When some of the men accused of killing Hennessy were acquitted, it angered the citizens of New Orleans and a lynch mob was formed. The mob hanged two and shot nine of the men who they thought was responsible for Hennessy's death. The contemporary Mafia image was set up; ethnically identifiable persons were responsible for the killing of Hennessy (Smith 1975, p. 29)!

The facts which preceded the Hennessy shooting are very confusing and a number of loose ends remain. One newspaper account stated that "Hennessy . . . incurred the hostility of a certain lawless Italian element here by arresting and sending on a steamer to New York the famous Bandit Esposito, who was sent back to his native land, tried, and convicted. Parties here who falsely swore that they had known Esposito as a law-abiding citizen of New Orleans for many years in order to prove an alibi, are among those suspected of the crime" (*New York Times*, October 17, 1890, p. 1).

An additional *New York Times* account (October 19, 1890, p. 1; cf. Albini 1971, pp. 159-67; Smith 1975 pp. 27-44; Albanese 1989, p. 18) suggests a business rivalry between two Italian families, the Matrangas and the Provenzanos. The Matrangas and the Provenzanos had fought over control of the New Orleans dock areas. Originally the Provenzanos had controlled the area. One evening while the Matrangas were returning from their work they were fired upon by the Provenzanos. Several of the Matrangas were wounded, including Tony Matranga, the leader. Chief Hennessy quickly arrested those who the Matrangas accused of this crime. Several of the Provenzanos were convicted but a new trial was ordered because of new evidence. Chief Hennessy had found out that the witnesses for the Matrangas had perjured themselves. The Matrangas were upset with Chief Hennessy who they thought was influential in getting the judge to set aside the original verdict. It was also believed that Hennessy had obtained the records of the Matrangas from Sicily. If these records were admitted into evidence then the Provenzanos would be acquitted. Hennessy was scheduled to testify against the Matrangas at the retrial. Hennessy was going to testify that the Matrangas were part of the "Mafia" in New

Orleans. His death, according to some, proved the existence of a "Mafia" in New Orleans. The issue of a Mafia in New Orleans was not brought up in the retrial of the Provenzanos. It seems that the need to believe in the existence of a local Mafia was present in the minds of the citizenry of New Orleans. This belief existed regardless of the fact that there was no evidence to support this conclusion (see Smith 1975, p. 32; Albanese 1989. p. 18).

A third explanation for the murder of Hennessy has been provided by Smith (1975, p. 33). Negative feelings against the local foreigners had already existed. The death of Hennessy intensified these negative feelings against foreigners. It did not matter which side Hennessy was on, the Matrangas or the Provenzanos. Nor did it matter what conclusions the facts might support. What did matter was that the dispute involved Sicilians and that his preference for one side led to his murder by the other side. No matter what, the New Orleans citizenry would see that justice was done. Whether that justice was legal justice or vigilante revenge did not matter.

It is uncertain if the principal issue was prejudice against the Italians. However, immigration restriction was a major concern of the time, and newspaper accounts appear to indicate that citizens believed criminality was a trait Italians brought with them to the New World. The following newspaper account from the *New York Times* (October 18, 1890) supports this view:

> A large majority of the immigrants arriving here are Italians and Sicilians, more than fifteen hundred having arrived here within the last twelve months. In a day or two 800 more are expected on the steamship Alicia from Palmero, Sicily, and 700 more are en route. The Italians have heretofore been allowed to land without a very strict examination, and some of them were paupers, brigands, or ex-convicts. The United States Collector of Customs stated today that the department, in view of the recent assassination, had determined to strictly enforce the immigration laws and send every one who could not pass a rigid examination back whence he came. (p. 1)

An additional *New York Times* (October 19, 1890) article reads, "It seems that the city is on the eve of a bloody race riot. . . . Public feeling is strongly aroused against the Italian colony, and the least thing would precipitate a riot. A steamship is now on her way up the river from Italy with over eight hundred immigrants on board, and a determination is expressed to prevent their landing" (p. 1).

It seems that as soon as Hennessy's murder was linked to Italians, a "Mafia" conclusion was inevitable. It did not matter what really happened (Smith 1975, p. 38). When Hennessy's murder was avenged, the local Mafia ceased to be a public issue. However, the issue was briefly revived in 1909 with the murder of New York City police lieutenant Joseph Petrosini. Historian William Moore (1974, pp. 8-9) suggests that Petrosini added credibility to the myth of a Mafia conspiracy. Petrosini was convinced that there was no nationally organized secret society but rather local extortionists who preyed on the fears of Italians who believed in legendary exploits of the Mafia or Black Hand in Sicily. Petrosini traveled to Italy and Sicily to gather information on certain immigrants. He was killed in Palmero, Sicily, by an unknown gunman. This unsolved murder, which was presented dramatically by the press, encouraged the belief in the very organization Petrosini was trying to disprove. The Hennessy and Petrosini murders had a great effect on the perception of organized crime in America. The deaths of these two men persuaded the American public that Italian crime was an organized conspiracy and not individual acts. The press took their time in converting the old Mafia image, of rebels using violence against the established order, into a contemporary alien conspiracy model. After all, the "Mafia" was a newsworthy subject! The conspiracy model fit in well with the fears of radicalism and ethnic conspiracies which were sweeping the country at the turn of the century. These fears prompted talks of immigration restriction. However, the long term effects of a belief in a conspiracy model was that this perception of organized crime endured for decades afterwards (Moore 1974, p. 9).

After these murders, the Mafia disappeared from view until the Kefauver hearings (1950-51). In its place appeared the Black Hand. After the Black Hand came an interest in a third Italian criminal organization, the Camorra, a Neapolitan secret society. The Camorra has its beginnings in the prisons of Naples during the early decades of the nineteenth century. Soon afterwards the Camorra formed an alliance with the Bourban government and the police. The Camorra was allowed to carry out its illegal activities as long as it helped to control the malcontents of the working class. During the revolution of 1860, the Camorra was given full authority to maintain public order. The Camorra became a powerful organization. Eventually it was destroyed by the very kingdom that had originally given it its power. By the early part of the twentieth century the Camorra was no longer the powerful organization it once was (see Nelli 1976, pp. 19-20; Albini 1971, pp. 119-23). What attracted attention to the Camorra in the United States was "a mass trial at Viterbo, Italy, of thirty-six alleged members of the Neapolitan criminal association for the murder, in 1906, of Gennaro Cuocolo and his wife Maria" (Smith 1975, p. 55). The trial lasted nearly two years. It concluded in July, 1912, with the conviction of twenty-six defendants.

The trial attracted press coverage from all major European papers and a stream of journalists and other observers from America. G. B. McClellan, former mayor of New York, and Arthur Train, former assistant district attorney for Manhattan, sent reports back to America. McClellan pushed the idea that the Camorra had created New York City's Black Hand. Train identified New York City's Italian criminals as linked to either the Camorra or the Mafia in southern Italy. However, he noted that the Mafia had a much more obvious influence in America than the Camorra (Smith 1975, p. 55).

Law enforcement agencies during the period from 1890 to 1915 considered secret criminal organizations to be a serious threat. Three names competed for the criminal label at the turn of the century and the Mafia label won out. As Smith (1975) suggests, "American commentators 'saw' only corruption in the Camorra and only violence in the Mafia. And it was the violence of the Mafia that survived as an almost subliminal base for today's images" (p. 61). Therefore, for all practical purposes, the labels Mafia, Camorra, and Black Hand were only archaic reminders of criminal activity prior to World War I. The Mafia label was reserved for specific persons (Italians) and events (violent ones) (Smith 1975, pp. 64-65). As Ianni and Ianni (1983) note, "The crimes in the early Italian colonies were those of the Mafia and Camorra— extortion through threats of physical violence, blood feuds (vendettas), and the kidnapping of brides" (p. 1099). These crimes were perpetrated by individuals or small groups. With the onset of Prohibition, crime became more organized and moved out of the ethnic neighborhoods. There was now an abundance of criminal activity to be labeled. Opportunities were available in bootlegging, prostitution, gambling, and usury (money lending). Second- generation Italians and non-Italians "became known as 'gangsters' or 'racketeers'" (Smith 1975, p. 64). The image of the gangster and the racketeer was depicted in novels and films of the period. The moving pictures generally ignored the issue of ethnicity and therefore the Mafia, Camorra, and Black Hand were not resurrected (see Smith 1975, p. 64; Golden 1980, p. 82). The press also seemed to ignore this issue of ethnicity. During the 1920s, Italians were heavily involved in violating Prohibition and gambling laws. Yet the press never focused on any ethnic conspiracy. Capone's power was attributed to the dissatisfaction born of Prohibition and not to any conspiratorial organization (Moore 1974, p. 20). Capone was known as a gangster and a racketeer (even mistakenly being credited for the origin of the latter term) (Smith 1975, p. 64). Barnes and Teeters (1943), in their criminology text *New Horizons in Criminology*, comment, "Whoever invented the term, or the practice [racketeering] . . . it is certain that Al Capone was the first conspicuous personage to bring it to public attention and to elevate it to the level of a leading American 'big business'" (p. 32). In any event, despite Capone's ethnic identification he was not known as a Cammorist or a Mafioso. These labels were just not very prevalent during the Prohibition era. In fact, Landesco's account of organized crime in Chicago, first published in 1929, gave the Mafia label little notice. Landesco did not equate the crimes of the Mafia in Sicily with the crimes of the American racketeer. Landesco (1968) states, "In Chicago there has developed a pattern like the Mafia among groups, such as 'Racketeer' organizations and trade associations, which did not import the pattern as an old-world trait" (p. 120).

The search for new names during the interwar period began with "gangster." "Gangster" needs to be distinguished from its root "gang." "Gang" referred to groups like Monk Eastman and Paul Kelly in New York and Mike McDonald in Chicago. It was these "gangs" which rose to prominence during Prohibition. There are two principal distinctions between "gangster" and "gang." The gangster was seen as a modern businessman. The gangs were made up of hooligans. Further, as the gangsters assumed the role of modern businessmen their behavior became less refined. Their main goal was profit and they would kill for it if they had to (Smith 1975, p. 65).

While the character of the gangster was reasonably clear, what was not clear was what he did. The gangster could be skillful at a number of activities, which included, but were not limited to, robbery, bootlegging, strike breaking, and extortion. "Occasionally, as a substitute for 'gangster,' he might be known as a 'mobster,' though the concept 'mob' has generally been reserved for riots and lynching" (Smith 1975, p. 66). The gangster label failed to account for all the activities that members of criminal associations might be involved in. Therefore, a new label was needed. This new label was "racketeer." This label encompassed a wider scope of criminal activities (Smith 1975, p. 66).

The word "racket" itself has a variety of origins, none of which are certain. Gurefin (1962, pp. 181-82) offers a number of plausible theories: (1) the term was used in 1885 when an official investigating a teamster's union said, "this is not a noise but a racket"; (2) the word caught on by way of the vaudeville stage where it once meant an easy way of getting along in the world, that is, through entertainment; and (3) the word was used to describe a loud noise, especially a party or good time, given by the social clubs of young men in New York City—these young men, and later local gangsters, pressured shopkeepers into buying tickets for these parties. Gurefin also suggests that the word became popular in Chicago during the 1920s, and was first used by gambling boss Timothy Murphy. Albini (1971) comments that "Gunther (1929) maintains that the term originated in Chicago during the 1920s and referred to the noise or racket made by hoodlums in the hangouts they frequented" (p. 29). The term later gained common usage when these individuals came to be referred to as "racketeers" by the newspapers. Courtney Terret (1930) maintains that the origin of the term comes from a mechanism of torture, the rack, indicating the racketeer's "slow and continuous method of inflicting pain without effecting the ultimate death of the victim" (Albini 1971, p. 29). Gordon Hostetter and Thomas Beesley published *It's A Racket!* in 1929. They define racket as "parasitic activity in which the racketeer lives from the industry of the victim, the latter being kept under control by he use of terror, force, and intimidation" (Albini 1971, p. 30). Barnes and Teeters (1943) state that "The word originally meant one's business, so that 'What business are you in?' was often asked thus: 'What's your racket?'" (p. 32). Landesco (1968) defined racketeering as "the exploitation for personal profit, by means of violence, of a business association or employees' organization" (p. 149). Landesco (1968, p. 149) quoting an article in the *Chicago Journal of Commerce*, December 17, 1927, states that the racketeer, through force and intimidation, organizes small business men into so-called protective associations, and is then able to collect dues, impose fines, and regulate prices and hours of work so that he will make a profit. During the 1920s and 1930s the newspapers gave various accounts of the origins of "racket" and "racketeering." One *New York Times* (November 20, 1927) article read:

> The public prosecutor of Cook County—which in effect means Chicago—has coined a new word and turned the attention of the law to Chicago's "racketeers." . . . All of Chicago and most of the rest of the world have known for years that certain colorful characters, whose criminal specialties ranged all the way from plain slugging to wholesale murder, have seized control of certain labor unions and business associations, and have operated them as private property. Now there is credible evidence to indicate that three or four gangsters operate a syndicate which does a wholesale business in organizing unions and

associations, or stealing those that are already organized, and plundering them scientifically. At least a score of such organizations seem to be under the control of this group. (p. 2)

An article in the *New York Times* (April 11, 1932), stated that Frank Loesh, head of the Chicago Crime Commission, defined the terms "racket" and "racketeer." "'Racketeers' are people who maintain themselves by working a racket. The racket is a scheme for making a dishonest livelihood by crooked, illegal, or criminal practices or all combined. The racket maintains itself by the industry of others" (p. 6). An additional *New York Times* (March 8, 1931) article suggests that "Troy was a racket; it levied tribute on the traders of its time. The feudal system was a racket; it made the peasant pay for protection. The Mafia was a racket; it exploited the landowner and the business man. Through the centuries, the fundamentals remain unchanged. Stripped of frills, the racket is nothing but extortion of a regular, fixed payment by threat of injury" (p. 6). One *New York Times* (August 9, 1931) article, discussing the origins of the "rackets" in Chicago states:

> Twenty-five years ago the use of "racket" as a slang term meant a sort of "shindig," a spree, a riotous party. To "stand the racket" meant to stand the consequence or expense. To say "What's the racket?" meant to inquire "What's it all about?"—meaning a party, plan, or proceeding. . . . It is quite clear that the use of the term to describe certain underworld activity became current four or five years ago in Chicago. Its use there was and is more exact than in most other American cities. A very pointed and illuminating definition of the term racket, . . . , is that of Colonel Robert Isham Randolph, president of the Chicago Association of Commerce and the leading figure in recent vigilante activity by business men of the city. He says that a racket is "a conspiracy to commit extortion by intimidation, force, violence, blackmail, arson, murder, kidnapping, bombing and undue influence." As the word has been taken over from Chicago however, it has become blurred beyond recognition until it has become the custom of even well-informed people to use it to describe all sort of undesirable conduct. (p. 1)

The term "racket" had multiple uses. Therefore the perception of the racketeer was unclear. However, as the concept developed in Chicago, it generally referred to organized illegal activity (extortion). The "rackets" and "racketeering" appear to have been public knowledge in Chicago as early as 1927. The focus of racketeering in Chicago was on the business or employee association.

For instance, when Hostetter and Beesley published *It's A Racket!* in 1929, they hardly made a reference to the bootlegging and gambling that was taking place in their hometown of Chicago. According to Hostetter and Beesley, the rackets were a defect of capitalism, rather than a gang phenomenon. There was a disrespect for the law and its observance. The consequence of the rackets was the alliance between politics, crime, and corruption. Barnes and Teeter (1943), discussing the business aspect of racketeering, suggest that "racketeering is mainly borderline crime. It often has a direct connection with legitimate business, making illegitimate gains out of legitimate industry . . . Violence is used only to secure acquiescence and to keep monopoly of a given racket. The top racketeers deplore violence and utilize it only as a last resort" (p. 60). In a similar vein Smith, (1975) writes that "The portrait of the racketeer was of a nouveau riche, almost vulgarly wealthy Beau Brummel. He was a businessman, not a criminal, and he rationalized his activity as being a service to other businesses" (p. 70). The image of the racketeer was expressively captured in one *New York Times* (August 18, 1929), article:

> . . . the racketeer is as nebulous as his business. He is likely to be the respectable man who lives next door to a detective in the suburbs. Quite often he occupies a suite in a fancy Broadway hotel. He moves in sedate circles with a quiet air and in rowdier ones with the more obvious attributes of the under-world character. Some of them "follow the horses," savor the salt breezes and rub elbows with the eminently respectable on the better known beaches. They loaf in all-night restaurants on Broadway and frequent the speakeasies in the Forties. When they are out of funds, they retreat to a furtive way of living and keep a wily eye open for the next job that will bring them "velvet." Their cars are sold. Their flashiness sobers down until they run into "luck" again. (p. 6)

In time, the image of racketeering split into two distinctive categories, labor racketeering and other forms of organized extortion. This distinction meant that the "racketeering" label was no longer an accurate term to describe criminal activities that were organized. A new, more inclusive term, was needed and that term was "organized crime." Organized crime became an umbrella term for all the organized criminal activities of the interwar period, including the organized criminal activities of the gangster and the activities of organized commercial vice (see Smith 1975, pp. 74-75). Originally the term was just a new name for continuing crimes. However, as indicated in chapter 1, the term eventually came to mean a formally structured nationwide conspiracy.

The publicity of the Murder Incorporated trials during the late 1930s and early 1940s increased the public's awareness of the phenomenon of organized crime. District Attorneys Thomas E. Dewey and William O'Dwyer exposed Murder Incorporated, which was a "ring of Jewish and Italian extortionists and murderers" (Ianni and Ianni 1972, p. 3). Once again the issue of a national conspiracy was brought to public attention. The national coverage given these crime fighters encouraged the American public to look for ethnic conspiracies. According to Moore (1974), because "academic criminologists, economists, and historians made no real effort to counter this tendency, . . . the study of organized crime became increasingly the province of prosecutors and sensationalists" (p. 24). In any event, the onset of World War II gave Americans something else to occupy their minds, that is, until the Kefauver committee hearings of 1951.

Before leaving this interwar period, it is important to discuss an additional criminal organization which gained prominence in the 1920s. This organization is the Unione Siciliane which helped the reemergence of the Mafia label in the 1950s. During the 1920s, the American Mafia became known also as the Unione Siciliane.

In 1895, a legitimate mutual-benefit society was formed in Chicago to assist immigrants with their social, financial, and economic needs. The "Mafia" gained control of the organization and members were forced to operate illegal stills in their homes, even before Prohibition. In 1925, some members tried to disassociate the name of the organization with crime by calling it the Italo-American National Union. The change in name did not help; the association was permanent in the minds of the public. During the 1920s, the name Unione Siciliane appeared in New York to identify the "Mafia." The exact date of change in names is unknown (Nelli 1976, p. 199). In the early 1960s the Unione was rediscovered as a benevolent society. Prior to this the Unione was given a primarily criminal description. Regardless of the Unione's earlier history, it became "a transitional label from the 'gangsters' of the twenties and thirties to the 'Mafiosi' of the fifties and sixties" (Smith 1975, p. 84).

Public perceptions of organized crime: 1950-94

The Mafia returned to public view in 1950 and 1951 (cf. Ianni and Ianni 1972, 1983; Moore 1974; Smith 1975; Woodiwiss 1987; Albanese 1989), when a special senate committee to investigate organized crime in the United States was active under the chairmanship of Senator Estes Kefauver of Tennessee.

Historian Michael Woodiwiss (1987) provides some historical background on Estes Kefauver. Kefauver hailed from a small town in Tennessee. He was elected to the House of Representatives in 1939 and became a senator in 1948. It is likely that his goal was to become president and to pave the way for his political ambitions he gained a reputation as a crime fighter.

Kefauver called for an investigation into crime in interstate commerce on January 1, 1950, and targeted interstate gambling activities and federal laws to control interstate gambling. Racing-news wire services, gambling operations, and gambling boss Frank Costello were the focus of the committee's work. The Kefauver hearings were televised in several cities. They began with New Orleans and ended in Chicago, the crime capital of the nation. Albini (1988) states that "Kefauver captured the imagination of the American public as the television camera for the first time gave America 'live coverage' of what the *Mafia* was like" (p. 344).

The Committee's perspective on gambling was already formed before the hearings began. Gambling was an immoral activity detrimental to other types of business. If the "Mafia" was at the root of America's organized crime problems, then enforcement of gambling laws, rather than regulation and control, was the only answer. Gambling, the major source of income for the "Mafia," would be eliminated through the Federal government's efforts (Woodiwiss 1987, p. 12).

The Kefauver committee concluded that the Sicilian Mafia was transplanted into America. The work of two journalists, Jack Lait and Lee Mortimer, columnists on the New York tabloid, the *Daily Mirror*, contributed to the Kefauver committee's Mafia conclusions. Lait and Mortimer produced a number of best-selling books beginning with *New York Confidential* in 1948, *Chicago Confidential* in 1950, *Washington Confidential* in 1951, and *U.S.A. Confidential* in 1952. Lait and Mortimer were the first of many journalists who would cash in on the naiveté of the public in matters concerned with organized crime. The *Confidential* books focused on communism and organized crime, two of the most important issues of post war America. The books played on the racist fears of the American public. It was an intolerant and hysterical period in American history. Black Americans and communists were vividly portrayed as our enemies. Coming from a small town and gullible about big city crime and vice, Kefauver believed the explanations of Lait and Mortimer. Organized crime had to be seen as something that developed on foreign shores and not something that developed inside the United States (Woodiwiss 1987, pp. 12-13).

The federal law enforcement agency which influenced the committee most was the Federal Bureau of Narcotics. Harold Anslinger, the Federal Bureau of Narcotics chief, developed a self-serving explanation for America's drug problem. Aliens were to blame for America's drug problem. Because the committee had already adopted a law enforcement rather than sociological view of crime, the committee readily accepted Anslinger's explanation (Moore 1974, p. 132). Addiction was not seen as the problem. The problem was that a criminal organization, known as the "Mafia," controlled the world's drug trade and the bulk of organized crime activities in America. The organization had to be attacked and the Federal Bureau of Narcotics was the agency to do just that.

Despite all of the efforts of the Kefauver committee, they never did prove that a criminal organization known as the Mafia was responsible for all the organized crime in the United States (see Albini 1971; Moore 1974; Smith 1975; Woodiwiss 1987; Albanese 1989). In truth, what the committee did find were Irish, Jewish, and Italian syndicate leaders who would cooperate in joint ventures when profitable to do so.

It appears that the sole intention of the Kefauver committee was to impose morality by tightening up enforcement of the existing legislation. Yet the United States today still produces gangsters. Drug prohibition offers much more to the gangsters of the future than unemployment or dead-end jobs. Gangsters who beat out the competition and escape detection continue to prosper (Woodiwiss 1987, p. 15).

While the Kefauver hearings advanced Kefauver's public career, the committee also contributed to a host of popular ideas about organized crime. The Committee adopted a law enforcement perspective rather than a sociological regulatory one. It did not even consider the economic, legal, and social conditions which give rise to organized crime. Instead, the committee implied that organized crime was forced on American society through an alien ethnic conspiracy (see Moore 1974, p. 237).

Academic and public interest began to turn to organized crime after the Kefauver hearings. For example, Smith (1975, p. 144) notes that the *New York Times Index* shows five Mafia citations for 1950 and eleven for 1951. After the Hennessy murder and before the Kefauver committee there was little interest in a "Mafia." Albanese (1989, p. 35) writes that the word "Mafia" during the period 1918 to 1943 could only be found in the *New York Times* four times. The bulk of the literature after the Kefauver hearings was highly sensational, primarily gangster biographies and law enforcement accounts of the Mafia and organized crime.

Robert Prall and Norton Mockridge published *This Is Costello* in 1951. Prall and Mockridge teamed up again in 1954 and published *The Big Fix*, which focused on police corruption in Brooklyn that was uncovered by investigating the Harry Gross gambling racket (Inciardi et al. 1977, p. 172).

Sid Feder, a journalist, worked with Joachim Joesten and published *The Luciano Story* (1954). This book is "a pro-Dewey account of the controversial commutation of Luciano's sentence" (Moore 1974, p. 250). Subsequently, in 1955 Joesten published *Dewey, Luciano and I*. Moore (1974, p. 250) comments that this book attacks the decision by the governor to commute Luciano's sentence based on the belief that the governor was afraid that Luciano could prove that he had framed him. Ed Reid's *Mafia* (1952), was the first of several journalistic accounts on the Mafia to appear after 1950. Reid cashed in on the Kefauver committee's publicity. Then, in 1953, Reid published *The Shame of New York*. The book was "an attempt to establish the criminal leadership of Thomas Luchese as America's leading 'Mafia Don' through the 1940s" (Inciardi et al. 1977, p. 172). Alston J. Smith published *Syndicate City* in 1954. Smith's was a journalistic account of the organized criminal underworld of Chicago. But unlike Virgil Peterson's *Barbarians in Our Midst* (1952), Smith refers to the Mafia. Peterson ignored the Mafia in his concern over the historic roots of gambling and politics (Smith 1975, pp. 146-47). Peterson's view was from the law enforcement perspective (Moore 1974, p. 249). Peterson focused on the relationship between politics, crime, and gang rule, just as Landesco did in *Organized Crime in Chicago* (1968). Both Peterson and Landesco explained the gangster as a natural product of his environment. Peterson however, began to use the term "organized crime" regularly in the chapters of his book written after the Kefauver committee hearings (Smith 1975, p. 147).

The principal journalistic critique of the Kefauver committee was Burton B. Turkus and Sid Feder, *Murder Inc.: The Story of 'The Syndicate'* (1953). *Murder Inc.* told of a series of murders in Brooklyn a decade earlier. Their story stands on the account of Abe ("Kid Twist") Reles, the informer whose testimony made possible the conviction and execution of seven men, most notably Louis ("Lepke") Buchalter. Turkus and Feder took exception to Reid's Mafia claim and to the Kefauver Committee conclusions. Turkus and Feder also took exception with the committee for confusing the Mafia and Black Hand (Moore 1974, p. 250).

Perhaps the strongest sociological criticism of the Kefauver committee was Daniel Bell's "Crime as an American Way of Life," which appeared in *The Antioch Review* in 1953 (see Ianni and Ianni 1972, p. 7; Smith 1975, p. 149; Fox 1989, p. 378; Albanese 1989, p. 37). Bell (1953) writes that "neither the Senate Crime Committee in its testimony, nor Kefauver in his book, presented any real evidence that the Mafia exists as a functioning organization" (p. 131). Bell provided an alternative explanation for the existence of organized crime in America. Bell (1953) argued that organized crime served as a way for immigrants to gain upward social mobility. Bell also believed that once these immigrants were well established in American life they would give up their careers in organized crime and enter conventional work.

The Mafia's role in organized crime remained uncertain as the Kefauver period came to a close (cf. Albini 1971, 1988; Ianni and Ianni 1972; Moore 1974; Smith 1975; Martens and Cunningham-Niederer 1985; Woodiwiss 1987; Albanese 1989). Ianni and Ianni (1972) state that "Even after the Kefauver Committee's investigations, the existence of a national organization of Italian-American criminals—whether *Mafia* or something else—remained a plausible but unproved contention of some law-enforcement agencies" (p. 3). Similarly Albini (1971) comments that the Kefauver committee did not prove the existence of the Mafia, they "merely presumed its existence" (p. 210). Albini (1988) comments that "Only one academic voice . . . Daniel Bell . . . took the Kefauver data to task and argued that Kefauver presented no real facts to prove the existence of *Mafia*" (p. 344). Albanese (1989) states "the independent investigations of Moore, Albini, and Bell could find no evidence of the alien conspiracy claimed to exist by the Kefauver Committee" (p. 38). Finally, Woodiwiss (1987) remarks, "When the Committee's conclusions were published in mid-1951 the press and the academic community, with only a few exceptions, failed to point out the almost complete absence of evidence and logic in the Committee's Mafia interpretation of organized crime and, in fact, confirmed large sections of the public in a belief that the Committee had 'proved' the existence of the all-powerful Mafia conspiracy" (p. 15).

The late 1950s and 1960s brought public attention to the "Mafia" again. The Apalachin Convention in 1957, the televised testimony of Joe Valachi, the pursuit by the late Robert F. Kennedy of organized crime members involved in illegal activities, and the formation of the Federal Strike Force in 1967 all focused attention on the "Mafia" as an identifiable organization once again. These events focused attention once again on organized crime as an exclusively Italian conspiracy. This image of organized crime has persisted to this day (cf. Smith 1975; Martens and Cunningham-Niederer 1985; Albanese 1989).

The Apalachin convention triggered another round of literature on the Mafia and organized crime. In 1958 there were eleven stories in the *New York Times* and ten more in 1959. Mafia stories even appeared in popular magazines. Eleven articles appeared under the Mafia label from 1957 to 1961 (Smith 1975, p. 181).

It was at this time that scholarly literature on organized crime began to appear. During the years 1962 and 1963, articles were published under the direction of the National Council On Crime and Delinquency, the American Academy of Political and Social Sciences, and the Notre Dame Law School. At the same time, an analysis by Earl Johnson, Jr., of the legal aspects of organized crime appeared in the *Journal of Criminal Law and Criminology and Police Science* (1962-63). These articles were indicative of the public's growing awareness of organized crime, but they contributed little to the public's understanding of the organized crime problem. Articles written by those in law enforcement focused on agency accomplishments. Those written by social scientists reinforced the earlier views of Thrasher and Landesco. Circulation of these articles was restricted and, as far as the Bureau of Narcotics was concerned, the comments from social scientists were better left hidden in obscure social science journals (Smith 1975, p. 182).

Two books of this period should not go unnoticed. *Brotherhood of Evil: The Mafia*, by Frederic Sondern, Jr., takes the position of the Narcotics Bureau and is based primarily on the Apalachin meeting of 1957 (Moore 1974, p. 251). The other book is Robert F. Kennedy's *The Enemy Within* (1960). This book focuses on the labor-management hearings of the late 1950s and is written from Kennedy's own biased perspective (cf. Moore 1974, p. 259; Smith 1975, pp. 182-83).

Two opposing voices were heard during this period. One was the voice of sociologist Gus Tyler and the other was the voice of Italian nationalist Giovanni Schiavo. In 1962, Gus Tyler edited *Organized Crime in America: A Book of Readings*. The book did not share the law enforcement perspective of its contemporaries. Tyler's introduction to the various parts of the book demonstrate his position that organized crime is a product and reflection of our national culture. Tyler looks at organized crime from the American tradition of gangs and demonstrates his thesis with stories from New York, Chicago, San Francisco, and other cities during the mid-1800s. Tyler (1962) states, "The roots of organized crime can be found in New York, in Kansas, Texas, and Missouri many decades before Volstead or Capone. The line of development from buccaneer to businessman, from fisticuffs to finance parallels the contour of the American economy" (p. 89). Tyler also disagreed with the contemporary view of the period that organized crime and Mafia were synonymous. Tyler (1962) writes, "While lurid journalism has made 'organized crime' and 'mafia' synonymous, this is a dangerous distortion of both the origin and nature of the underworld. Organized crime in America is not an import, 'Made in Sicily.' It is American, risen out of a native matrix of lawlessness, different but not dissimilar from that of Sicily. The underworld is not an Italian organization, but a vast syndicate of many ethnic and native groups" (p. 336). Smith (1975, p. 183) felt that Tyler's edited volume had limited impact since it did not share the popular law enforcement perspective which the American public was exposed to.

Giovanni Schiavo, published *The Truth About the Mafia and Organized Crime in America* in 1962. Schiavo especially attacks the Federal Bureau of Narcotics and Frederic Sondern, Jr., for fostering the myth of an America mafia.

The testimony of Joe Valachi before the McClellan committee in 1963 placed Mafia in the public's vocabulary permanently (see Smith 1975, p. 240; Albanese 1989, pp. 43-46). Valachi also gave the organization a new name, Cosa Nostra. Valachi consistently made newspaper headlines during his testimony. An article in the *New York Times* (September 28, 1963) relays the following:

> Joseph M. Valachi, the underworld killer turned informer, publicly identified today the men he said were chiefs of organized crime in the United States. . . . The witness described the crime organization as consisting of "borgatas" or families, each under the leadership of a "capo," or boss. Each boss had a "caporegima," or lieutenant, who was in charge of the "regime," or

"crew," consisting of "soldiers." In his first public appearance before the Senate Permanent Subcommittee on Investigations, Valachi described extortion, murder, assault and other depredations as the stock in trade of what he called Cosa Nostra, the crime syndicate, which is also known as the Mafia. (p. 1)

A subsequent *New York Times* (October 2, 1963, p. 1) headline read, "Valachi Names 5 As Crime Chiefs in New York Area." The article continues to say that Valachi "identified the leaders of New York's five Cosa Nostra 'families' as Vito Genovese, Carlo Gambino, Joseph Magliocco, Joseph Bonanno, and Thomas Luchese" (ibid. , p. 1).

With the testimony of Valachi there was a renewed interest in Mafia and organized crime. After Valachi testified Mafia or Cosa Nostra articles in the *New York Times* numbered sixty-seven in 1963, fifty-seven in 1964, eighty-one in 1965, ninety-eight in 1966, and 148 in 1967. Between the period of Kefauver and Apalachin there were only nineteen items listed in the *New York Times Index* of Mafia significance. In the period from Apalachin to the first public statement by Valachi there were a total of thirty-five items of Mafia significance (Smith 1975, pp. 240-241). In short, Valachi's testimony sparked a wave of organized crime literature, not only in newspapers, but also in popular journals and books.

In the period beginning in the mid-sixties and ending in 1967, *Life* and *The Saturday Evening Post* had a series of exposes on the Mafia and organized crime (Smith 1975, p. 241). Journalistic accounts include Ed Reid and Ovid Demaris who published *The Green Felt Jungle* in 1963. The book is a disclosure of the control of Las Vegas gambling by outsiders (Moore 1974, p. 250). Fred J. Cook, a newspaper reporter, published *The Secret Rulers* in 1966. The book discusses Valachi's testimony about Joe Adonis and the New Jersey underworld during the late 1940s and 1950s. *The Conspiracy of Death*, co-authored by George Redston, was published in 1965. The book concentrates on the California life-styles of Mickey Cohen, Bugsy Siegel, and Virginia Hill. The story of the Gallo-Profacci gang war was told by Raymond V. Martin who published *Revolt in the Mafia* in 1963. The Cleveland gambling syndicate is the focus of journalist Wallace Turner's *Gambler's Money: The New Force in American Life* (1965) (Moore 1974, pp. 250-52).

What is significant about these accounts is that they are not scholarly accounts to be shared with academics. Like the literature that came after the Kefauver hearings, the literature published after Valachi testified was also for popular consumption. Therefore, "the conspiracy message circulated more widely than would have been likely in a conventional academic mode" (Smith 1975, p. 242).

After the President's Crime Commission in 1967, Mario Puzo's *The Godfather* (1969), and Peter Maas's *The Valachi Papers* (1968), there were major increases in the interest of organized crime. Journalists continued their interest in organized crime with a furor but the newcomers were the sociologists. As Albini (1988) states, the period of the mid-1960s "saw the beginnings of academic interest and research concerning the area of organized crime" (p. 339). The period from 1950 to 1969 primarily produced literature written from a law enforcement perspective. When a few academics tried to counter this tendency, their work was ignored by Mafia advocates. In 1969, sociologist Donald Cressey, working for the President's Crime Commission, produced "The Functions and Structure of Criminal Syndicates." Cressey hoped other social scientists would continue to explore the world of organized crime by asking new questions. However, when Cressey published *Theft of the Nation* in 1969 the book was nothing more than a rehash of the same old myths and stereotypes, though based on new evidence, about organized crime. When some social scientists tried to challenge Cressey's findings they were ignored by Mafia advocates (see Smith 1975, p. 291, pp. 309-10; Albini 1988, p. 345, 350). Albini (1988) argues that Cressey, in his consultant paper "The Functions and Structure of Criminal Syndicates," proposed that the data on organized crime contained in government files should be available to social scientists so that new questions could be asked. Yet, when Cressey published his 1969 *Theft of the Nation,* there was no such proposal. Likewise, Ianni and Ianni (1972) write:

> ...perhaps we have asked the wrong questions about the *Mafia* and the role of Italian-Americans in organized crime in America, so that we have searched for answers which were inevitably misleading. . . . The focus of the agency studies has been on criminal activity rather than on the organization through which the activity occurs. For this reason, they failed to ask the kinds of questions about organized-crime groups among Italian-Americans that lead to an understanding of how and why they exist and persist. (p. 8)

As previously indicated, two best-sellers, *The Godfather* by Mario Puzo and *The Valachi Papers* by Peter Maas, inspired others to write about the Mafia and organized crime. Journalists, especially, jumped on the bandwagon. Journalists often retold old news stories in biographic form. The following are just some examples of the literature that followed Puzo's *The Godfather* and Maas's *The Valachi Papers*: Dean Jennings, *We Only Kill Each Other: The Life and Times of Bugsy Siegel* (1968); Joseph Volz and Peter J. Bridge, *The Mafia Talks* (1969); Jimmy Breslin, *The Gang That Couldn't Shoot Straight* (1969); Ed Reid, *The Grim Reapers: The Anatomy of Organized Crime in America* (1969); Charles Durbin, *Vendetta: A Novel of the Mafia* (1970); Paul Sann, *Kill the Dutchman! The Story of Dutch Schultz* (1971); Gay Talese, *Honor Thy Father* (1971); Hank Messick, *Lansky* 1971; Nicholas Gage, *Mafia U.S.A.* (1972); Nicholas Gage, *The Mafia is not An Equal Opportunity Employer* (1972); Ed Reid, *The Mistress and the Mafia: The Virginia Hill Story* (1972); Clark Molenhoff, *Strike Force: Organized Crime and the Government* (1972); Hank Messick and Burt Goldblatt, *The Mobs and the Mafia* (1972); Paul Meskil, *Don Carlo: Boss of Bosses* (1973); Fred Cook, *Mafia* (1973); and George Wolf, *Frank Costello: Prime Minister of the Underworld* (1974). There are probably a number of Mafia novels that could be listed here. Significantly absent from these publications is the scholarly work of sociologists. However, after 1967, sociologists do enter the picture in increasing numbers.

During the period between Landesco's (1929) study of organized crime in Chicago and the President's Crime Commission Report of 1967, there appeared very little empirically objective research into the real nature of organized crime (see Smith

1975, p. 306; Albanese 1989, p. 94; 1991, pp. 203-04). The President's Crime Commission Report of 1967 was the first attempt to define and explain the problem of organized crime to the American public. Cressey provided the academic credibility necessary for the alien conspiracy theory of organized crime.

As we have already noted, Cressey challenged social scientists to ask new questions, which are not ordinarily asked by law enforcement personnel. Some members of the academic community did respond, but Cressey was really the first to answer his own challenge. In 1969, he published *Theft of the Nation* and defined organized crime as:

> A nationwide alliance of at least twenty-four tightly knit "families" of criminals. . . . The members of these "families" are all Italians and Sicilians, or of Italian and Sicilian descent, and those on the Eastern Seaboard, especially, call the entire system "Cosa Nostra." Each participant thinks of himself as a "member" of a specific "family" and of Cosa Nostra (or some equivalent term). . . . The "families" are linked to each other, and to non-Cosa Nostra syndicates, by understandings, agreements and "treaties," and by mutual deference to a "commission" made up of the "families." (Cressey 1969, pp. x-xi)

Sociologist Joseph Albini (1988, pp. 338-54) has offered an evaluation of Cressey's contributions to organized crime. Albini criticized Cressey for blindly accepting the government's data as true. But the two most important criticisms which Albini offers, in this writer's opinion, are Cressey's lack of an adequate definition of organized crime and his ahistorical analysis of organized crime in America. With regard to the first criticism, Albini (1988, p. 346) comments that Cressey begins with an insufficient definition of organized crime. When Cressey wrote his consultant paper, "The Function and Structure of Criminal Syndicates," he suggested an unbiased or nonethnic term to describe organized crime. The term was "confederation." However, in *Theft of the Nation*, the term he chooses to use to describe organized crime is "Cosa Nostra." In fact, Cressey does not give a definition of organized crime at all but gives a description of a criminal organization which he calls Cosa Nostra (Albini 1988, pp. 345-346; cf. Smith 1975, pp. 308-309).

Albini (1988, p. 347) states that Cressey's ahistorical analysis of organized crime is a result of his preoccupation with Cosa Nostra and Cressey's attempt to explain the genesis of that organization. Therefore, Cressey's analysis is limited to the time period when Italian and Sicilian immigrants came to America. The period in American history prior to Italian and Sicilian immigration is missing from Cressey's analysis. Hence, Cressey neglected to explain that organized crime had been in existence in America before the great wave of Italian and Sicilian immigration and that it operated in much the same way as later organized crime activities by Italians, Sicilians and other ethnic groups.

In addition to these criticisms, Albini (1988, pp. 338-54) also writes that Cressey ignored blatant inconsistencies in Valachi's testimony, became swept away by the notion of a Mafia conspiracy, and failed to question the way the government collected the data which subsequently became the foundation for his own analysis of organized crime. However, in all fairness to Cressey, there are some positive contributions that should not go unnoticed. Researchers now have a model of organized crime which can be compared to other models. By comparing and analyzing the strengths and weaknesses of different models of organized crime, researchers can add to the understanding of organized crime in American society (see Albanese 1989, pp. 89-104). Further, Cressey was one of the first contemporary social scientists to explore the nature of organized crime. Like most other researchers and academics of the time, Cressey's lack of research experience in studying organized crime could not prepare him for the methodological problems which lay ahead. Cressey's research has also demonstrated the vast amount of problems that social scientists face when they agree to be consultants for government agencies. In chapter 8 we will examine the methodological problems organized crime researchers encounter, as well as the problems which confront researchers who agree to work for government agencies.

Public perceptions of organized crime during the 1960s, then, focused on Italian crime families which were believed to be the backbone of organized crime. Cressey's perspective, although based on new data, replaced the image of both Landesco's real-world gangster and W. R. Burnett's fictional gangster. In time, contemporary social scientists returned to the kinds of questions Landesco asked (Smith 1975, p. 315).

Among the best contemporary work on organized crime are "revisionist" writings which question the so-called Italian/Sicilian dominance of organized crime. Much of this revisionist work debunks the alien conspiracy theory, attacks the "formal" structure of the so-called Mafia, and suggests socioeconomic inequalities as responsible for organized crime (Moore 1974, p. 254). It is certainly true that many sociologists, because of their liberal vision, are often supporters of the Mafia-as-myth literature. Sociologists generally think of society as being shaped by social forces, not by individual choices or personalities. Organized crime is not an individual choice, it is a result of circumstances forced upon individuals. Organized crime is not viewed as morally right or wrong, rather social scientists are "objective" researchers and do not make such judgments. Organized crime is seen as functional to American society. It provides society's members with goods and services which are in demand. The "Mafia" is a convenient scapegoat for a society which needs to undergo fundamental changes (Fox 1989, p. 377). This explanation helps us to understand why sociologists have ignored organized crime for so long and why they had to explore other perspectives on organized crime when the Mafia theory appeared. This is a point which will be further developed in chapter 8. For now, let us turn to an examination of some of this revisionist work by sociologists.

Landesco's *Organized Crime in Chicago*, lost inside the voluminous *Illinois Crime Survey* of 1929, was reestablished in 1968 by the University of Chicago Press. This work, as already mentioned, does not share the law enforcement perspective on organized crime. According to Inciardi et al. (1977), Landesco's *Organized Crime in Chicago* "remains the finest book on Chicago crime to this date" (p. 174). The organized crime era of which Landesco wrote bore little resemblance to the organized crime era of the late 1960s. However, it is very likely that Landesco's study was published as a refutation of the then on-going work of the President's Crime Commission and because it was timely to reestablish the work, a point which will be further examined later in this book.

In 1971, Joseph Albini published *The American Mafia: Genesis of A Legend*. In his study of organized crime Albini (1971, pp. 11-13) relied on historical data, government publications, newspaper and journal articles, and informants on both sides of the law. Albini (1988, p. 341) states that if he had not made contact with informants on both sides of the law, it is very possible that he would have come to many of the same conclusions as Cressey had about organized crime. However, his informants presented him with information that contradicted that of the President's Crime Commission. Albini (1988, p. 341) comments that it was this data that caused him to disregard the government's model of organized crime.

Albini's perspective is that of a structural-functionalist. As Albini (1971) states, "the goal of this work is to describe the structure of the criminal syndicate as well as how it performs its functions" (p. 11). Further, he argues that syndicate crime exists because the public demands its services and the syndicate criminal is offered immunity and protection from various government officials (Albini 1971, p. 14).

Albini was able to demonstrate that organized crime existed in America prior to the massive immigration of Italians to America. Albini (1971, pp. 183-89) cites the nineteenth century Irish syndicates of Mike McDonald in Chicago and John Morrisey in New York as evidence of this. Organized crime, for Albini, consisted of a number of overlapping associations which he called patron-client relationships. Valachi's testimony, of exotic organizational charts, was not taken seriously by Albini. Albini (1971) defined organized crime as "any criminal activity involving two or more individuals, specialized or non-specialized, encompassing some form of social structure, with some form of leadership, utilizing certain modes of operation, in which the ultimate purposes of the organization is found in the enterprises of the particular group" (p. 37).

Anthropologists Francis A. J. Ianni and Elizabeth Reuss-Ianni published *A Family Business: Kinship and Social Control in Organized Crime* in 1972. The Iannis studied the Lupollo crime family of Brooklyn, New York. (The book jacket reveals that Lupollo is a "pseudonym for an Italian-American crime family which has operated in New York since the turn of the century.") The Iannis conducted a participatory field study of the Lupollo family over two and one-half years. The Iannis found no evidence of a national crime commission ruling over all organized crime in the United States. Similar to Albini, the Iannis (1972) state that organized crime groups are not formal organizations with hierarchical positions, they are "patterns of relationships among individuals" (p. 153).

The Mafia Mystique, by Dwight C. Smith, was published in 1975. In this book Smith questions the belief in the Mafia origins of organized crime. Smith demonstrates that America's perceptions of the underworld have been based on our anxieties and fears about certain persons and events throughout American history.

Smith believed that organized crime was the fault of American society; organized criminals and good citizens engaged in mutually agreed upon illegal activities. Corruption and collusion were widespread. In this view, the gangster was not a predatory criminal, he was just another American businessman.

The themes of corruption and collusion between the underworld and legitimate society, first identified by Landesco in 1929, are also taken up by William Chambliss in his study of organized crime in Rainfall West. Rainfall West is a fictitious name for Seattle, Washington. The study was first published in 1971 as "Vice, Corruption, Bureaucracy and Power," in the *Wisconsin Law Review*.

The data for the study of Rainfall West was collected over a period of seven years, from 1962 to 1969. The data came from interviews with persons who were members of the vice syndicates, law enforcement agencies, or both. Chambliss conducted a participatory field study of vice in Rainfall West. Chambliss (1973, p. 354) found that the business of vice was strongly correlated with the political and economic structure of the community. More important, Chambliss (1973, pp. 377-78) found that the leaders of organized crime in Rainfall West were of various ethnic backgrounds. Finally, organized crime in Rainfall West was sustained through the corruption of the political and legal institutions of the city.

Subsequently, in 1981, Alan A. Block and William J. Chambliss published *Organizing Crime*. Their perspective towards organized crime is unique. The authors (1981) state, "this book seeks to apply the perspective of the new criminology to the study of organized crime" (p. 12). The authors recognize the problem of acceptable definitions of organized crime within the American academic community. They suggest the following definition of organized crime: "those illegal activities involving the management and coordination of racketeering (organized extortion) and vice (illegal drugs, illegal gambling, usury, and prostitution)" (Block and Chambliss 1981, p. 12). According to Block and Chambliss (1981) this definition "does not suggest who is involved, thereby leaving that question open for research, nor does it include a wide range of activities thereby rendering the definition meaningless" (p. 12). Block and Chambliss study organized crime by examining the political and economic environment in which it takes place.

In 1978 Alan Block published "History and the Study of Organized Crime," which appeared in *Urban Life*. In this article Block demonstrates how the history of organized crime has been misinterpreted and distorted by the sociologist's reliance on government data and a belief in the conspiracy doctrine. The article primarily discredits the accepted account of the Castellamarese war in which thirty to forty old-time gangsters (the Mustache Petes, as they were called) lost their lives. The so-called purge of the greasers was going to clear the way for a new breed of Americanized gangsters. An additional article which deserves mention is Gordon Hawkins's "God and the Mafia," which appeared in *The Public Interest* in 1969. This article discredits the conclusions of the Kefauver and McClellan committees. While Hawkins readily admits the presence of Italian Americans in organized crime he is highly skeptical of a national crime syndicate. Hawkins likens the belief in the Mafia to the belief in the existence of God, both rely on faith for their existence because both are based on unprovable assumptions.

Sociologist Howard Abadinsky has studied the Gambino crime family (*The Mafia in America*, 1981c) and the Genovese crime family (*The Criminal Elite*, 1983). Abadinsky based his conclusions on others' research and his own interviews with New York crime figures. Abadinsky (1983) concludes that "Italian-American organized crime is more accurately conceived of in terms of patrimonial organizations and patron-client networks (patrito) than by bureaucratic analogies" (p. 109).

When Cressey called for new questions to be asked, some sociologists did answer the call. The revisionist work of many of these scholars challenged the prevailing law enforcement perspective of organized crime. These studies presented an alternative view of organized crime, one that emphasized social, political, and economic forces. They contributed much to our understanding of organized crime. However, between the period 1929 and 1969, there were only two major studies of organized crime by sociologists: Landesco's *Organized Crime in Chicago* and Cressey's *Theft of the Nation*. Landesco's study was buried inside the *Illinois Crime Survey* until its separate publication in 1968. With Cressey's work for the President's Crime Commission and his subsequent publication of *Theft of the Nation* it seems that sociological interests turned to organized crime. As already indicated, much of this work was revisionist in nature. This has much to do with sociologists' general view of the relationship between crime and society and will be considered in our final chapter. In short, prior to the 1960s, organized crime was the province of journalists and law enforcers, not sociologists!

The depiction of gangsters in film: public perceptions and objective realities

INTRODUCTION

The public's view of crime and criminal justice is rarely the result of direct experiences. Instead, what the public learns about crime and criminal justice often comes from the print and electronic media. Print media includes newspapers, books, and magazines. The electronic media consists of film, radio, video, and television. In short, views about crime and criminal justice are formed from secondhand experiences, not from direct observation.

Surette (1992, pp. 4-5) writes that the media is one of four knowledge sources that helps to shape our social realities. The other three knowledge sources include personal experiences, significant others, and other social groups and institutions. From these four knowledge sources we construct our social worlds and act accordingly. However, it is the media, in industrialized societies, that has the most profound influence in shaping the attitudes and opinions of the public. It is the media that is responsible for disseminating large amounts of information to social organizations and institutions. In fact, the mass media has been "singled out as the most common and pervasive source of shared information on crime and justice"

(Surette 1994, p. 5). The present discussion is limited to a special type of electronic media, namely, film. In particular, we will examine how gangsterism and organized crime have been depicted in film and how these depictions have influenced and shaped the American public's perception of these same phenomena. Before we speak specifically about what has been called the "gangster film," a discussion of the media in relation to crime and criminal justice will be useful.

Movies are part of popular culture, that is, they occupy peoples' time when they are not working or sleeping (Anderson and Howard 1994, p. 127). In short, they are a leisure activity made possible by our technological capabilities. Movies emerged on the American social landscape at the turn of the century. For the first time Americans of all economic strata, races, geographical locations, and ethnic groups were able to share substantial amounts of information. In fact, movies have historically been easily accessible to the American public. When first produced, silent movies cost very little and did not require that one understood English. Unlike the print media, movies did not require a literate audience. Movies are a mass medium and have created a mass culture (Surette 1994, p. 25).

Surette (1994, pp. 2-6) has stated that there are several important reasons to study the media, crime, and criminal justice: (1) there are few academic works that present a comprehensive discussion of the media's effects on the three major components of the criminal justice system (courts, corrections, and law enforcement); (2) the media's pervasiveness is felt by millions of Americans, thereby influencing people's perceptions of crime and criminal justice (e.g., the media helps to socially construct our reality); (3) the media has been viewed as having both a positive and negative influence on crime control; and (4) studying the media, crime, and criminal justice gives one the unique opportunity to comprehend American society. While all of these reasons are sound, it is the second and fourth reasons that seem to have the most applicability to the present discussion. A society's idea of itself, and in particular, its ideas of crime and social justice, are eloquently reflected in the media. Perhaps this is especially true in movies where visual images have a long-lasting effect and are not as easily dismissed as the written word. Movies are strong cultural objects with powerful messages about success, failure, humanity, the social structure, the American Dream, free will, and political ideologies. Movies reveal a lot about what is going on in a particular society. Movies about crime and justice are especially ripe for the sociological analysis of society!

Themes of crime and justice have long been a part of the entertainment media. Crime, by its very nature and necessity, is hidden and secretive. The more dangerous the crime the more secretive it is. Therefore, a curious public is allowed to take a peek at the dangerous underside of American life while safely seated in a movie theatre. People are afforded a glimpse into something new, exciting, and forbidden without ever breaking any conventional rules of society. At the turn of the century large-scale immigration, urbanization, and industrialization resulted in cities that were plagued by social problems; including poverty, unemployment, family disintegration, and most important, crime. The American people were worried about the increasing crime problem and a popular image of crime and the criminal was born (Surette 1994, p. 22). The criminal was a foreign-born, ethnic immigrant, who lived in the urban slums of our great cities. Surprisingly, the early gangster films did not really focus on the issue of ethnicity. Nevertheless, this image would later come to dominate themes of crime and justice in movies and television, images which are still to be found in the electronic media today.

The demographic transition of America from a rural to an urban people resulted in a change in the pursuit of popular cultural activities. Movies, along with radio and newspapers, broadened the concerns and interests of Americans culminating in a new national mass culture. Mass culture brought new socializing agents with strong influences, especially on our youth. As a socializing agent the movies had managed, for the first time ever, to have a stronger influence on people than traditional social institutions like the family, religion, and education. Movies had the ability to directly reach individuals; the movies were becoming a major source of social information (Surette 1994, p. 26).

Through film, the American public was confronted with a collective vision of society. Movies contained powerful messages about society itself and the types of individuals who lived in that society. Recurring themes about crime and justice appeared in film after film. Themes about crime and justice evolve to correspond with the changes taking place in American society. In the discussion to follow, a comparison of gangster films from different periods in American history demonstrates how the image of the gangster was transformed from the hero of the late 1920s and early 1930s, to the villain of the 1940s and 1950s. Such a transformation paralleled changes in America's cultural views concerning organized crime and gangsterism. The film criminal of the late 1920s and early 1930s was portrayed as a bootlegger who worked hard for a living. By the 1950s the film criminal became a modern syndicate chief. As we will see, these screen transformations reflected the changes taking place in the American social landscape.

The present discussion of gangster movies intends to use the review of gangster movies and their history to document the extent to which gangsters, the social actors at the center of organized crime, were part of the popular imagination, part of common knowledge and imagery in America at the time the Chicago sociologists were writing their works.

THE HOLLYWOOD GANGSTER MOVIE

The first Hollywood gangster movie was D. W. Griffith's *Musketeers of Pig Alley* (1912) (Earley 1978, p. 127; Cashman 1981, p. 171; Raeburn 1988, p. 47). However, it was Joseph Von Sternberg's silent film *Underworld* (1927), which "triggered the gangster film cycle of the Prohibition years" (Earley 1978, p. 127). *Underworld* became the model for almost all of the gangster movies which followed. Gangster films belong to a specific genre. A genre is "A term for any group of motion pictures which follows similar stylistic, thematic, and structural interests" (Beaver 1983, p. 514).

Large-scale gangsterism was a product of the Chicago Prohibition era. Prohibition required a good deal of organization and cooperation and transformed the "crook" into the "gangster" (Raeburn 1988, p. 47). The men who supplied alcohol, to an otherwise law-abiding public, were admired. The news media and the film industry both capitalized on the activities of these men (cf. Raeburn 1988, p. 47; Powers 1983, p. 4).

The setting for the early gangster films was the city (cf. Shadoian 1977; Earley 1978; Cashman 1981; Raeburn 1988). The city is where the gangster comes to make it big. The gangster will either succeed or be destroyed in the city. The city imposes its own will upon its inhabitants. The city exposed the contradictions between WASPS and ethnics, middle class and working class, and urban and rural. Cultural conditions were right for the emergence of the gangster film genre. However, it was the advent of sound in film which launched the gangster genre. Raeburn (1988) writes that "The city the gangster hero must traverse and dominate is a dense, crowded, noisy place, and the throbbing motor and squealing tires of his automobile and the staccato of his guns confirms his sovereignty" (p. 48). Directors quickly learned that "the splinter of tommy-gun bullets, the squealing tires of speeding cars, the music from the honky-tonks, and the torch songs of nightclub singers" (Earley 1978, p. 127) greatly enhanced the gangster film.

The model for the gangster film was Al Capone (cf. Shadoian 1977; Earley 1978; Cashman 1981; Powers 1983; Raeburn 1988). As Shadoian (1977) states "Capone; the first and greatest gangster—the man whose name is synonymous with 'gangster'—was the model, and everyone knew it" (p. 20). Al Capone, undoubtedly the most famous organized criminal, has been chronicled in several biographies and films. The image of Capone as the prototypical gangster and the city of Chicago as the crime capital of the world is still with us. In 1987, the film *The Untouchables* was shot on location in Chicago. Robert De Niro played Al Capone and Kevin Costner played Eliot Ness in the film. The movie did very well at the box office. However, the city of Chicago was torn between putting the bang-bang image behind them or cashing in on the money and jobs the film would provide. They chose the latter. An article in the *New York Times* (September 20, 1987) discusses this dilemma which has confronted Chicagoans since the 1920s:

> ... how can the city erase its image abroad as a place infested with gun-toting gangsters—or better yet, capitalize on it. Over the years, a constant flow of books, magazine articles, television dramas and films, including this summer's hit movie "The Untouchables," have cashed in on Chicago's legacy of Prohibition violence, and some believe that gritty reputation is chasing away foreign tourist dollars. ... It might have been a half-century ago, but the memories of gangland mayhem die hard in a town where John Dillinger was shot down and Al Capone ruled; where Eliot Ness and his G-men waged war against rum runners, and Bugs Moran's boys were lined up against the wall of a Clark Street garage on St. Valentine's Day in 1929, and machine gunned to death. (p. 26)

The article goes on to say that the chairman of the International Visitor's Center, the director of the Chicago Crime Commission, and the mayor all believe that

Chicago still has the "rat-atat-tat" or "bang-bang" image. The chairman of the International Visitor's Center states, "I've been to more than 100 foreign cities, and every place I go, as soon as I tell people I'm from Chicago, I get the same response, . . . Chicago? Bang-bang. Al Capone" (ibid., p. 26).

Some of the books which chronicle the career of Capone are: *Al Capone: The Biography of A Self-Made Man* (Palsey, 1931); *The Bootleggers: The Story of Prohibition* (Allsop 1968); *Capone: The Life and World of Al Capone* (Kobler 1971); and *Johnny Torrio: First of the Gang Lords* (McPhaul, 1970). Some of the films which chronicle Capone's career include: *Scarface: Shame of A Nation* (1932); *Al Capone* (1958); *The St. Valentine's Day Massacre* (1967); and *The Untouchables* (1987). Periodically, Capone's career has been revived through literature and film. Interestingly, in what purports to be an interview with Capone himself in 1931 (*New York Times*, July 30), Capone tells us that publishers and movie makers had promised him a bundle for a book or a part:

> I've been offered $2 000 000 to write a book but I won't do it. . . . I've had lots of offers from moving picture producers, but I feel about that as I do about books. You know these gang pictures that's terrible kid stuff. Why they ought to take all of them and throw them into the lake. They're doing nothing but harm to the younger element of this country. I don't blame the censors for trying to bar them. . . . these gang movies are making a lot of kids want to be tough guys, and they don't serve any useful purpose. (p. 12)

Nevertheless, Al Capone was the model for the gangster film. The gangster lived in an anonymous city, hung out in nightclubs, and was surrounded by an interesting array of characters, lawyers, racketeers, gun molls, bodyguards, and usually a blond goldigger. The gangster rarely drank and indulged himself with mercenary women. The loyal errand boy would listen intently to the boss's ramblings (Earley 1978, p. 127). This image of the gangster is eloquently described in the *New York Times* article "The Willow-The-Wisps of The Underworld" (August 18, 1929, pp. 6-7). The article discusses the hangouts of the racketeer (nightclubs and speakeasies) and the girlfriends of the racketeer (who are often visible participants in the night life). Also discussed are the racketeer's associates, the errand boy, the bodyguard, and the "mouthpiece" (lawyer).

The gangster hero was extremely popular during the early years of the Great Depression. Earley (1978, p. 135) and others (Powers 1983; Raeburn 1988: Kooistra 1989) have suggested a number of reasons why this was so. It was a period in American history when Americans were antiestablishment. Financial worries and unemployment preoccupied the minds of most Americans. Moviegoers admired the gangster who solved his problems with violence and guns. Crime, during this era, was one way to show the world how you felt, not about law and order, but about the weakening economy.

The earliest gangster films include *Underworld* (1927), *Dragnet* (1928), *The Lights of New York* (1928), *The Racket* (1929), and *Quick Millions* (1931). But the "classic" gangster film trio included *Little Caesar* (1930), *Public Enemy* (1931), and *Scarface* (1932). *Lights of*

New York, released by Warners, showed how an innocent young man got involved in "Prohibition-era gangsterism" and the "illegal activities of bootleggers" (Beaver 1983, p. 237). Its success as one of the first all-talking pictures, catapulted Warner Brothers to a key position within the industry.

W. R. Burnett wrote his novel *Little Caesar* after he arrived in Chicago. Burnett's earliest opinions of the city were of violence, corruption, and indifference to the concerns of the common citizen. While shocked, Burnett was absorbed in, and resolved to write about, the dangerous city. In his introduction to the 1958 edition of *Little Caesar*, Burnett writes that there were three influences on the development of his novel. One influence was an acquaintance who was a police reporter, another was Thrasher's *The Gang* (1927), and yet another was a young Italian-American man, on the North Side, who was a pay-off man for the biggest mob on the North Side. (Smith 1975, p. 104). It was not until Burnett read Thrasher's account "of the rise and fall of the Sam Cardinelli gang" (Smith 1975, p. 104) that Burnett's writing efforts became fruitful. Burnett adopted the rise and fall of the Sam Cardinelli gang as the plot for *Little Caesar*. Like the work of Landesco, ethnicity is notably absent from Burnett's novel. "There was no Mafia in Little Caesar's World" (Smith 1975, p. 104). Smith (1975) writes that Burnett's effort was "a second hand rewriting of the Sam Cardinelli story in North Side argot. He did not create an image: he captured in vivid style a generally held public image of the Chicago gangster" (pp. 104-05). Thus the gangsters in Landesco's *Organized Crime in Chicago* and Burnett's *Little Caesar* were remarkably similar.

Mervyn Le Roy both adapted *Little Caesar* for the big screen and directed it. Actor, Edward G. Robinson gave an outstanding performance as the cocky killer, Rico Bandello. *Little Caesar* was the first genuine gangster film that focused on the gangster's character and the gangster's relationship to the larger social structure (again, a similar theme is found in Landesco's *Organized Crime in Chicago*). Rico, like real-world gangsters, is a character the culture both admires and scorns. As Shadoian (1977) remarks, "Ethical matters related to success are diverted by the positive, ambitious actions of powerful men, who though powerful, die and thus express, fatalitstically, an inversion of the American dream" (p. 22).

Rico's one goal is to rise to the top. He comes to the city from somewhere in the West in order to achieve success. Rico joins a gang and it is his "determination, self-discipline . . . , and superior business acumen" (Raeburn 1988, p. 49) which propels him to the top. Each step up the ladder of success is accompanied by bigger and better material things. The city which Rico traverses has no name, Rico calls it "The Big Town" (Raeburn 1988, p. 49).

Rico's success captures the American dream. A man of lowly origins rises to the top of his profession. As Shadoian (1977) remarks:

> The theme of success is perhaps the most insistent in American cinema, a cinema that reflects, whether it means to or not, the crucial dilemma of a capitalist democracy. The illusion of unlimited possibility for achieving wealth and position (power) and the culture's inducement of individual triumph create several moral

and psychological strains. The gangster film contains the clearest exposition of this disturbance, the extremities of success and failure–exhilarating, top-of-the-heap life and brutal death–being its (initial) stock in trade. (p. 5)

Despite Rico's achievements there are limits to his success. He can get only so far, then the wrong class or ethnic background gets in the way and trips him up. For example, in one scene Rico is called to "The Big Boy's" apartment for a conference. Immediately one senses how uncomfortable Rico is in this environment. His limitations are readily apparent and they are limitations we all can identify with. Rico's fumbling with the butter, his naiveté about the gold frame costing fifteen thousand dollars, and the way he seats himself on an expensive chair are all faux pas we can easily identify with. Even his flicking of ashes on an expensive rug are understandable to us. (Shadoian 1977, p. 33; cf. Raeburn 1988, p. 49).

When Rico arrived in "The Big Town" he had a sidekick, Joe Massara. Joe was his accomplice in petty crimes in the town from which they came. Rico, more than money, wants power. Rico wants to have the ability to tell people what to do and to have his own way. Joe has other goals. He wants to be a dancer and make a lot of money. Joe will dance for a price. Rico, on the other hand, is not for sale, he cannot be bought. However, Rico is able to get Joe's help in a heist at a nightclub where Joe performs. Yet throughout the film Joe tries hard to free himself from his relationship with Rico. Rico on the other hand tries to maintain the relationship. Joe falls in love with Olga, his dancing partner. Rico cannot believe that Joe prefers another to himself. This shows that even Rico needs closeness and friendship. Some scholars of film history have seen the relationship between Rico and Joe as a "covertly homosexual one." However, while that may have been the case, even more interesting, is the way the relationship exposes a conflict in American society between individualism and community (Raeburn 1988, p. 50).

Rico dies on an unknown street in the city. Rico rightly suspects that Joe is going to betray him, but he cannot shoot Joe at point-blank range, when he has the opportunity. The law finally catches up to him and his famous dying words are "Mother of Mercy, is this the end of Rico?" Rico cannot believe that he cannot triumph over death (Raeburn 1988, p. 50).

Public Enemy (1931), directed by William Wellman, was "the first film to examine seriously the causes of criminal behavior and to portray the gangster as a product of his environment" (Earley 1978, p. 129), a viewpoint widely held by the Chicago school sociologists. The film is a peek at the conditions of American society and culture during the 1920s and early 1930s (Jowett 1979, p. 58). It is a realistic drama. Warners had hired newspapermen "familiar with big-city gangsterism, to help authenticate the studio's crime films" (Beaver 1983, p. 239; cf. Earley 1978, p. 128). Ben Hecht, John Bright, and Kubec Glasmon came to Warner Brothers from Chicago newspapers. The scenes written for the film were inspired by the stories dominating the front pages of the newspapers. They also introduced such colloquialisms as "on the spot," "So what?," and "taken for a ride" (Beaver 1983, p. 239).

John Bright and Kubec Glasmon wrote the novel *Blood and Beer* (later the film was retitled *Public Enemy*). In Chicago, Bright had worked for Glasmon in a drugstore which was frequented by gangsters and young hoodlums. They used this background to write their novel *Blood and Beer* (Jowett 1979, p. 59).

James Cagney's role as Tom Powers, in *Public Enemy*, established the actor as a star. His performance has been describes as both "sinister and honest" (Beaver 1983, p. 238). Beaver (1983) describes Cagney's character as "that of a cold-blooded killer who intimidates and inflicts cruelty on all who cross his path" (p. 238). Women, except for his mother, do not fare any better. The film is memorable for the scene where Cagney shoves a grapefruit into the face of his girlfriend, played by Mae Clarke. It is not difficult to figure why this scene had such impact. The gesture had shock value; it was both sudden and brutal. The grapefruit pushed in her face was a gratuitous act. The scene also showed the gangster as a bruiser of women (except for his mother)—a theme played up in Cagney's *White Heat*. The misogynous feature of gangster films has been discussed by Raeburn (1988, p. 52) who speculated that this theme revealed the conflicting views of American men about the "new women" who were replacing their Victorian mothers. Undoubtedly, the portraits of the gangsters and their women were important aspects of their powerful appeal.

Public Enemy, the story of the rise and fall of the small-time hoodlum, is told in a series of sequences. The final sequence, 1920, shows actual newsreel footage of the hours before Prohibition on January 16, 1920. Prohibition provides the opportunity for Tom, and his friend Matt, to move up in the criminal hierarchy. Tom and Matt become salesmen for an illegal beer operation run by Paddy Ryan, "Nails" Nathan, and a crooked brewery owner, Leeman. Gang wars over the liquor rackets cause the demise of Tom. At the end of the film Tom's bullet-ridden body is sprawled on his mother's doorstep (Jowett 1979, pp. 62-64). *Public Enemy* attempts to show the sociological and psychological reasons Tom Powers is a deviant. The principle reason is remarkably similar to that of the Chicago school theorists, Tom Powers is a product of his environment.

The third classic gangster film, *Scarface* (1932), was directed by Howard Hawks. The complete title is *Scarface: Shame of a Nation*. Paul Muni was perfectly cast as the ruthless killer Tony Camonte. "It was Hawks' idea to show that the ruthless Al Capone and his henchmen controlled Chicago with all the cunning, treachery, and violence of the powerful Borgia family of fifteenth-century Italy " (Earley 1978, p. 129).

A common thread for these three classic gangster films of the early 1930s was that the principle actors all had immigrant backgrounds. Rico Bandello, Tom Powers, and Tony Camonte all start from humble beginnings to pursue the American dream. This theme of success, of making it in America, is evident as well in Landesco's *Organized Crime in Chicago*. Gangsters were immigrants, not native-born Americans. As already indicated, the WASPS of the city of Chicago during the 1920s held deep fears about the criminal inclinations of immigrants. They had good reason to believe their fears. "Of the 108 'directors' of the Chicago underworld, 30 percent were of Italian ancestry, 29 percent were Irish, 20 percent were Jewish, and 12 percent were black" (Jowett 1979, p. 68).

Throughout American film history the image of Italians is the dominant gangster prototype. We witness this from the early thirties, (*Little Caesar*), to the mid-seventies, (*The Godfather*). Italians were initially ridiculed or feared for the way they looked, for their strong emotions, and for their religious beliefs. In fact, much of the early anti-Italianism was really directed at Italians because of their Catholicism. Although Italian gangsters were trying to achieve the American dream of economic success and material well-being, they were still feared as a danger to American capitalism (Golden 1980, pp. 77-78).

"Italians were not the first gangsters, either in reality or in film" (Golden 1980, p. 78). It was a sequence of historical and cultural events which propelled them to the top as the gangster prototype. Of utmost importance was Prohibition and the rise of Al Capone in Chicago (Golden 1980, p. 78; cf. Earley 1978; Powers 1983). Capone received a lot of publicity from the tabloid press. Capone loved publicity and welcomed inquiring journalists who would feed his legend (Fox 1989, p. 45; cf. Powers 1983; Woodiwiss 1987). In fact, receiving too much publicity caused Capone's downfall. Capone became an embarrassment to the Hoover administration. "By 1930 Al Capone was known around the world as the new symbol of crime in America—crime accepted matter-of-factly as an intrinsic part of society, a force in American life that government was powerless to control " (Powers 1983, p. 6). Mounting political pressure forced Hoover to do something about Capone (Powers 1983, p. 8; cf. Woodiwiss 1987, p. 8). Hoover wanted to demonstrate his promise to enforce the liquor laws and Capone was the target of his promise. Because of the national attention Capone received in newspapers, books, and film he became the target of Hoover's obsession (Woodiwiss 1987, p. 8). In fact, during the period between 1929 and 1931, seven books were published chronicling Capone's life (Powers 1983, p. 6). Capone's life story was also told in several films. These films, along with others portraying underworld figures such as Johnny Torrio and Big Jim Colosimo, led to a belief in the association of Italians with organized crime.

"The crucial complicating factor in the image of the Italian criminal entrepreneur is, of course, the notion of the 'Mafia,' the almost mythical Italian subculture" (Golden 1980, p. 79). The Mafia family portrayed in film is often envied by the American public. They are jealous that Italian criminals can call upon their extended family for aid and that they can pursue the American dream without having to do it on their own. Most Americans feel isolated and alone in their quest for success, they are excluded from the inner circle. Italian criminals have a large network of relationships to draw from in their pursuit of the American dream (Golden 1980, pp. 79-80).

Yet ethnicity is missing from the early gangster films. It was only later, when the Mafia label was present, that the presence of Italian ethnicity in a film was erroneously interpreted to mean Mafia. As Smith (1975) writes "For the most part, Rico offers the unfortunate paradigm for the Italian-American gangster film stereotype, enough cultural signature to be affixed as Italian, but little if anything of that ethnic group's familial structures and codes of behavior and belief" (p. 115).

Therefore, the presence of the Italian-American gangster in the early films did not mean a Mafia association. The early gangsters could just as readily have been of some other ethnicity.

Little Caesar, The Public Enemy, and *Scarface* are "part of a trio that serves as the paradigm of what may be called the 'classic' gangster film'" (Jowett 1979, p. 58; cf. Earley 1978, p. 128; Raeburn 1988, p. 48). The early gangster films relied on the public's fascination with actual criminals and their fascinating activities. The young kids portrayed in these early gangster films were first-generation immigrants who were members of organized crime. They tried hard to succeed but were victims of their environments and their heritage. Society was to blame for their criminality. Their criminality was a matter of chance, not choice! This liberal vision of the criminal portrayed in the early gangster films is remarkably similar to the points of view expressed by the Chicago school theorists. Given this fact, and the fact that the gangster was very much in the public's consciousness during the 1920s and early 1930s, it is interesting that the Chicago school theorists would ignore this symbol of American culture. These sociologists did nothing to either confirm or discredit the image of the gangster in American film.

The heyday of these early gangster films was relatively short-lived. By 1933, various community organizations were protesting the brutal gangster films. *Scarface* especially received unwanted attention from pressure groups who prompted censors to stop the production of such films. "The fate of *Scarface* . . . shows how aware the censors were of the gangster movies' significance. *Scarface* served up forty-three murders as it followed Al Capone's career from the death of Big Jim Colosimo through the Saint Valentine's Day Massacre. . . . It was so violent and amoral that the Motion Picture Production Code . . . withheld its seal of approval" (Powers 1983, p. 18). Producer Howard Hughes released *Scarface* anyway and the censors made Hughes add the phrase "Shame of A Nation" to the film title, and also changed the film's ending (Powers 1983, p. 18).

Two events seemed to have set off the protests of gangster films by various organizations: the Lindbergh kidnapping case and the repeal of Prohibition in 1933. The Lindbergh case alerted the public that gangsters were a dangerous breed. The Lindbergh case was seen as an act against legitimate and civilized society by the underworld. In addition, while the gangster may have been an admired hero during Prohibition, providing a service to customers, after Prohibition the gangster continued to engage in criminal activities, and this was not viewed favorably by most of the American public (Earley 1978, p. 130; Powers 1983, p. 8).

With the repeal of Prohibition "the 1920's-style gangster became obsolete" (Earley 1978, p. 130). The gangster did not leave the big screen, he just appeared in a lesser role. By 1935, "G-men replaced 'public enemies' as the tough guys at Warners; this reversal of emphasis projected a clear-cut conflict between good and evil and was, therefore, considered more acceptable to the censors" (Beaver 1983, p. 241). The violence in these films remained the same, just the stars changed. Thus the censors, as well as the public, were satisfied. Popular films at this time included *G-Men* (1935),

Bullets or Ballots (1936), and *I Am the Law* (1938), in which crime fighters are the stars (Earley 1978, pp. 130-31).

Gangsters reemerged in the thirties with movies like Michael Curtiz's *Angels With Dirty Faces* (1939). The screenplay was written by Roland Brown and there was a distinguished cast that included of Pat O' Brien, James Cagney, Humphrey Bogart, George Bancroft, and the Dead End kids. The main character of the film is Rocky, played by James Cagney. Rocky grew up in the slums and becomes an important gangster. When he returns to the slums, the neighborhood kids treat him like a hero. Rocky's boyhood friend has escaped the negative influences of slum living and is now a priest. The priest, Father Jerry, is concerned that the young boys in the neighborhood will follow in Rocky's footsteps. The priest pleads with Rocky, who is condemned to die in the electric chair to tell the neighborhood kids that crime does not pay. Rocky does tell the boys and he dies apologizing for his criminal life-style (Earley 1978, p. 131).

Another effort to bring back the "lawless decade" was Raoul Walsh's *The Roaring Twenties* (1939). The film shows three young World War I veterans who enter the world of petty crime because they cannot find legitimate work. All three veterans are hired by the syndicate and they become powerful leaders in the illicit liquor industry during Prohibition. Scenes in the film include sleazy streets, dark warehouses, speakeasies and gang warfare. (Earley 1978, p. 131). The film is a "nostalgic farewell to the 'bathtub gin' era" (Earley 1978, p. 131).

By the 1940s the ruthless killer image was assumed by Humphrey Bogart who became a star after *High Sierra* (1941). His role as Roy Earle, was originally turned down by Paul Muni and George Raft, who no longer wanted to be cast as ruthless killers. Bogart plays an emotionally complex character in *High Sierra*, one who is very much at odds with the society in which he lives (Earley 1978, p. 131).

The fascination with the gangster/G-men films had subsided by the mid-1940s. However, these films did not completely leave the big screen. Occasionally the gangster/G-men theme resurfaced in such films as Henry Hathaway's *Kiss of Death* (1947), William Keighley's *Street With No Name* (1948), and Robert Sidmak's *Cry of the City* (1948). These films added little to the genre (Earley 1978, p. 132). Earley (1978, p. 132) and Raeburn (1988, p. 54) both agree that Raoul Walsh's *White Heat* (1949) was perhaps the most outstanding film of the period.

By the end of the 1940s, then, the gangster genre seems to have ended. There were occasional gangster films like *Force of Evil* (1948), *Al Capone* (1958), *Murder, Inc.* (1960), *The Rise and Fall of Legs Diamond* (1960), and the *St. Valentine's Day Massacre* (1967), but for the most part the genre was neglected (Earley 1978, p. 136). It is interesting to note that these films were released during a period in which there was great public interest in organized crime. The release coinciding with the Kefauver hearings, Apalachin meeting, and the testimony of Joe Valachi.

The gangster genre had a second revival in the late 1960s, of which the finest examples are *Bonnie and Clyde* (1967) and *The Godfather, I* and *II* (1972 and 1974). These films were made during the Vietnam era, a time characterized by uncertainty and the questioning of American values. The normative society was unable to meet the needs of its members; instead, people turned to criminal societies to find love, intimacy, enjoyment, and fulfillment (Raeburn 1988, p. 55).

Bonnie and Clyde has been accurately described as a "countercultural youth film" (Beaver 1983, p. 468). The film was tremendously popular with young people who identified with its main protagonists. Bonnie and Clyde are two people at odds with society. All they have is each other. During the 1960s, a period characterized by war protests, race riots, and a growing generation gap between young and old, many of America's youth knew just what Bonnie and Clyde were feeling.

Critics of *Bonnie and Clyde* argue that producers of the film, Arthur Penn and Warren Beatty, romanticized the characters of Bonnie and Clyde rather than portraying them as they really were, amoral and callous killers (cf. Earley 1978, p. 133; Beaver 1983; Raeburn 1988). Beaver (1983) writes, "Penn's folk-hero treatment of social misfits and his poetic rendering of violence left an indelible mark on developing American cinema. The effort brought focus on a new wave of violence-based motion pictures which in 1967 suddenly seemed to be coming from every direction" (p. 469).

Mario Puzo wrote *The Godfather* in 1969. Paramount studios assigned Francis Ford Coppola to direct Puzo's *The Godfather* for the screen. The film traces the life of the Corleones, a Mafia family, from 1945 to 1955. The main character in the film is Marlon Brando's "godfather." As godfather he has the power to grant favors and to control crime, law enforcement officers, judges, politicians, and union officials. When the godfather is wounded, his sons take over. In *Godfather II* the youngest son, Michael, becomes the Mafia boss. *Godfather II* sees Michael change from a young godfather to a crazed American gangster (Earley 1978, p. 134; Beaver 1983, p. 473). Raeburn (1988) writes that the *Godfather* films are "the richest, most complex and ambitious gangster films ever made" (p. 56).

Film critic David Sterritt (1985) writes, "Gangster movies are back in style" (p. 1004) and Karen Jaehne (1991), in her review of *Goodfellas* (1991), writes that "The mob film, a subcategory of the gangster film, is currently enjoying a popular revival" (p. 44). Yes, we are presently witnessing a revival of the gangster genre which began in the mid-1980s with such films as *Once Upon A Time In America* (1984), *The Pope of Greenwich Village* (1984), *Prizzi's Honor* (1985), *Year of the Dragon* (1985), *The Untouchables* (1987), *Godfather III* (1990), *Goodfellas* (1991), *Bugsy* (1991), and *A Bronx Tale* (1994). Many of these films, *Once Upon A Time in America*, *The Pope of Greenwich Village*, *The Untouchables*, and *Bugsy*, are set in the early years of the twentieth century and retell the development of organized crime in America.

Once Upon A Time in America is the story of first-generation Americans growing up on the Lower East Side. The story traces the development of these youngsters "from their initial rebellion against their parents' European values through petty thievery, small-time protection and eventually big-time gangsterism, owning politicians and labor leaders" (Anderson 1985, p. 1005). The film is told in a series of sequences from the 1920s to the 1960s. According to Sterritt (1985, p. 1004), *The Pope of Greenwich Village* is a less ambitious film, about a couple of petty criminals who commit a burglary and unknowingly become targets of the mob.

Perhaps a film which more closely resembles *The Godfather* (only with humor) is *Prizzi's Honor*. *Prizzi's Honor* "can be seen as a deadpan spoof" (Denby 1986, p. 1001) of *The Godfather*. *Prizzi's Honor* "is *The Godfather* with laughs" (Reed 1986, p. 1002). However, on a more serious note, perhaps the most significant of all the recent gangster films is *Goodfellas* because it is based on the life of Henry Hill, real-life mob informant. Henry Hill's life is chronicled in Nicholas Pileggi's book *Wise Guy* (1985). Hill was a successful wise guy for Mafia boss Paul Vario from 1963 to 1980. Hill lost the backing of Vario when he was arrested for dealing drugs and enrolled in the Federal Witness Protection Program. Hill's testimony led to the convictions of Paul Vario and Jimmy Burke.

The evolution of gangster films has paralleled an increase in sociological depth. The earlier gangster films tended to analyze and moralize. The films of the thirties portrayed "the good guy going wrong" (Jarvie 1970, p. 169). This theory views the gangster "more as a victim of his situation than creator of it" (Jarvie 1970, p. 169). It is a liberal theory and one that most classical and contemporary theorists would endorse. The forties and fifties focused on the psychological problems of the gangster, looking for individual reasons to explain the character's criminality. For example, the reason for Cody Jarrett's pathological behavior in *White Heat* is largely because he was a mama's boy. Modern gangsters are not products of their environment nor are they psychologically crippled. They are "members of an under-class with its own deviant norms" (Jarvie 1970, p. 169). The subcultural theories of Walter Miller, Albert Cohen, and Richard Cloward and Lloyd Ohlin could be applied here. Contemporary portraits of gangsters are gangsters by choice not circumstance. For instance, in the movie *Goodfellas* (1991) the voice-over of Henry Hill says, "As far back as I can remember, I always wanted to be a gangster" (Jaehne 1991, p. 47). Today, some contemporary theorists do endorse rational choice theory. This theory suggests that people will make a rational decision to choose criminality if the potential benefits of their criminality will outweigh the potential consequences (e.g., the risk involved, the possibility of arrest and conviction). The theory has its roots in classical criminology.

In sum, gangster films used the screen to examine why individuals turn to crime. Often these reasons were because of economic and environmental conditions; circumstances that were often beyond the control of the individual. Society was at fault, not the criminal. These pictures made film audiences aware of the sociological problems that existed in their contemporary worlds. It would seem that was more than America's sociologists were doing!

Concluding remarks

In this chapter we have documented that public knowledge of and interest in organized crime has been constant from the 1920s to the 1990s. Dissemination of public knowledge about organized crime is not always accurate, but the American public usually accepts it as such. We have seen how the "gangster" and "racketeer" of the 1920s and 1930s became the Mafiosi of the 1950s and 1960s. Changes in public perception came about through governmental studies and commissions, films, newspaper accounts, and journalistic exposes which depicted organized crime and organized criminals. The chapter also shows that while governmental studies and commissions, journalistic exposes, and films have done much to stimulate the public's imagination about organized crime, the scholarly approach has done little. This is particularly true during the critical phase in the development of American sociology, 1920 to 1940, when gangsters, the social actors in organized crime, were very much a part of the popular imagination. Gangsterism and organized crime were very much part of the American landscape yet the Chicago school sociologists, and others after them, chose to ignore or deny their existence. As documented earlier in chapter 3, against the backdrop of organized crime, the Chicago school sociologists were studying other urban social problems. When did organized crime become a part of the subject matter of sociology? This question will be answered in chapter 7.

NOTES

1. The writer had originally wanted to utilize the principal Chicago newspapers of the period for this chapter but was unable to do so. The principal Chicago newspapers were not available at university and public libraries in New Jersey and New York until approximately the 1940s. Therefore, the writer decided to mainly utilize the *New York Times*, since articles written in the 1920s and 1930s could be easily located through the *New York Times Index*.

7

Organized crime as a topic of sociological interest

Introduction

THIS CHAPTER contains three sections which consider when and how organized crime became part of the field of sociology of crime and delinquency. Section one will briefly review the place of criminology in the development of American sociology. A second section will examine the contents of some early criminology textbooks in order to document the lack of interest by the early criminologists in the subjects of vice, racketeering, and gangsterism. Finally, we will examine critically some criminology textbooks with sections or chapters on organized crime. A further explanation of the methodology of this examination will be provided at that time.

The primary purpose of this chapter is to document that during the critical phase in the development of American sociology, 1920 to 1940, vice, racketeering, and gangsterism were not part of the subject matter of sociology and criminology; in fact, that a substantive discussion of organized crime did not appear in a criminology textbook until 1943. Furthermore, sociologists, in the past, and even today, too often rely on official documents and journalistic accounts for their information about organized crime. In short, this chapter confirms the book's thesis that vice, racketeering, and gangsterism played a marginal role in the development of American sociology, until relatively recently, even though these activities were, in a significant way, part of the popular imagination.

Criminology in American sociology: a brief review

Most scholars, who refer to themselves as criminologists, have been trained in sociology. In fact, most contributors to the theory of crime causation have been sociological criminologists. Modern criminology is a product of America and is a subdiscipline of sociology. Most of the literature in the field of criminology has been written by sociologists; American criminology and sociology have developed together.

Yet we must caution ourselves not to neglect the contributions of other countries and other academic disciplines to the field of criminology. A strong "criminological enterprise" can be found in England, Scandinavia, Australia, Japan and other countries. And while it is true that many American criminological concepts have been borrowed by foreign nations to help their criminological endeavors, it would be wrong to view the criminological enterprise in those foreign countries as "cheap copies of a made-in-America product" (Gibbons 1992, p. 29).

Criminology is a field of study which has received contributions from a variety of disciplines. Those fields contributing to the knowledge base of criminology have included history, law, political science, anthropology, economics, psychology, and psychiatry among others. Sociologists are not the principal owners of criminology. However, it is within sociology that the subdiscipline of criminology, has been most fully developed.

There is no specific date when American criminology was born. Crime and delinquency books first appeared before the turn of the century. Most of these books expressed the view that criminality had a biological basis. Theories of crime which were social in nature developed at a slower pace. The first comprehensive textbook in criminology was published in 1918 by Maurice Parmelee (see Clinard 1951, p. 549; Gibbons 1992, p. 30). It could be said, then, that criminology was born in 1918 with the Parmelee text. Subsequent criminology texts, written by sociologists, aided in the development of criminology. In fact, today, criminology is a standard course in most sociology departments. The most well-known and extensively used criminology textbooks have been written by sociologists.

Criminology paralleled the development of sociology. Both, in their early stages, were simple, moralistic, and discriminating. As sociology became more specialized so did criminology. As new theoretical perspectives and research methodologies were developed in sociology they were later borrowed by criminology.

The influence of sociological criminology was clearly felt in the United States during the 1920s. It was during the period 1920 to 1940 that criminology truly became a part of the American academy. As we have already indicated, it was at this time that the Chicago school sociologists developed their ecological model of the city and their theoretical perspective of social disorganization to explain the urban social problems in their hometown of Chicago. Thus the work of the Chicago sociologists in this area of crime and delinquency was actually linked to a larger theoretical interest in the sociology of deviance and urban social problems. American sociology from its beginning until about World War II adopted a reformist stance focusing on such urban social problems as delinquency, alcoholism, mental illness, racial and religious minorities, and family disorganization. The focus on crime and delinquency was part of a larger interest in why some people disregard the norms of rural, middle-class, white society and others obey them (Mills, 1943). What causes some people to deviate? As stated in chapter 2, the answer, for the Chicago school sociologists, was to be found in its theory of deviance as social disorganization. The

Chicago school sociologists, applying its ecological model to the study of urban social problems, concluded that the highest rates of deviance were found in the disorganized areas of the city. The study of crime per se was not yet a distinct specialty within sociology.

Sociological criminology in the United States, then, was a product of the Chicago school. The men who contributed to this field (Thrasher, Shaw, McKay, and Sutherland) of sociology were white, male, Anglo-Saxon, Protestant liberals who hailed from the rural Midwest. The liberal visions of these men influenced their views of the United States, and more important, their views of crime causation. All of these men basically approved of the United States. The United States was an egalitarian democracy. Therefore, if crime was not caused by the social order, which was essentially good, and it was not found within the individual, then the causes of crime must lie elsewhere. For Shaw and McKay, the causes of crime were found in certain urban neighborhoods and the conditions within these neighborhoods; for Sutherland, it was the social relationships within these neighborhoods (Snodgrass 1972, p. 20). As Snodgrass (1972) remarks, "The neighborhoods themselves were entities which existed almost independent of American political and economic history and structure. . . .Given the assumption of the overall quality in American society, they could not entertain historical, structural, institutional, class, political or economic theoretical notions. The causes of crime were always understood in terms of what were not the causes" (p. 20).

This insightful comment by Snodgrass helps to explain why the Chicago school criminologists could not expose organized crime. To do so would have meant exposing wider collusive agreements between criminals and "good citizens." American society was too perfect to engage in such behavior. It would have meant looking at the wider political, economic, and class structure to explain organized crime and the Chicago school criminologists did not look beyond the immediate neighborhood. Imperfections did not lie in the social structure, they argued, but in the immediate environment of the neighborhood.

In short, the underlying assumption of this school of criminal sociology is that unfavorable environmental conditions move a person into delinquency and crime. Of course, the theory cannot account for those individuals who live in unfavorable environmental conditions and yet lead law-abiding lives, reformers, then, in the period between the two world wars, focused on social disorganization in the slum areas as the major source of crime.

Edwin Sutherland, while probably best known for his theory of differential association, has also made important contributions to criminology with his studies of professional theft and white-collar criminality, all three of which were developed principally during the 1930s and 1940s. Sutherland introduced his theory of differential association in the 1939 edition of *Principles of Criminology*. The theory has two principal ideas: first, people are more likely to commit crimes when they have an excess of definitions favorable to law violation than not favorable to law violation; second, individuals learn crime in the same way that one learns any other behavior.

With regard to this second idea is the role social environment plays in crime causation. In other words, it is the social environment and not an individual's personal characteristics that are criminogenic. Sutherland linked crime and delinquency to faulty or improper socialization.

Sutherland's theory of differential association was influenced by another sociological perspective which was developing at the University of Chicago during the 1920s, symbolic interactionism. This perspective, which is grounded in social psychology, was largely developed by Chicago sociologists George Herbert Mead, Charles Horton Cooley, and William I. Thomas. Siegel (1992) has summarized the three main tenants of this position, "People act according to their own interpretations of reality, according to the meaning things have for them, . . . they learn the meaning of a thing from the way others react to it, . . . and . . . according to the meaning and symbols they have learned from others" (p. 16). The ecological or socialization view was adopted by most criminologists by 1950. The mix of biological, psychological, economic, and sociological factors that had formerly characterized theoretical criminology was giving way to a more specialized social psychological approach (Clinnard 1951, p. 550).

During the 1940s an increasing number of researchers began to emphasize anomie. As initially developed by Emile Durkheim, anomie was a condition of relative normlessness in a society or group. Anomie was a property of the social structure, not a property of the individual in relation to the society. Anomic conditions arise when the social structure no longer has control over individuals' wants and desires. The emphasis on anomie demonstrates that crime occurs in all social classes including the white-collar crime of business leaders which Sutherland analyzed in 1949.

Anomie theory, as developed by Robert Merton, stresses that the ultimate American goal is economic success and material well-being. When the institutional means are not available to achieve these culturally approved goals, then individuals will either scale down their ambitions, withdraw, or turn to deviant behavior to obtain their desired goals. The chosen path of deviance depends on opportunity and environment. For example, a youth in an urban slum may steal to get what he desires or a business executive may resort to stock fraud. This adaptation to alienation or stress is what Merton called innovation. The adaptation of innovation is most clearly associated with deviant behavior.

A relationship between organized crime and anomie theory was examined earlier in chapter 5. As indicated then, most theories of crime causation have been directed at juvenile delinquency, not adult criminality, so that theories of organized crime have "been mostly a by-product of work directed primarily toward juvenile delinquency or the study of social structures" (Moore 1974, p. viii). In fact, although the Chicago school criminologists did not acknowledge it, their work with youth gangs suggests that these theorists already had some knowledge of anomie. As we already know, the Chicago school theorists made no attempt to apply their theories to adult criminals. As Moore (1974) suggests "Although John Landesco published his valuable *Organized Crime in Chicago* in 1929, most sociologists continued to concentrate on juvenile delinquency and related problems. Despite their limited appreciation of the modern theory of anomie, researchers had certainly demonstrated by 1950 an organic relationship between those engaged in organized criminal activities and the social conditions in urban slums" (p. viii).

As noted earlier in chapter 4, various state crime surveys were undertaken in the 1920s. These state crime surveys, with the exception of Landesco's work, devoted little to an understanding of the socioeconomic causes of crime in general, or to organized crime in particular. We have already commented that Thrasher's and Landesco's understanding of organized crime were similar. Organized crime was the environment in which underworld figures associated. This, at least, was an alternative approach to the law enforcement perspective of the state crime surveys. Because the state crime surveys of the 1920s and the Wickersham Crime Commission of 1931 paid little attention to the existence and threat of organized crime and racketeering, the academic point of view on environment lost out to the law enforcement perspective (Moore 1974, p. 14).

Mainstream criminology has its roots in the work of Shaw, McKay, Sutherland, and Merton. But until the end of World War II, sociologists in general, and criminologists in particular, were a small lot. The major growth period for both sociology and sociological criminology occurred after World War II. Departments of sociology were firmly established on campuses across the United States by the 1940s and 1950s. During the 1940s and 1950s, the continued development of academic sociology took root in the East, at Harvard and Columbia Universities. The premier sociologist of this time was Talcott Parsons and his theoretical perspective was structural-functionalism. The basic premise of structural-functionalism is that society is made up of interdependent parts and that these parts work together as one to produce consensus and stability within the society. These interdependent parts include social relationships, social institutions, and social organizations.

Sociologist Alvin Gouldner (1970, p. 23), in *The Coming Crisis of Western Sociology,* writes that the development of American sociology after World War II was directly linked to the emerging welfare state. The regional shift of academic sociology from the Midwest to the eastern United States was accompanied by a cultural shift as well. Gouldner (1970) comments that the "Eastern Seaboard culture tends to be somewhat less localistic, parochial, isolationist, and less 'down to earth'; . . . more 'intellectualistic,' more national and more international in its orientations" (p. 145).

The needs of the emerging welfare state were met by sociologists. The welfare state provided the academic discipline of sociology with the opportunity to become institutionalized. The American middle class generally believes that the institutions of American society are sound and only minor adjustments need to be made. A radical transformation of American society is not necessary. Therefore, social problems could be solved "with expert services, research, and advice, and a modest amount of income redistribution" (Gouldner 1970, p. 161). Sociologists are the university-based specialists who will address the social problems of crime, deviance, delinquency, and poverty. Just as the theory of social disorganization was responsive to the needs of the state during the 1920s and 1930s, the theory of structural-functionalism was responsive to the needs of the welfare state during the 1940s and 1950s. Both theoretical perspectives gave support to the academic discipline of sociology.

The factors which were responsible for the growth of sociology after World War II were also responsible for the growth of criminology. But in the case of criminology there were additional factors at work. The 1960s was a period when the "crime problem" occupied the minds of most Americans. This preoccupation, would, in a significant way, lead to the further development of American criminology. On July 25, 1965, President Johnson established the President's Crime Commission on Law Enforcement and Administration of Justice and waged a "war on crime." Although not known by Americans, or even the president himself, the new Crime Commission ushered in a new era for criminal justice in the United States.

A series of task force reports were released by the President's Crime Commission in 1967. The various reports were summarized in a work entitled *The Challenge of Crime In A Free Society* (1967). A major finding of the report was that local agencies were totally ill equipped to deal with the problems of crime and its control. This prompted the federal government to channel moneys into reforming the criminal justice system, through its Omnibus Crime Control and Safe Streets Act.

Prior to 1967 and the President's Crime Commission Report, the term and the concept "criminal justice," did not even exist (J. Martin, personal communication, April 23, 1991). The President's Crime Commission defined criminal justice as "the structure, functions, and decision processes of those agencies that deal with the management of crime—the police, the courts, and corrections" (Inciardi 1990, p. 24).

One important by-product of the Omnibus Crime Control and Safe Streets Act was the creation of an agency called the Law Enforcement Assistance Administration (LEAA) which was directly responsible for the Law Enforcement Education Program (LEEP). The Law Enforcement Education Program had a significant impact on the development of American criminology. LEEP funds were now available for criminal justice personnel to return to school and pursue further course work and degrees. The result was an increase in college students pursuing criminal justice studies. Before long programs in criminal justice and criminology were being developed in institutions across the United States. These programs went by a variety of names: "criminal justice," "law enforcement," "police science," "criminology," and "administration of justice" to name a few.

There was another development that was occurring in American sociology during the late 1960s and early 1970s that also had impacted American sociology and criminology. New theoretical perspectives were once again on the rise. Social changes in the 1960s and 1970s prompted criminologists and sociologists to ask new questions. This led to a growth in conflict perspectives (see Block and Chambliss 1981).

The legal definition of crime was no longer prevalent. A social definition of crime was replacing it. As Howard Becker (1963) suggests, "the deviant is one to whom that label has successfully been applied; deviant behavior is behavior so labeled"

(p. 9). During the 1960s there was a movement within criminology to develop a sociology of law. The criminal law, its application and formulation, was no longer taken as a given by criminologists. The development of a sociology of criminal law has been guided by the work of Quinney, Shur, Turk, and Chambliss (Jeffery 1972, p. 494).

Criminology underwent a "paradigm revolution" in the words of Thomas Kuhn; the crimes of the powerful were increasingly examined. This new criminology, also known as radical, critical, Marxist, and conflict criminology, began to develop in the 1960s (Block and Chambliss 1981, p. 2). The perspective of the "new criminology" and the social changes that brought this perspective about are considered in greater detail in chapter 8.

One more point has to be made before we leave this section on the place of criminology in sociology. Today it is not unusual to find attorneys, political scientists, psychologists, biologists, and others among the faculty in criminology departments. It is becoming increasingly incorrect to identify criminology as a specialized field of inquiry within sociology.

Textbooks in American criminology: 1920-40

As an academic subject of study, criminology was taken over by American sociologists. This is probably because the study of social problems was the jurisdiction of sociologists, and crime and delinquency were conceived as social problems. These sociologists wrote the textbooks and offered courses in criminology.

In 1973, Walter Reckless reviewed some of the important criminology textbooks written by American sociologists between 1920 and 1940. It will be useful to review the topics in these early textbooks to document that organized crime was not considered a part of the subject matter of crime and delinquency during this early period.

Maurice Parmelee wrote the first textbook in criminology for academic use in 1920 (others have cited the date as 1918, e.g., Clinnard 1951; Gibbons 1992). The text was titled *Criminology*. The contents included the following topics: criminology as a hybrid science; crime related to social control; the effect of the physical environment; the urban-rural, economic, and political base of crime; the influence of civilization on crime; the organic and mental bases of crime; feebleminded and psychopathic offenders; types of criminals; juvenile criminality; female criminality; criminal jurisprudence; evolution of punishment; individualization of punishment; and the prison system. Many of these topics are still included in contemporary texts.

In 1924, Edwin H. Sutherland published *Criminology*. The text was the most widely used textbook on criminology for sociology classes. The contents included the following: laws and crime; statistics; victims; composition of the criminal population; causes; police; courts; prisons; punishment; and prevention.

John L. Gillin published *Criminology and Penology* in 1926. The following topics were included in the text: definition of offending behavior; the physiognomy; factors in the physical environment influencing crime; physical characteristics of criminals; mental heredity; economic and social factors in crime; history of punishment; modern penal institutions; and the machinery of justice.

Crime and the Criminal was published in 1929 by Philip A. Parsons. His coverage included the following topics: who is the criminal; theories of crime; classification of criminals; the anatomical and psychological factors; the clinical approach to the study of the criminal; the nature of crime; the operation of the physical and social environment in causation; the functioning of the police and the public; theories of punishment; penal institutions; and new conceptions of treatment.

Fred E. Haynes published *Criminology* in 1930. Topics included the following: the scientific study of the criminal; types of criminals; social control; criminal law and procedure; punishment; jails and prisons; probation; and parole.

Crime: Criminals and Criminal Justice was published by Nathaniel F. Cantor in 1932. His chapters include the following: criminology as a social science; the nature of crime; the search for causes; "making the criminal mind"; the administration of justice; and penology.

Clayton J. Ettinger, a psychiatrist and sociologist, published *The Problem of Crime* in 1932. Topic coverage included the following: the cost of crime; the mechanics of crime; economic and political factors; the psychiatric approach; the machinery of justice; jails; prisons; probation; and parole.

In 1934, Albert Morris published *Criminology*. The contents of his text included the following: criminal behavior as an interplay of focuses unique in every man; childhood and the foundations of behavior; expanding horizons of the person; the criminal habit; prevention; police; criminal justice; and treatment of criminals.

Lastly, Walter Reckless published *Criminal Behavior* in 1940. The coverage included the following: the nature of criminal behavior; relationship of crime to social disorganization; area and regional differences in crime; sex, age, and race variations in crime; the development of criminal careers; the search for causes; the nature of punishment; prisons and reformatories; relapse and the result of treatment; and crime prevention.

We can see that, although gangsterism and organized crime was public knowledge during the period, the textbook writers did not choose to include the subject matter of organized crime in the forms of racketeering, gangsterism, and vice in their books. Organized crime was not considered part of the subject matter of crime and delinquency during this time period. However, contemporary criminology texts almost always include organized crime as part of their subject matter. When did this change take place? The answer, as we will see, was in 1943. Our analysis of criminology textbooks in the following section will document this.

American textbooks in criminology with chapters or sections on organized crime: 1941-92

In 1974, John Galliher and James Cain published "Citation Support for the Mafia Myth in Criminology Textbooks." The present analysis borrows heavily on the methodology of Galliher and Cain[1]. However, the present analysis does not claim to be as rigorous as the original research of Galliher and Cain; nor does it claim to be a replication of the Galliher and Cain study. The writer has randomly selected nineteen criminology textbooks, written by American sociologists, during the period 1940 to 1992[2]. The texts were selected from library shelves and personal collections. Some texts have gone through several editions. Where this is the case we have tried to use the most recent edition. However, the most recent edition was not always available to the writer. All of the texts selected made reference to organized crime. Yet some texts devoted only minor attention to the topic.

Each reference on the chapters or sections of organized crime were recorded and placed into categories. The categories included: official documents (hearings and commission reports on the city, state, or federal level; city, federal, and state statutes; court cases and laws; and government issued pamphlets and books); articles and books based on official documents; journalistic accounts (articles and books); legalistic accounts (law journals and ABA publications); criminology and social problems textbooks; and social science accounts (articles and books). If a reference was cited by the same author more than once, it was not counted again. Table 2, below, lists the criminology texts selected for analysis.

Table 2. Textbooks With Sections or Chapters On Organized Crime

Author	Title	Year
Elgius Weir	Criminology	1941
Harry Elmer Barnes and Negley K. Teeters	New Horizons in Criminology, 2nd edition	1951
Mabel Elliot	Crime in Modern Society	1952
Donald R. Taft and Ralph W. England	Criminology, 4th edition	1964
Herbert A. Bloch and Gilbert Geis	Men, Crime and Society	1965
Walter Reckless	The Crime Problem, 5th edition	1973
Martin R. Haskell and Lewis Yablonsky	Criminology: Crime and Criminality	1974
Richard Quinney	Criminology	1975
Edwin Sutherland and Donald Cressey	Criminology, 10th edition	1978
Gresham M. Sykes	Criminology	1978
Harold J. Vetter and Ira J. Silverman	Criminology and Crime: An Introduction	1986
George Vold and Thomas Bernard	Theoretical Criminology, 3rd edition	1986
*Alex Thio	Deviant Behavior, 3rd edition	1988
John Conklin	Criminology, 3rd edition	1989
Hugh Barlow	Criminology, 5th edition	1990
Ruth Masters and Cliff Roberson	Inside Criminology	1990
Sue Titus Reid	Crime and Criminology, 6th edition	1991
Don C. Gibbons	Society, Crime and Criminal Behavior, 6th edition	1991
Larry J. Siegel	Criminology, 4th edition	1992

* This is a combination criminology/social problems text. It is used here because there is a detailed chapter on organized crime in his text.

Our first text selected, *Criminology*, by Weir, contains a three-page discussion of organized crime-racketeering. In actuality, the discussion is of racketeering and vice in industrial areas. Racketeering was very much in the public's mind in 1941. So it is not surprising that Weir would include a discussion of racketeering in his text. However, Weir does not provide the reader with any citations to his text material. It should also be noted that Weir was trained in religion and philosophy, not sociology.

The first discussion of organized crime, of any substance, is found in Barnes and Teeters, *New Horizons in Criminology*, published in 1943. The topics in the 1943 edition which refer to the activities of organized crime include the following: the relation of the something-for-nothing psychology and competitive capitalism to organized crime and racketeering; the evolution of racketeering, lotteries and organized gambling; leading types and characteristic methods of racketeering and organized crime; and political graft, racketeers, and politicians. The second edition of this text, published in 1951, " takes account of the new trends during the war decade, such as shifts in the character of organized crime and racketeering, the recent development and political infiltration of syndicated gambling and criminality" (Barnes and Teeters 1951, p. vii). Their discussion of organized crime is quite sophisticated for its time. However, the heavy reliance on journalistic accounts of organized crime (42 citations) lends credence to the belief that sociologists often rely on secondary data for their accounts of organized crime. Of course, in 1951, there were few accounts about organized crime written by sociologists.

Also significant is the text by Masters and Robinson (1990). This text devotes a whole three pages to the topic of organized crime. The only two citations are both official government documents. The first citation is from the Law Enforcement Assistance Administration, Task Force Report on Organized Crime, 1967. This document is used to give a definition of organized crime. It is remarkable that a 1990 criminology textbook would have only three pages devoted to organized crime.

The text with the most social science citations (48) was Gibbons's *Society, Crime and Criminal Behavior* (1992). In contrast, Haskell and Yablonsky (1974) contain no social science citations in their chapter on organized crime. While they do cite Cressey's *Theft of the Nation*, this text is, in actuality, a result of his work for the President's Crime Commission in 1967. Therefore, the book is categorized as a book based on an official document. Table 3, below lists the total citations to organized crime in criminology textbooks by type of document.

Observation of table 3 tells us that sociologists do rely heavily on journalistic accounts and official documents for their information on organized crime. Consistent with the findings of Galliher and Cain, overall more citations are taken from social science and journalistic accounts than from official documents. When we examine the citations more closely, we find that official documents are often used to give a general description of organized crime (definition, structure, characteristics of organized crime). However, journalistic and social science accounts often deal with specific subjects (illegal gambling, illegal drugs, racketeering, prostitution,

Table 3. Total Citations To Organized Crime in Criminology Textbooks by Type
of Document: 1941-92

Type of Document Cited	Number of Times Cited
Social Science Accounts	198
Journalistic Accounts	166
Official documents	70
Books Based On Official Documents	25
Criminology and Social Problems Textbooks	9
Legalistic Accounts	5

corruption, political collusion, the existence of the Mafia, leaders in organized crime). Again, this is a finding consistent with the research of Galliher and Cain.

However, one of the most significant findings of this analysis, unlike the original research of Galliher and Cain, is that a handful of writers (Sykes 1978; Thio 1988; Conklin 1989; Reid 1991; Gibbons 1992; Siegel 1992) provide both a law enforcement and a sociological orientation to organized crime. In doing so, they have cited much of the revisionist work discussed earlier in this book (Bell 1953; Albini 1971; Ianni and Ianni 1972; Chambliss 1973; Smith 1975). As Inciardi et al. (1977) note, "it is the preoccupation with a Mafia mystique that has been the stifling of serious work on the social world of organized crime" (p. 15). Likewise, Moore (1974) writes that the concern over the existence of the Mafia has "led the public to ask the wrong questions" and to ignore the "legal, social, and economic problems that give rise to organized crime."

In sum, it appears that most contemporary criminology textbook writers are utilizing more social science accounts. This is because more social science accounts are now available and organized crime has recently become a problem which sociologists are studying. As we have documented, prior to the work of the President's Crime Commission, not much research on organized crime was generated by sociologists. They, therefore, were almost forced to utilize data sources based on official documents and journalistic accounts. It is encouraging to see some change in this area. Lastly, table 4, below lists the three most frequently cited sources in criminology textbooks to organized crime.

Two of the most frequently cited sources include a book based on an official document and an official document (which, we might add, are both dated). This finding is not surprising. However, the social science citation by Bell, as a most frequently cited source, is not consistent with what we might expect. Yet in this analysis we have found several social science accounts which were cited four or five times. For example, the Ianni's (1972) *A Family Business* was cited five times. In contrast, only one journalistic account, Sondern's (1959), *Brotherhood of Evil*, was cited four times. These findings differ from those of Galliher and Cain and can be interpreted to mean that organized crime has slowly become a subject that sociologists are studying. It might also be interpreted to mean that sociologists prefer

Table 4. Most Frequently Cited Sources In Criminology Textbooks To Organized
Crime: 1941-1992

Cressey, Donald R. 1969. *Theft of the Nation*. NY:Harper and Row.	10
Bell, Daniel. 1953. "Crime As An American Way of Life," *Antioch Review*, 13 (June):131-54 (this account also includes Bell's expansion of this article in his 1962 book *The End of Ideology: On the Exhaustion of Political Ideology in the Fifties*).	8
Task Force Report: Organized Crime: 1967 Washington, D.C.: U.S. GPO.	7

a sociological, rather than law enforcement orientation, to organized crime.
However, it should also be noted that two additional books based on official
documents were cited five times and six times respectively. These books were Robert
Kennedy's (1960) *The Enemy Within* and Estes Kefauver's (1951) *Crime In America*.
Also cited six times was the Third Interim Report of the Kefauver committee
hearings. In short, while sociologists are beginning to generate their own research
into organized crime, there still appears to be a heavy reliance on journalistic
accounts and official documents.

Concluding remarks

This chapter began with a brief review of the place of criminology in American
sociology. It was pointed out that sociological criminology in the United States had
its roots in the Chicago school. We then examined the contents of a number of the
early criminology texts, from 1920 to 1940, and found that these books did not
address the topic of organized crime in the forms of vice, gangsterism, and
racketeering that were so prevalent then. Finally, we noted that a substantive
discussion of organized crime did not appear in a criminology textbook until 1943.
Furthermore, we found that even today, many sociologists still rely on official
documents and journalistic accounts for their information regarding organized
crime. However, in the late 1960s sociologists did turn to the study of organized
crime. Our final chapter will address the question why the Chicago school ignored
or denied the existence of organized crime and why, after decades of systematic
neglect, sociologists began to study organized crime in the late 1960s.

NOTES

1. For a complete discussion of the research of John Galliher and James Cain, see:
   Galliher, John and James Cain. 1974. "Citation Support for the Mafia Myth in
   Criminology Textbooks," *American Sociologist* 9:68-74.
2. The Barnes and Teeters textbook, *New Horizons In Criminology*, was not randomly
   selected. It was known to be the first instance where organized crime is discussed, in
   any depth, in a criminology textbook. This information was provided by Dr. John
   Martin of the Department of Sociology and Anthropology at Fordham University,
   Bronx, N.Y.

8

Academic inattention toward the
study of organized crime by
American sociologists:
some reasons why

O UR FINAL chapter will inquire into the sources of sociology's inattention
to the phenomenon of racketeering and gangsterism during the period of
its development and flourishing at Chicago. This inquiry will extend into
the period when it became "organized crime" and when sociologists finally began to
recognize it as an object worthy of its attention. The chapter will deal with
sociologists' and criminologists' seeming neglect of the subject, with the research
methods used in its study, and the ideological and theoretical trends which
predisposed social scientists to ignore or minimize the problem.

This chapter will consist of three main sections and some concluding remarks.
Sections one and two will offer some reasons why sociologists and criminologists
ignored or denied the existence of organized crime. The focus of the first section is
the Chicago school sociologists and criminologists; the focus of the second is
contemporary American sociologists and criminologists. We will see that the
Chicago school theorists shared many of the same values and assumptions held by
today's mainstream sociologists and criminologists. These ideological, theoretical,
and methodological assumptions have predisposed sociologists and criminologists
to study the crimes of the powerless and to neglect the crimes of the powerful; or even
to neglect crime when it becomes a lucrative organized industry and business. A third
section will document the critical events in American society during the late 1960s
and early 1970s that influenced the study of the crimes of the powerful, and the
introduction of a new theoretical perspective, critical criminology, to study these
crimes.

The Chicago school's inattention to the study of organized crime: some reasons why

As previously documented, sociological criminology in the United States had its origins with the Chicago school theorists. The period of the Chicago school was critical to the development of American sociology. Bramson (1961) cites the distinguishing features of the period as "an expansion of academic sociology, a large increase in the number of students and faculty, the beginnings of specialization and differentiation within sociology, the search for a methodology which would guarantee the scientific status of the discipline, and the connection of leadership in the Department of Sociology at the University of Chicago" (p. 86).

These early pioneers were positivist criminologists. They studied delinquency and crime by applying the scientific method, they believed they were avoiding the intrusion of their own personal values. Therefore, they believed that their theories of crime causation were value-free (see Snodgrass 1972, p. 22). Yet, as many have demonstrated, "positivism is itself ideological . . . it is rooted in an ideology of rational technocratic control over the world and its people" (Pfohl 1985, p. 355).

Further, one premise dominated their thinking: American society was primarily good. The Chicago school theorists shared a "central commitment to the American way, an ideal of living whose validity and attainability was taken for granted" (Smith 1988, p. 33). Because society was considered to be so good, it did not need to be examined for any imperfections. The good society "could not therefore be conceptually related to delinquency" (Snodgrass 1972, p. 23) or, we might add any organized or structurally based system of criminal activity. "The good society could not cause the evil offender" (Snodgrass 1972, p. 23). A "good society" would not have organized crime, let alone cause its existence. Perhaps, more than any other writer and critic, economist Gerald E. Caiden (1985) has persuasively argued that the very things that make up the social body of the criminological industry—its blood and guts, so to speak—violates the common conceptions of who and what America is:

> While organized crime may be pure entrepreneurship unfettered by noneconomic considerations, its ethic of "making it," its rip-off mentality, its disregard for social costs, its crass materialism, its reliance on intimidation and violence, all run counter to the basic moral tenets of Western society. The contrasting ethical system creates conflict and confusion, corrupts the socialization process, and turns traditional Judeo-Christian morality upside down. It mocks social responsibility. It deliberately caters to the baser instincts and gratifies aberrations. It cheapens life. It worships power. Where does organized crime take society? What is its image of the good society? What future does it envisage for humanity? (p. 154)

Caiden goes on to reason that to study and expose this kind of crime took a different kind of stand toward America than prevailed at that time. Apparently, a more sober, a more dismal view of power and capitalism would have to wait for a later era when people could imagine such things and when violence was more digestible for more of us.

The exposure of organized crime makes society look closely at itself. What is portrayed may not be at all flattering to social self-images. It will show many blemishes in the nature of prevailing ethical standards and morals, in the state of the laws, lawlessness, and law enforcement, in the conduct of public business and official behavior, in the effectiveness of social controls, government regulation, and communal policing, and in the willingness of public authorities, established institutions and professional crime fighters to organized crime. It paints a dismal, frightening, and disillusioning picture. Either we leave it as it is and permit organized crime to gnaw at society, or we do something about it, reminding people that the good society is unattainable until organized crime is eradicated. (Caiden 1985, pp. 154-55)

Furthermore, it also seems clear that the Chicago school theorists, like many social scientists today, were reluctant to study organized crime because to do so meant to expose the business relationships between the underworld and the upper world, a group of people that included professional sociologists themselves. This was clearly documented in chapter 4, where the relationships of Burgess, Shaw, and Landesco to the Illinois Association for Criminal Justice placed them in close contact with professional groups such as police, judges, and politicians. The Chicago school theorists were well aware that the underworld could not wield the influence it did if it were not for the financial and political alliances with the inhabitants of Chicago's upper world (see Pearce 1981; Smith 1988). Further, given their belief in free expression and free enterprise, it is not surprising that sociologists and criminologists would not interfere in the "business of organized crime." A case in point: both Burgess and Shaw had excellent contacts with leaders in the community who often sponsored social science research (cf. Snodgrass 1972, 1976; Carey 1975; Bulmer 1984; Kurtz 1984; Smith 1988). Shaw often worked closely with the political and economic leaders of the community in order to secure cooperation and funding for community organizations (Snodgrass 1972, p. 7).

The sociological criminologists typically adopted a legal definition of crime. This meant that crime and delinquency were behavior that violated the criminal law. The state, then, defined what behavior was criminal, and criminologists thus aligned themselves with official state definitions of crime. The state defined what was right or wrong on the basis of what was advantageous to the state. With this conception of delinquency and crime the theorist could be "loyal to the society from which he gained respectability" (Snodgrass 1972, p. 30). Platt (1975) concurs, the legal code is the "reference-point" for those sociologists who "assume a State definition of crime" (p. 96). The concern of criminology has long been to reform and control those individuals who have been legally defined and prosecuted as criminals. By accepting a state and legal definition of crime much behavior is excluded from study. "In accepting the State and legal definition of crime, the scope of analysis has been constrained to exclude behavior which is not legally defined as 'crime' (for example, imperialism, exploitation, racism, and sexism) as well as behaviour which is not typically prosecuted (for example, tax evasion, price fixing, consumer fraud, government corruption, police homicides, etc.)" (Platt 1975, p. 6).

Furthermore, because of the emphasis on "rehabilitation" sociological criminologists have been reluctant to study and expose the official agencies of justice to
systematic investigation. Kurtz (1984) also states as much saying that the "Chicago
sociologists were more likely to cooperate with and in some cases attempt to affect
political institutions than to perceive of them as subject matter for research" (pp. 78-
79). Kurtz cites the work of Landesco (1929), Sutherland (1937), and Shaw and
McKay (1942) to support this view. These sociologists all studied the criminal rather
than the official agencies of justice.

From many respects it is obvious that the Chicago school theorists had a vested
interest in maintaining cooperation with the leaders of the community and their
respective institutions in order to obtain funding for their research and promote the
academic discipline of sociology. By 1929, many of the wealthy organizations in
Chicago had already signed research contracts with Chicago school sociologists to
study the problems of the city which were of interest to the various groups (Smith
1988, p. 24; cf. Carey 1975; Bulmer 1984; Kurtz 1984). Platt (1975, pp. 100-101; cf.
Thio 1973; Quinney 1970) comments that criminological research is often agency-
determined, that is, research questions and the specifications of funding are decided
by the research agency, rather than by the social scientist. Moreover, criminological
research supports the status quo by ignoring issues which may lead to structural
criticisms of the society.

Therefore, due to the relationship between the Chicago theorists and the
established and elite agencies and institutions within the community, it was unlikely
that the Chicagoans would be inclined to be critical of such institutions when they
worked side by side with their directors and professional employees. They certainly
would not be engaged in research which would portray such institutions in an
unfavorable light, not so much because they lacked interest in studying these
institutions, but because to do so would put their own activities and the functions
they served into a questionable light. This surely influenced the fact that they did not
examine the courts, the police, the probation, and parole systems. These systems were
all exempt from analysis.

It is also significant that the Chicago theorists made no attempt to examine the
Volstead Act itself. Laws were accepted as a given. There was no consideration that
laws often reflect the interests and values of the ruling class. Because of the
criminologists' reform orientation they were not interested in studying law and
society. Knowledge of law and society will not help the criminologist reform the
criminal. If the science of criminology was to be a success, then the criminologists
must be able to reform the criminal. If one considers the history of American
sociology, then it is not surprising that many criminologists have accepted the
positivist position with respect to the definition of crime and the focus on the
individual offender. The problem that did preoccupy the sociologists was that of
socialization and "personality development" (Jeffery 1972, p. 467). The early
theorists, W. I. Thomas, G. H. Mead, John Dewey, and C. H. Cooley, were not as
interested in the question of social structure and social institutions as were later

theorists. The issues of social structure and social institutions gained greater prominence in the late 1930s when American sociologists became more interested in the work of such great European thinkers as Weber, Durkheim, and Tönnies (Jeffery 1972, p. 467). In other words, the early criminologists maintained an individual, psychological bias, as opposed to a structural orientation, of crime and its control. This bias undoubtedly contributed, however remotely, to their neglect of organized crime.

However, the fact that institutions and the lawmaking process were not subjected to study is not the only problem with accepting official definitions of crime. Official offenders, those who have been arrested and convicted, are not representative of all offenders. Much crime goes undetected and unreported. Then, as now, the vast majority of official criminals came from the lowest social classes. As Haller (1970) noted, "most of the people processed by the criminal justice system were the unorganized offenders" (p. 620). The "unorganized offenders" included juvenile delinquents, drunkards, wife-beaters, and amateur thieves. Organized offenders included professional thieves, business or labor racketeers, and participants in organized crime. Landesco (1932) also noted the "relative immunity to punishment of gangsters engaged in organized crime" (p. 127).

Given the fact that criminologists often study their subjects in artificial environments, such as prisons, jails, or probation and parole offices, it is not surprising that they do not find organized criminals in these settings. As Polsky (1967) pointedly comments, "sociologists find it too difficult or distasteful to get near adult criminals except in jails or other anti-crime settings, such as the courts and probation and parole systems" (p. 119). Polsky (1967) continues, "there is a misguided 'democratic' notion that a society's official acts and public definitions really tell us what a society is all about, and that the sociologist's main job is to count and codify them" (p. 119). Criminologists have traditionally studied conventional criminals in conventional settings, like prisons and jails. These conventional criminals, while readily accessible to the criminologist, are not representative of the full spectrum of criminality. And as Foster (1977) tells us, "prisons are one of the least likely places in which to find full-fledged members of the major crime bureaucracies" (p. 15). Criminologists, Polsky (1967) suggests, should "get out of the jails and courts and into the field" (p. 120).

In addition to organized criminals' relative immunity from prosecution, they also wield a great deal of power and influence within the community. This was certainly true during the reign of Al Capone. "Al Capone's mob . . . were able to maintain over a wide area of Chicago's business life a hegemony upon which the Rockefeller Foundation and its subsidiaries made relatively little impact. Big business had to operate cheek by jowl with the criminal underworld" (Smith 1988, p. 23).

Organized criminals within the Chicago community were on their guard against unsympathetic scientific investigation. Smith (1988) comments that it was much harder for Burgess and his students "to study the powerful than the weak within Chicago society" (p. 25). As sociologist Solomon Kobrin (personal communication, June 1, 1991) writes, the theory of urban sociology developed by Robert Park and his students focused on "spatially segregated moral worlds," and "none of Park's followers had or could obtain access to the world of organized crime." As another example of the limited access to the world of organized crime by the Chicago sociologists this present writer cites the personal recollections of sociologist John Martin (personal communication, April 23, 1991) while he was a graduate student of Frederic Thrasher's at New York University. Professor Martin recalls that one day in class Thrasher showed the class a newspaper headline, from one of the Chicago papers, which read, "Professor Predicts Gang Wars," and the newspaper article named Thrasher. The "gang wars happened" and Thrasher was "told it was time to leave, so he left" Chicago for New York (J. Martin, personal communication, April 23, 1991). It appears that Thrasher had been warned to refrain from studying the world of organized crime in Chicago.

One final illustration of the Chicago school's inability to obtain access to the world of organized crime comes from Chicago school scholars Solomon Kobrin (personal communication, June 1, 1991) and Daniel Glaser (personal communication, January 24, 1992). Both of these men relay an incident about sociologist Joseph Lohman, who began working for Clifford Shaw on the Chicago Area Projects in the late 1930s. Lohman was assigned to the Near North Side of Chicago, a predominantly Italian area. Lohman's job was to get to know the important leaders of the community so that these leaders would help organize programs to reform delinquents and prevent delinquency. Many of the important community leaders had contacts with organized crime and organized criminals. In the late 1930s or early 1940s, "Lohman wrote and presented at the annual meeting of the American Sociological Society . . . a paper describing a segment of the vice industry in Chicago's Near North area as an example of the fruitfulness of the participant-observation method" (S. Kobrin, personal communication, June 1, 1991). In the crowd was a newspaper reporter who thought that Lohman's presentation would make an exciting organized crime story. The following day the story was published in the Chicago newspapers and "Shaw then received a phone call from a dentist on the Near North Side, . . . who told Shaw that if he didn't get Lohman out of the area they would not be responsible for what happened to him" (D. Glaser, personal communication, January 24, 1992). Shaw relayed the story to Lohman who did not take it seriously. Shaw evidently did and reassigned Lohman to another area. Lohman refused the assignment and resigned from the Chicago Area Project.

Reformers, while successful in their efforts with juvenile delinquents, had almost no success with adult criminals. Because "success" was more easily achieved with juvenile delinquents than with organized criminals, social scientists turned their attention to "reforming" them. The sociologist sought to correct individuals or conditions in the marginal groups. The aim was "to bring the offender or his group over to the theorist's side" to "the shared standards of the larger, conventional order" (Snodgrass 1972, p. 49).

Mills (1943, p. 169) explains that "social pathologists" (his term for a whole host of social scientists of the city's ills) define problems as those things which deviate from the norm. The norms are standards set by conventional society, particularly the norms of rural middle-class white Protestant men. The pathologists do not question the origins of these norms. The norms are taken as a given and the pathologists often sanction them. Because there is no examination of the norms themselves, there is no examination of the normative structure or of the political implications of the normative structure.

The terms "treatment," "reformation," "rehabilitation," "correction" meant conversion or conventionalization. It was much easier to manipulate the juvenile delinquent or his environment than the organized criminal or his environment, or expect as much from the delinquents themselves. The ultimate goal was social control. Social control was seen, by the Chicago sociologists, as the central problem of sociology (Kurtz 1984, p. 57). "Social control is always an exercise in power" (Pfohl 1985, p. 333).

Reform is an important component of positivist thought. However, one must distinguish between liberal reform and other anti capitalist criticisms of American society. Liberal reform is the "belief that it is possible to create a well-regulated, stable and humanitarian system of criminal justice under the present economic and political arrangements" (Platt 1975, p. 97). As Platt (1975) argues, "Liberal reformism in criminology supports the extension of welfare state capitalism and gradual programmes of amelioration, whilst rejecting radical and violent forms of social political change" (p. 97). Positive social change will occur gradually through the work of technocratic problem-solvers, not through the work of the oppressed themselves.

Indeed, this is the type of reform liberalism carried out by the Chicago school theorists (see Schwendinger and Schwendinger, 1974). An example of this type of reform liberalism is Shaw's Chicago Area Project (a delinquency prevention program). "The Chicago Area Project was first and foremost a disciplinary force, designed to inculcate values, socialise behaviour, and to achieve an accommodation of slum residents to the conventional order" (Snodgrass 1972, p. 17). In actuality, the Chicago Area Project was a way to maintain social control over the local youth. In addition, Shaw and McKay's ecological analysis of delinquency stopped at the community level. They looked inward to the delinquents' primary groups within the community. Business, industry, and the larger social structure were immune from investigation. They were not considered in the etiology of crime (Snodgrass 1972, p. 35; cf. Pfohl 1985).

Because the criminologist saw American society as only "mildly flawed," crime could be controlled through modest social changes. These sociologists were not interested in examining society itself or even in explaining why the society has crime. They were only interested in explaining why the individual offender was motivated to commit crime. The conception of the "good society" made it impossible to locate the cause of crime within the social structure of the society itself. There was no need to examine the history, culture, political system, economic system, or stratification system of society or of society's social institutions, because these things did not cause crime in society (Snodgrass 1972, pp. 33-34).

Much of the work of the Chicago school was ahistorical and apolitical (see Snodgrass 1972; Pfohl 1985). However, this criticism is not really totally appropriate for Landesco's work on organized crime in Chicago. It is likely that this is why Landesco's work was not given much attention by the Chicago school sociologists. His study uncovered facts and relationships that might be better left hidden. All societies have topics which are considered taboo, and organized crime in American society is one of these taboo subjects. No one likes to admit that organized crime exists and people avoid talking about it (Caiden 1985, pp. 148-49). Caiden (1985) in his address to the first National Conference on Organized Crime held on November 8-9, 1979, relates the following:

> organized crime was sustained by collusion, corruption, and complacency. Too many of us wanted what organized crime was prepared to supply at a price we, as individuals, were willing to pay. It was already so big that established institutions had come to terms with it and were prepared to accommodate it as long as the public was kept in ignorance about its extent. We would rather not talk about such things because we knew we did wrong but were too weak to do anything about them. The taboo on organized crime covered our shame and weakness and hid the harm we did to the ethical basis of civilized society. I accused academia of going along with the taboo and in so doing damaging its credibility and ignoring its moral obligation to remind society of things it would prefer not to know about. I referred to the current crop of textbooks on United States public policy and administration where one looks in vain for any account of public immorality, official lawlessness, bureaucratic deceit, administrative corruption, and the subversion of government by special interests. None of these topics was listed in an index. . . . It seemed that the authors were reluctant to admit that anything but honesty and goodness prevailed in the conduct of public affairs. (p. 149)

Caiden spoke these words in 1979 but the year could just as easily have been 1929. Notwithstanding the social and academic taboos, studying organized crime was still a difficult process . Caiden (1985) suggests the following reasons for this difficulty: (1) "restrictive access policies" made the collection of foreign materials difficult; (2) there were also "restrictive access policies" in the United States; (3) public agencies in charge of "public security and safety" would not disclose what they knew to the public; (4) research in the area of crime itself was given low status by funding agencies and therefore organized crime research was not encouraged or supported either; and (5) there were numerous "methodological problems" (pp. 149-50). In summarizing, Caiden (1985) stated that there were many reasons why organized crime was left hidden:

> There were a great many other topics that occupied people's attention, that were more central to their concerns, and that commanded official support for investigation. Relatively few persons were willing or able to bring organized crime out of the closet, at least not for the personal risks involved, the official discouragements encountered, and the practical obstacles which had to be

> overcome. As it was illegal and conspiratorial, investigation ought to be left to public authorities, which were in a better position to uncover the facts by matching organized crime in sophistication without being compromised. Simplest of all was not to get involved, ignoring the phenomenon and pretending it did not exist. (pp. 150-51)

In fact, it seems that the Chicago school sociologists took just this attitude in their own view of organized crime research. As Solomon Kobrin (personal communication, June 1, 1991) remarks, "My recollection of both the tone and the content of treatment was to take the existence of organized crime for granted , . . . and to account for its durability by reference to the phenomenon of 'entrenchment' brought about by the corruptibility of public officials. With this, attention moved to other matters."

Many of the difficulties discussed by Caiden have been with social scientists from the beginning. Yet it must be understood that Caiden, and other social scientists, who have really wanted to know about organized crime in the United States, have been successful in finding out a great deal about it. They have read official documents and popular authors on the subject, they have cut out important organized crime articles in newspapers and magazines, and have talked with investigators of organized crime. In more recent years they have read textbooks on organized crime written by social scientists, attended trials of mob bosses, and have engaged in their own primary research (see Caiden 1985, p. 151). The point to be made is that social scientists often rationalize their not studying organized crime by claiming the difficulties suggested by Caiden and others.

Furthermore, it is also important to note that members of the Chicago school did not employ the concepts of social class and economic conditions in their discussion of crime causation. They were opposed to any ideas of Marxism or economic determinism. In fact, after World War I, Marxist scholarship was disapproved of in all the social sciences. University posts held by some radical scholars were lost. Research funding was provided only to those scholars who were not viewed as an intellectual threat to the economic and political systems of the United States (Greenberg 1981, p. 1). Criminologists were opposed to the concepts of social class and economic conditions because they did not see the social world in which they lived as marked by class distinctions. The causes of crime were not due to differences of class and wealth (Snodgrass 1972, p. 38). These assumptions about crime, social class, and economic conditions have precluded sociologists and criminologists, until recently, from attempting to explain the roots of organized crime in these terms.

An additional assumption made by the positivists was that if society is "good" then offenders must be "bad." The offender and the offended were from two different social worlds. Criminals had qualities which made them different from conventional folk. These negative qualities placed them on a lower level than the criminologists. The criminologists were aligned with society, therefore they were separated from their research subjects (Snodgrass 1972, p. 41). As Thio (1973) states, "the sociologists of deviance may be said to tacitly support the power elite because both their research and analysis imply that the powerful are not only morally superior but should not be held responsible for causing deviance within their society" (p. 1). A common criticism of the Chicago school sociologists is their middle-class bias. That is, the Chicago school sociologists believed that deviance was a characteristic of the lower social classes. And that these so-called deviants were "disorganized" because their behavior was at odds with the "respectable" members of the white middle class. They would, for example, single out the streetwalker but ignore the behavior of the middle-class call girl.

By ignoring the behavior of the middle and upper classes the Chicago sociologists were making a value judgment that crime is a lower-class phenomenon. Further, they were condoning the class structure which places certain individuals in places of power. It was as if "natural" occurrences placed some people in positions of power and leadership.

The criminologists and the power elite shared a fondness for American society and therefore had a stake in its survival. The aim of the criminologist and the power elite was to protect and preserve society. Criminologists had to protect society from those forces which destroyed it. It was the ethic of "societal defense" which closely aligned the criminologists with the power elite (Snodgrass 1972, p. 52).

The Marxist criminologists Herman and Julia Schwendinger (1974), in *The Sociologists of the Chair*, argue that sociology has served capitalism at the expense of democracy. The Schwendingers argue that the early sociologists maintained an ideology of corporate liberalism. "Corporate liberalism accepted that intervention by the capitalist state was needed as one means of managing the relationships of large-scale organized labour and gigantic business monopolies" (Smith 1988, p. 14).

The Schwendingers (1974) state, "American sociologists during the formative years played a significant role in constructing 'scientific' theories of urban community life that were eventually used to justify the domination, by white middle-and-upper-class families, of American cities" (p. 482). They utilize Zorbaugh's study of *The Gold Coast and the Slum* as one example of "technography as justification for class domination" (Schwendinger and Schwendinger 1974, p. 484). The Schwendingers remark that Zorbaugh's technography was based on Darwinian notions. According to these notions the better individuals would naturally rise to the top and would assume positions of power and leadership in the society. Leadership could not come from the poorer residential districts because these residents were "disorganized." Instead of discussing how the poorer residents struggle to have a voice in the government of their city, Zorbaugh chose to justify why certain individuals are in positions of power and leadership within the city government. "Zorbaugh's study was little more than a sociological apologetic for the upper-class political domination of Chicago" (Schwendinger and Schwendinger 1974, p. 485).

This theme of sociologists as servants of the power elite has also been echoed by Thio (1973), Quinney (1970), and Platt (1975). Quinney (1970, pp. 26-28) writes that the primary purpose of scientific criminology has been to support the status quo of society, while established social structures, institutions, and laws are taken for granted. The motives of the state are rarely questioned and attention is focused on reforming the law violator, not the state. In short, as servants of the state criminologists provide information to the powerful members of society on how to control the dangerous classes. This relationship is not a plot, it exists because both the criminologist and the state have an interest in preserving the established order.

Although Shaw and McKay worked for the state of Illinois, they were not "conscious conspirators who were aware of the political context of their criminology" (Snodgrass 1972, p. 52). Bramson (1961) similarly states "The sociologists of the second generation were often 'unconscious' liberals who were concerned over the 'disorganizing' aspects of American life under the impact of industrialization and urbanism. They were often as unaware of their liberalism, . . . as they were of the conservative implications of some of the concepts they employed to analyze the society around them" (p. 91).

In sum, the Chicago sociologists were aligned with the very institutions of authority which guided their research endeavors. In the interest of turning their field into a profession they served their master well. Their theories of crime causation and control have justified the positions of power and privilege held by the dominant classes. Thio (1973, p. 9) argues that the very reason the sociology of deviance has continued in the same direction is because the sociologist's alignment with the state severely narrows the subject matter to be studied. As a result, the secretive and hidden forms of deviance of the powerful have been ignored and neglected.

Contemporary American sociologists' inattention to the study of organized crime: some reasons why

Thus far our discussion has focused primarily on the theoretical and ideological assumptions of the Chicago school sociologists and criminologists. At this time we will turn to more contemporary explanations for the neglect of organized crime by American sociologists. However, it is important to remember that many of these explanations are also appropriate in explaining the negligence in studying organized crime by the Chicago school theorists. Positivism has dominated criminological thought until the late 1960s. Even today, relatively few sociologists and criminologists reject positivism completely.

Foster (1977) wrote that "with the possible exception of corporate crime, no major form of criminal activity is as poorly understood by the American people or as routinely avoided, denied, minimized or rationalized, by the nation's academics as organized crime" (p. 1). Foster suggests that there is very little treatment of organized crime in contemporary criminology textbooks. The topic is "almost routinely omitted from the syllabi of college-level courses in criminology, corrections, and social problems" (Foster 1977, p. 2). Of course, Foster was writing in 1977 and his comments are no longer completely accurate. As we saw earlier in chapter 7, most contemporary criminology texts do contain chapters or sections on organized crime.

Furthermore, Foster (1977, p. 2) and others (Albini 1971; Ianni and Ianni 1972; Smith 1975; Martens and Cunningham-Niederer, 1985) argue that the media coverage of organized crime is highly sensationalized; government publications are often unavailable to researchers, and, if available, may be of questionable validity, and popular books on the subject are often highly romanticized. This leads to a misinformed public and worse, avoidance, denial, or minimization of the phenomenon by social scientists. Foster (1977) states "given the scope of organized crime as a social problem and given the extent of popular interest in the subject, . . . the omissions of the textbook and journal writers are indeed curious and, . . . are not accidental" (p. 1).

Foster offers a number of methodological obstacles, and theoretical, and ideological trends which predispose criminologists and other social scientists to ignore or minimize the phenomenon of organized crime, or to offer rationalizations for its existence. We will consider some of Foster's observations and the observations of other social scientists below.

It has already been suggested that there are problems in looking for organized criminals in conventional settings (jails, prisons, probation and parole offices). Very few organized criminals will be found in these settings, especially not the most successful and powerful ones. Yet there has been a long-standing tradition in American criminology that criminals are those that have been convicted in court. Of course, this tradition is rooted in the constitutional principle of innocent until proven guilty. This view, that criminals are those that have been convicted in court, may have contributed as a theoretical deterrent to the study of organized crime (Foster 1977, p. 16).

An additional view which has contributed as a deterrent to the study of organized crime is our image of who the criminal is and what constitutes a crime. From the beginning, crime has been viewed, by the public and most criminologists, as a lower-class phenomenon. The "Typical Criminal is a young lower-class male" and the "Typical Crime is *one-on-one* harm" (Reiman 1984, p. 46). Harm is interpreted as "either physical injury or loss of something valuable or both" (Reiman 1984, p. 46). It might be said, then, that harm is direct and purposeful. These "one-on-one" crimes are often quite visible to the public. They are often conceptualized as "street crimes," "illegal acts designed to prey on the public through theft, damage and violence" (Siegel 1989, p. 552). These are the crimes that we believe to be the most dangerous and threatening to the individual and society. Our moral sensibilities tell us that these crimes are more evil than indirect harm (e.g., harm through occupational hazards, corporate crime, or organized crime). These "one-on-one" crimes are imposed on their victims against their will. We rationalize the presence of organized crime in society by arguing that the public demands its services. In sum, "Because we accept the belief . . . that the model for crime is one person specifically intending to harm another, we accept a legal system that leaves us unprotected against much greater dangers to our lives and well-being than those threatened by the Typical Criminal" (Reiman 1984, p. 47).

It is Foster's (1977, p. 5) opinion that the rationalization of organized crime detracts from its socially destructive nature. He argues that there is the incorrect assumption that organized crime is functional for society, because it provides Americans with desired goods and services. However, this assumption ignores the fact that organized crime is also harmful to society, providing it with unwanted activities—extortion, securities market manipulation, pension fund raiding, and the bilking of legitimate business.

Foster (1977) is also critical of the ethnic succession theory of organized crime, which has "long served as a functional-type explanation of how crime aids disadvantaged minority groups in their struggles for economic and political equality" (p. 6). While he readily admits that organized crime did present opportunities for success for the earlier ethnic immigrants, he is not convinced that contemporary immigrants are experiencing this same success. Today's ethnic immigrants have not been able to assume positions of power and leadership within established criminal organizations nor are they establishing strong rival organizations.

While it is true that many ethnic groups are involved in organized crime today, none of these groups seems to have amassed the power and control of organized crime that Italian Americans have. Italian Americans seem to make up a kind of "criminal power elite," which controls most organized urban crime (Foster 1977, p. 9). This fact, the identification of gangsterism with Italian and Irish immigrants, is yet another instance where the Chicago sociologists' views and assumptions ran up against some inconvenient social facts, facts that were incompatible not only with their sociology, but also with their liberal vision (a sometimes highly romanticized one) of the ethnic and the immigrant. In today's terms, a hard and truly "value-free" look at Italian mobsters would have been "politically incorrect"!

The positive and liberal orientations of many criminologists also predisposed them to believe that individuals entered organized crime because of circumstance and not choice. And yet this was rarely true. Entrance into organized crime was often a rational choice. This argument is aptly demonstrated in Lupsha's (1981) article, *Individual Choice, Material Culture and Organized Crime*.

Methodological obstacles to studying organized crime are many, but they can be overcome. Data collection is often a long and tedious process. Data is often accumulated from "official documents, media reports, eyewitness accounts, court proceedings, social events, biographies, and so forth" (Foster 1977, p. 16). This type of data collection more closely resembles "intelligence gathering," than social scientific research, and may make many social scientists uncomfortable. The data may also be off limits to social scientists, faulty, or sensationalistic. More important, professional journals often seek "hard data," not "soft data" which may produce ambiguous research results. Positivistic criminologists often utilize "standard measuring instruments" to study their subjects directly. Furthermore, ambiguous research results may make the social scientist fearful of reprisals, legal and extra legal (Foster 1977, p. 16).

However, many social scientists agree, that the best research on organized crime has come from the field. Witness the work of Landesco (1929), Albini (1971), Ianni and Ianni (1972), and Chambliss (1973). There is a moral dilemma confronting the social scientist who engages in field research of organized criminals. The social scientist will be privy to criminal acts engaged in by organized criminals. The social scientist will have to make decisions as to what life-styles and subcultures he or she will disclose and not disclose (Polsky 1967, p. 140). They must try and obtain the complete trust of their subjects. Further, social scientists must try and remain objective. They cannot show moral condemnation toward their subjects. They should not try and "reform" or "rehabilitate" their subjects. This will be a very difficult task for the positivist criminologist (Polsky 1967, p. 144).

As others have pointed out, criminologists often have an "anti-criminal moral code" (Polsky 1967, p. 146). The moral code often prohibits the criminologist from engaging in field research. For these reasons they pass up the field study of criminals, invent rationalizations for avoiding it, exaggerate its difficulties, and neglect some fairly obvious techniques for avoiding these difficulties (Polsky 1967, p. 146). This "anti-criminal moral code" has long been with the criminologist. As Snodgrass (1972) stated of the Chicago school theorists, "whatever the criminal was the theorist was not" (p. 45). In rather pointed prose, Polsky (1967, p. 147) claims that unless criminologists surrender the safety of positivistic studies of crime, they will remain "veranda anthropologists," comfortably removed from the "cannibals and head-hunters" they purport to study and describe. Until then they will remain "jailhouse" or "courthouse" sociologists, "unable to produce anything like a genuinely scientific picture of crime" (Polsky 1967, p. 147).

Cressey (1969) suggests that one reason there is a lack of understanding about organized crime is "the proclivity of our society, and even social scientists, to view criminality as an individual matter rather than as an organizational matter" (pp. 65-70). This inclination to view criminality as an individual matter is peculiarly American, steeped in it s special brand of moralistic individualism. Of special importance to positivism is that its focus was on the individual criminal. Theoretical perspectives of criminality, whether biological, psychological, or sociological in nature, have continued to focus on the individual offender and not on the crime itself (Jeffery 1972, p. 471).

According to this view, criminality is seen as a problem of individual maladjustment or improper socialization. Criminality is not often viewed as a consequence of participation in a social system (Cressey 1969, p. 67). The theoretical models needed to study organized crime are often lacking. As sociologist John Martin (personal communication, April 23, 1991) remarks "We don't have good organizational models for the study of crime . . . as soon as you conceptualize crime as an organizational behavior rather than the behavior of individuals . . . you're getting into an area of sociological theory where we don't have a lot of experience in applying organizational analysis. . . . how do you organize something that officially doesn't exist? . . . where you can't study its records, or its annual reports, or its advertising." Even the courts have been designed for the trials of individuals, not organizations.

For these reasons criminologists have only recently begun to examine and explain the criminality of organizations and corporations. The change undoubtedly represents a change in our assumptions.

Foster (1977, p. 17) also identifies some dominant ideological beliefs which predispose social scientists to ignore or minimize the problem of organized crime, or to offer functional rationalizations for its existence. These ideological beliefs include democracy, egalitarianism, populism, and civil libertarianism. The belief in egalitarianism and democracy often prohibits the social scientist from accepting evidence which may imply that disadvantaged racial, ethnic, or cultural groups are morally inferior. Therefore, they choose not to focus on the organized criminal activity of these groups. Further, civil libertarianism precludes social scientists from interfering in the activities of criminal bureaucracies. Lastly, social scientists often minimize the importance of organized crime because they are often suspicious of governmental explanations of crime.

Despite all of the methodological, theoretical, and ideological explanations discussed thus far, some sociologists and criminologists have overcome these obstacles and trends to studying organized crime. This has come about particularly during the past two decades. Critical events in the wider social context of American society prompted sociologists and criminologists to study the crimes of the powerful, including organized crime. As Thio (1973, pp. 10-11) has indicated, the conservative sociology that has traditionally been practiced by sociologists needs to become more conflict oriented. Conservative sociology has allowed the sociologist to explore the behavior of the powerless but has failed to allow the sociologist to study the hidden behaviors of the powerful. The sociology of deviance as a field of study will always be suspect unless it explores the behaviors of all its citizens.

While Cressey published *Theft of the Nation* in 1969, many of his contemporaries were skeptical of Cressey's mainstream orientation and his affiliation with the 1967 President's Crime Commission. This was expressed in Quinney's Marxist insights (1970, pp. 60-61) that the commission's members represented dominant class interests. Quinney linked the commission's acceptance of the standard definitions of crime as a problem that threatens the status quo, to the commission's own self-conception as an organization serving the public interest, meaning the interests of the dominant class. Albini (1988, p. 352) also agrees that social scientists should be leery of working for governmental commissions. According to Albini (1988), it is often true that "governmental commissions have already drawn their conclusions before their investigations begin; hence, ... consultants are ... often selected in terms of those who are more likely to lend agreement to the Commission's findings" (p. 352). While Albini did not say that this was the case with Cressey's research, he did imply as much.

The emergence of a critical perspective

The theoretical perspectives of the Chicago school and the theories of Merton and Durkheim have been the dominant theoretical perspectives of the century.

However, a new perspective exploded onto the American scene during the late 1960s and early 1970s. This new school of thought has been known as "Marxist," "radical," or "critical," theory. This new perspective on crime and deviance challenged existing theories and drew on the intuitions of the New Left.

But the issues and concerns of the "new criminology" were not invented or created by sociologists. The "new criminology" reflected the interests and concerns of journalists, politicians, and the citizenry. These issues and concerns were those which dominated American society during the late 1960s and early 1970s.

Sociologists and criminologists sought to find explanations and research methodologies which could be applied to the issues. Block and Chambliss (1981) note that the "new criminology" raises questions that were asked in the past, but which were largely ignored in the 1950s. The authors (1981) pose the following questions which the "new criminology" attempts to answer:

1. Why are some acts defined as criminal while others are not?

2. Why are some people who commit acts defined as criminal punished while others are not?

3. Are the incidence and distribution of criminal acts explicable in terms of political and economic factors?

4. Are law and crime best understood as a reflection of shared values or as a reflection of social conflict?

5. To what extent does political and economic power determine the workings of the law, its creation, and its implementation? (p. 3)

However, what is significant is not that "radical ideas on crime and deviance . . . have fluctuated across different historical periods" (Cullen 1983, pp. 148-49), but that the perspective of the "new criminology" took hold because it was timely. The perspective of the "new criminology" emerged at a time when radical explanations seemed more creditable, given the American social landscape at that time. In the late 1960s the perspective became accepted as a legitimate school of deviance theory (Cullen 1983, p. 148).

Let us review the social context of America during this critical period in American history. The crisis in American society can be traced to a long history of racial and economic oppression of some groups of people. Groups who wanted and were promised a piece of the American pie, but who instead faced mostly opposition and discrimination. After World War II many American blacks were optimistic and struggled for social equality. Their rising expectations were not immediately met in the aftermath of the war. By the mid-1960s blacks made modest gains in formal legal equality. Yet many young blacks were still angry. They still had a long way to go in their fight for social equality. The anger was fueled by acts of police brutality and the assassination of civil rights leader Martin Luther King, in 1968. After King's death, rioting erupted in the black ghettos of the nation's largest cities. It was evident that America was made up of two societies, one white, one black, separate but unequal. This was the finding of the Kerner Commission Report which investigated rioting in America's major cities. The organization of power in America was decidedly lopsided (Pfohl 1985, pp. 335-41).

Political protests of inmates in America's prisons also occurred. These inmates who were legally defined as criminals by the state came to see themselves as victims of social oppression by the state. They fought the "hierarchically organized" prison "power structure" (Pfohl 1985, p. 336). The result was that prison administrators employed even more repressive measures against the inmates. Some inmates involved in prisoner rights met untimely deaths, including the over forty inmates and guards killed at New York's Attica State Prison (Pfohl 1985, p. 336). Pfohl (1985) asks, "Why were these politicized prisoners so feared by those in power? (p. 336) Pfohl states the answer is simple, "They had connected their crimes and criminality to a struggle for power within society as a whole" (p. 336).

Black politics, prisoners' uprisings, and the Vietnam War were all major impetuses for the new criminology (Pfohl 1985, p. 386). As protest and resistance against the war escalated, many young Americans went to jail as draft resisters or fled the country. The political turbulence was especially acute on college campuses where the war and struggles over racial equality upset the daily routines of these institutions. As Greenberg (1981) states, "By the early 1970s, radicalized graduate students and college faculty began to draw on the World View they had developed in the New Left to criticize ideas in the social sciences. . . . Opposition to racism, war, and imperialism were central issues" (p. 5). A new way of looking at the social order was demanded. The "critical perspective" was born out of this demand.

Furthermore, the postwar baby boom produced a large subculture of middle-class youth. These young people grew up believing in the validity of the American dream. Yet, they were also faced with images of racial discrimination and the violent, imperialist war in Vietnam. These images contrasted with the image of a dignified and good America. Many young people became disillusioned, some rebelled, some dropped out. They contrasted with mainstream American culture by wearing long hair, opposing the work ethic and the war in Vietnam. They experimented with new drugs and new forms of sexual expression. They also challenged the viewpoints of many mainstream professors. The college classroom became an environment for conflict and opposition. Students would act up in class, take over administrative offices on the campus, or leave their classrooms in disgust. Some mainstream professors struck back at their students. But other professors became radicalized. A generation of critical sociologists was born. These critical sociologists saw a connection between the powerless members of society who were drafted to fight the war in Vietnam, the young minorities who filled our prisons, Black Panther members who were killed by police bullets, the rioting in our urban ghettos, and those who were arrested for criticizing the policies of the American government. They all lacked the power to initiate change! Critical sociologists of deviance began to view deviance and its control as linked to social justice. Deviance in American society could only be studied as a political phenomenon, which meant an analysis of the role of power in American society was necessary (Pfohl 1985, pp. 337-338).

Soon after, radical professors and their students were singled out for "surveil-lance and control," "spied on," and "beaten by police" (Pfohl 1985, p. 338). Some radical professors were not granted tenure. In 1970, students at Jackson State College in Mississippi and Kent State University in Ohio were fired on while protesting. Vietnam, Kent State, and Attica altered the image of the state as dispensing only goodwill. The state was now viewed as a coercive instrument of social control (Cullen 1983, p. 149).

Sociologists of deviance began to understand more clearly the role that conflict and power plays in society. While the conditions were ripe for the new criminology, the growth of the paradigm did not happen overnight. In fact, the conflict theorists borrowed heavily from the issues and concerns of the labeling school. In the beginning, the critical criminologists simply added to their writings the power dimension which was lacking in the societal reaction school (labeling school). The labeling school strongly believed in nonintervention. In other words, young delinquents who were charged with acts of delinquency would be better off if they were not "treated" or punished. "Treatment" and punishment would stigmatize these youngsters as "delinquents," which would negatively effect there self-esteem. This in turn would lead to further criminality on the part of these "delinquents." Because treatment programs did not work anyway, it was better to intervene as little as possible in the lives of these youngsters (see Greenberg 1981, p. 3; Cullen 1983, p.150)

Critical criminologists, then, building on the work of the labeling theorists, added another dimension to the crime problem. Labeling theorists failed to recognize the relationship between inequalities in power and social control. In other words, while labeling theorists have paid attention to micro interactions between labeling and deviants, they have spent less time studying the relationship between social control and macro structural features of society as a whole. The labeling perspective fails to see deviance as originating from the "master institutions of the larger society" (Pfohl 1985, pp. 321-22).

During the period between the 1960s and the 1970s, the American New Left faced some difficulties. The United States withdrew from Vietnam. There was postwar defeatism. The American economy was slumping. The oil-producing nations were rising in economic power. Japan and West Germany were gaining in technological domination. Throughout the 1980s we witnessed inflation, recession, and high unemployment. A new conservative mood enveloped the country. Many Americans wondered what happened to America's power and influence. Many Americans ignored the problems of those whose ascribed social characteristics prevented them from sharing in the American dream. The romanticism of the young was replaced with the responsibilities of a career and family (Pfohl 1985, p. 339). "Only the women's movement, and to a more limited extent, the gay movement, remained capable of energizing and mobilizing the large numbers of people on behalf of left causes the way the antiwar and civil rights/black power movements had done" (Greenberg 1981, p. 10). Thus the critical perspective in recent years has been nurtured by the feminist movement, gay rights movement, and the increased attention to deviance by the powerful.

During the 1960s, C. Wright Mills nurtured the development of a critical perspective with his essays on the "power elite" of society. Mills challenged his sociological colleagues to address the unequal and often unnoticed hierarchical power structure of American society. His challenge was not answered by sociologists of deviance until almost a decade later. Why had it taken so long for sociologists to turn their attention to the deviance of the powerful? According to Liazos (1972), American sociologists were preoccupied with the deviance of "nuts, sluts, and perverts." Therefore, "the unethical, illegal and destructive actions of powerful groups, individuals and institutions" (Liazos, 1972) went unnoticed.

During the 1960s, the theories of functionalism, social learning, and anomie generated government funds to study lower-class crime and deviance. There was very little money to study crimes of business or deviance of the powerful. In the 1970s, sociologists witnessed Watergate, fraud, corruption, alliances between organized criminals and the government, illegal wire tapping of American citizens, and a host of other objectionable activities by the government. Witnessing these activities made sociologists of deviance realize the importance of researching the crimes of the powerful. This interest in the critical perspective is reflected in a number of theoretical and empirical studies. Many of these studies examined the social stratification and hierarchical organization of American life (Pfohl 1985, p. 370, 374).

In 1973, Taylor, Walton, and Young, authors of *The New Criminology*, explained what would be necessary for a radical theory of crime and delinquency. However, their primary purpose for writing their text was to critique existing theoretical perspectives (Cullen 1983, p. 152). Quinney (1977) "has offered an extended discussion of 'crime and capitalism,' . . . . while others have provided insights into the etiology of delinquency (Schwendinger and Schwendinger 1976, 1982; Greenberg 1977), organized crime (Pearce 1976), corporate crime (Barnett 1981), street crime (Gordon 1973; Wallace and Humphries 1980), and sex offenses (cf. Balkan et. al. 1980; Thio 1978)" (Cullen 1983, pp. 152-53).

Greenberg (1977) locates delinquency in terms of the "contradictory and structurally blocked aspirations of youths subordinated by the compound power hierarchies of age, class, and race" (Pfohl 1985, p. 370). Wallace and Humphries (1980) "use multiple-regression analysis to analyze the impact of capitalist accumulation (the production of higher rates of profit or surplus value when compared to wage value of labor returned to workers) on rates of urban crime" (Pfohl 1985, p. 371). Frank Pearce (1976), in *Crimes of the Powerful*, examines the links between big business, government, and organized crime in breaking up strikes and fighting communism in the international community.

These are just a few examples of critical inquiries aimed at those in positions of power. It should also be noted that radical theorists have also called attention to such violations of human rights as war, racism, sexism, and poverty. They argue that these acts should be labeled as crimes and their origins investigated (Schwendinger and

Schwendinger, 1975).

The diverse viewpoints of radical criminologists make it difficult to summarize their work. Yet, a number of common themes do emerge. Radical scholars reject the legal definition of crime. Instead, they propose a radical, human-rights definition of crime (see Platt, 1975, p. 103). A human rights definition of crime allows the researcher to examine systems of exploitation—racism, sexism, capitalism , and imperialism. Radical criminologists also critique mainstream criminology, observe the relationship between power and law, critique liberal reform, note the relationship between crime and politics, investigate ideologies of crime and stress radical action (Greenberg 1981, pp. 5-10).

As already indicated, Taylor, Walton, and Young (1973) critiqued a number of the leading theories of crime causation. They wanted criminologists to examine the unequal power structure in American society. Quinney (1970) attacked positivist criminology and Platt (1975) argued that criminology has served the capitalistic state.

Critical theorists also observed the role of power in shaping laws. Institutional discrimination, the unequal treatment of minorities and the poor, and the discriminatory use of discretion by police, prosecutors, judges, and paroling authorities became common themes in the literature written by critical criminologists (Greenberg 1981, p. 8).

Critical criminologists "sought to abolish the distinction between crime and politics" (Greenberg 1981, p. 8). "Crime itself" was thought to be "invested with political meaning" as a "protest against oppressive social conditions" (Greenberg 1981, p. 9) or as a rejection of the established order. Liberal reform was also critiqued. Platt's (1969) analysis of the juvenile court movement and the invention of delinquency is an excellent example of this type of study. Platt argues that the founding of the juvenile justice system in the late 1800s was an attempt on the part of white, middle-class women to control the "disorganized" youth living in the urban slums of Chicago. It was an attempt on the part of these women to reaffirm parental authority, home education, rural life, and traditional institutions because these things seemed to be threatened by the rapid industrialization, urbanization, and immigration which was occurring at the time (Platt 1977 p. 98).

Radical criminologists also began to "investigate the content and the social sources of beliefs about crime, law and criminal justice in the mass media, in government propaganda and even in the writings of criminologists" (Greenberg 1981, p. 9). Many of these beliefs were seen to be false. Radical scholars argued that these beliefs reinforced capitalistic values. They also argued that there was a "manufactured consensus" about what crime is (Greenberg 1981, p. 9).

Finally, radical criminologists believe in radical action. Radical criminologists must become actively involved in fighting for the disadvantaged members of society, ending the death penalty, stopping police brutality, and supporting the rights of political and indigent prisoners (Greenberg 1981, p. 10).

Concluding remarks

We have discussed the methodological obstacles, and the theoretical and ideological trends which have predisposed sociologists and criminologists to ignore or minimize the phenomenon of organized crime. While our initial focus was on the theorists of the Chicago school, we came to see that contemporary theorists often shared the same methodological, theoretical, and ideological assumptions of the Chicago school. These shared assumptions were often the result of a belief in positivist and liberal criminology. Let us review some of the reasons why sociologists and criminologists continue to ignore or minimize the importance of organized crime which have been addressed in this book: (1) the assumption that crime is a lower-class phenomenon; (2) the belief that the crimes of the powerless are more harmful than the crimes of the powerful; (3) the tendency to view crime as an individual act and to view the criminal as someone who needs to be reformed; (4) a belief in a legal definition of crime and the belief that a criminal is one who has been convicted in court; (5) the ability to manipulate and control the powerless rather than the powerful; (6) the rationalization that the public wants the services of organized crime; (7) the belief that American society is primarily good and the hesitancy to expose anything which might tarnish the image of American society; (8) the tendency of much research to be agency-determined; (9) the tendency to study criminals in conventional settings and to shy away from field research; (10) the repression of Marxist criminology in American universities; (12) the tendency to study individual offenders and not criminal or corporate organizations; and (13) a belief in the values of democracy, egalitarianism, populism, and civil libertarianism. All of these have persuaded sociologists and criminologists to ignore or minimize the phenomenon of organized crime.

In the final analysis, the most critical factors in accounting for sociologists reluctance to study organized crime are (1) the class and status positions of the sociologists themselves; and (2) their positivist methods. Both of these two factors are interrelated. Their positivist methods support and reinforce their class perspectives and interests. These liberal sociologists hold relative positions of power and influence in America's elite universities. Their class and identity is tied to the very institutions that make up American society, a society which they hold in high esteem. The liberalism of the sociologists dictates their belief in the fundamental values of America's institutions. Therefore, America's institutions and agencies do not cause the social problems found in the society. In fact, the possibility that organized crime was sustained through its links with official agencies and institutions was hardly even entertained by sociologists until relatively recently. In short, sociologists often study those individuals who are considered to be marginal members of the society and who are seen by the power elite, including the sociologists themselves, to be disruptive to the status quo. These are often individuals who are weak and powerless and who can be easily manipulated by their investigators.

However, criminology is the sign of the times. And these factors no longer seemed valid to sociologists and criminologists in the late 1960s and early 1970s. A new perspective was needed to view crime and deviance. That new perspective was critical criminology. Yet as Cullen (1983) remarks, "the potential for the new criminology to yield significant insights into the causes of wayward conduct—whether in the upper world or (especially) in our streets—remains largely undeveloped" (p. 153).

Even today, when organized crime is such a public issue, sociologists continue to ignore this phenomenon. As an example of sociologists' lack of attention to the phenomenon of organized crime, we can refer to the recent trial of the boss of the Gambino crime family, John Gotti. The American public has been made aware of this trial through the media. For several months the newspaper headlines have been filled with stories about Gotti's trial and subsequent conviction. Some of these recent headlines which appeared in *The Star Ledger* newspaper included the following: "Prosecutor Accuses Gotti of Shooting His Way to Top of Gambino Family" (February 13, 1992, p. 20); "A Don Behind the Times" (February 20, 1992, p. 17); "Gotti Deputy Turned Informant Testifies on the Castellano 'Hit'" (March 3, 1992, p. 1); "Trial Shows Gotti Broke Underworld's Basic Rules" (March 23, 1992, p. 11; "Gotti, Judge Clash in Court" (March 21, 1992, p. 2); "Gotti Guilty on all Counts, Faces A Life Prison Sentence" (April 3, 1992, p. 1); "Murder Trial Scratches the Surface of the Teflon Don's Many Faces" (April 3, 1992, p. 8). In addition, a headline in *Newsweek* (April 13, 1992, pp. 34-35) read "The 'Velcro Don': Wiseguys Finish Last." The point to be made is that these are articles written by journalists, not sociologists. The phenomenon of organized crime, as documented in Chapter 7, has been identified with journalism, law enforcement, and film. The American public is made aware of the phenomenon of organized crime through the media (newspapers, films, television, popular books). As one newspaper journalist pointedly wrote about John Gotti, "The flashy mobster captured the public imagination like no mobster since Al Capone" (*The Star Ledger*, April 3, 1992, p. 8).

As documented in chapter 7, even social scientists depend on journalists for their information on organized crime. There are very few well-known sociologists who study organized crime (a notable exception is Howard Abadinsky). There are very few organized crime articles found in sociology and criminology journals. Organized crime has always been and still is, to a large extent, the province of law enforcers, journalists, and film producers. When social scientists do study organized crime they are frequently identified as historians, economists, and political scientists, not as sociologists. In recent years, those social scientists who have studied organized crime have frequently been white ethnics who (1) have had some experience in urban environments; and (2) are dissatisfied with existing explanations of organized crime. For instance, as Howard Abadinsky (personal communication, September 6, 1990b) writes, "My own interest in organized crime developed out of my limited involvement with the phenomenon as a parole officer in the Redhook section of Brooklyn." In short, all social scientists, including sociologists, are encouraged to study the fascinating yet little understood phenomenon of organized crime.

References

Abadinsky, Howard. 1981a. *Organized Crime*. Massachusetts: Allyn and Bacon Incorporated.
_____ 1981b. "Researching Organized Crime: Methodological Problems." Paper presented at the Academy of Criminal Justice Sciences, Philadelphia, PA, March.
_____. 1981c. *The Mafia in America: An Oral History*. New York: Praeger.
_____. 1983. *The Criminal Elite: Professional and Organized Crime*. Connecticut: Greenwood Press.
_____. 1990a. *Organized Crime* (3rd ed.). Chicago, Illinois: Nelson-Hall Incorporated.
_____. 1990b, September 6. Letter to Marylee Reynolds.
Albanese, Jay. 1989. *Organized Crime in America* (2nd ed.). Cincinnati, Ohio: Anderson Publishing Company.
_____. 1991. "Organized Crime: The Mafia Mystique." Pp. 200-217 in *Criminology*, edited by Joseph F. Sheley. Belmont, CA: Wadsworth Publishing Company.
Albini, Joseph L. 1971. *The American Mafia Genesis of a Legend*. New York: Appleton-Century-Crofts.
_____. 1988. "Donald Cressey's Contributions to the Study of Organized Crime: An Evaluation." *Crime and Delinquency* 34:338-354.
Alihan, Milla Aissa. 1938. *Social Ecology: A Critical Analysis*. New York: Cooper Square Publishers.
Allsop, Kenneth. [1961] 1968. *The Bootleggers*. New Rochelle, NY: Arlington House.
Anderson, Nels. [1923] 1961. *The Hobo: The Sociology of the Homeless Man*. Chicago: University of Chicago Press.
Anderson, Pat. 1985. [Review of *Once Upon A Time in America*]. p. 1005 in *Film Review Annual*, edited by Jerome S. Ozer. Englewood, NJ: Jerome S. Ozer, Publisher.
Anderson, Sean. and Gregory J. Howard. 1994. "Crime, Criminal Justice, and Popular Culture." *Journal of Criminal Justice Education* 5:123-131.
Barlow, Hugh D. 1990. *Introduction to Criminology* (5th ed.). Illinois: Scott, Foresman and Company.
Barnes, Harry Elmer and Negley K. Teeters. 1943. *New Horizons In Criminology*. New Jersey: Prentice-Hall.
_____. 1951. *New Horizons In Criminology* (2nd ed.). New Jersey: Prentice-Hall.
Beaver, Frank E. 1983. *On Film: A History of the Motion Picture*. New York: McGraw-Hill Book Company.
Becker, Howard. 1963. *Outsiders: Studies in the Sociology of Deviance*. Glencoe, Illinois: The Free

Press.

Bell, Daniel. 1953. "Crime as an American Way of Life." *The Antioch Review* 13:131-154.

_____. 1962. *The End of Ideology.* Glencoe, Illinois: The Free Press.

Bennett, James. 1981. *Oral History and Delinquency.* Chicago: Unoversity of Chicago Press.

Berger, Peter L. and Brigitte Berger. 1972. "Deviance." Pp. 303-323 in *Sociology: A Biographical Approach,* (2nd ed.)., by Peter Berger and Brigitte Berger. NY: Basic Books.

Bloch, Herbert and Gilbert Geis. 1965. *Man, Crime, and Society* (4th ed.). NY: Random House.

Block, Alan A. 1978. "History and the Study of Organized Crime." *Urban Life* 6:455-74.

_____. 1983. *East Side/West Side.* NJ: Transaction Books.

Block, Alan A. and William J. Chambliss. 1981. *Organizing Crime.* NY: Elsevier North Holland Incorporated.

Bramson, Leon. 1961. *The Political Context of Sociology.* NJ: Princeton University Press.

Bruce, Andrew. [1929] 1968. "Introduction to Survey of Organized Crime." Pp. 1-7 in *Organized Crime in Chicago,* by John Landesco. Chicago: University of Chicago Press.

Bulmer, Martin. 1984. *The Chicago School of Sociology Institutionalization, Diversity and the Rise of Sociological Research.* Chicago: University of Chicago Press.

Burgess, Ernest W. [1925] 1967. "The Growth of the City: An Introduction to A Research Project." Pp. 47-62 in *The City,* edited by R. E. Park and E. W. Burgess. Chicago: University of Chicago Press.

_____. 1926. *The Urban Community.* Chicago: University of Chicago Press.

_____. [1929] 1968. "Summary and Recommendations." Pp. 227-286 in *Organized Crime in Chicago,* by John Landesco. Chicago: University of Chicago Press.

Burgess, Ernest W. and Donald J. Bogue. 1964. "Research in Urban Society: A Long View." Pp. 1-14 in *Contributions to Urban Sociology,* edited by Ernest W. Burgess and Donald J. Bogue. Chicago: University of Chicago Press.

Caiden, Gerald E. 1985. "What Should be Done About Organized Crime." Pp. 145-164 in *The Politics and Economics of Organized Crime,* edited by Herbert E. Alexander and Gerald E. Caiden. Lexington, MA: D. C. Heath and Company.

"Capone Moralizes on Eve of Sentence." 1931, July 30. *The New York Times,* p. 12.

Carey, James T. 1975. *Sociology and Public Affairs: The Chicago School.* Beverly Hills, CA: Sage Publications.

Cashman, Sean Dennis. 1981. *Prohibition: The Lie of the Land.* NY: The Free Press.

Cavan, Ruth. 1928. *Suicide.* Chicago: University of Chicago Press.

_____. 1983. "The Chicago School of Sociology, 1918-1933." *Urban Life* 11:407-419.

Chambliss, William J. 1973. "Vice, Corruption, Bureaucracy and Power." Pp. 353-379 in *Sociological Readings in the Conflict Perspective,* edited by William J. Chambliss. Reading, MA: Addison-Wesley.

Chambliss, William J. and R. B. Seidman. 1971. *Law, Order and Power.* Reading, MA: Addison Wesley.

Clinard, Marshall B. "Sociologists and American Criminology." *Journal of Criminal Law and Criminology* 41:549-77.

Cohen, Stanley. 1970. [Review of *Organized Crime in Chicago*]. *British Journal of Criminology* 10:92.

Conklin, John E. 1973. "Introduction: Organized Crime and American Society." Pp. 1-24 in *The Crime Establishment,* edited by John E. Conklin. NJ: Prentice-Hall.

_____. 1989. *Criminology* (3rd ed.). NY: MacMillan.

Cressey, Donald R. 1969. *Theft of the Nation.* NY: Harper and Rpw.

Cressey, Paul G. 1932. *The Taxi-Dance Hall: A Sociological Study in Commercialized Recreation and*

City Life. Chicago: University of Chicago Press.

_____. 1971. "The Taxi-Dance Hall." Pp. 193-209 in *The Social Fabric of the Metropolis: Contributions of the Chicago School of Urban Sociology*, edited by James F. Short, Jr. Chicago: University of Chicago Press.

"Crimes of the Mafias." 1890, October 20. *The New York Times*, p. 1.

Cullen, Francis T. 1983. *Rethinking Crime and Deviance Theory.* NJ: Rowman and Allanheld.

Deegan, Mary Jo. 1991, May 11. Letter to Marylee Reynolds.

Denby, David. 1986. [Review of *Prizzi's Honor*]. p. 1009 in *Film Review Annual*, edited by Jerome S. Ozer. Englewood, NJ: Jerome S. Ozer, Publisher.

Earley, Steven C. 1978. *An Introduction to American Movies.* NY: A Mentor Book.

Elliot, Mabel A. 1952. *Crime in Modern Society.* NY: Harper and Brothers.

"Ethnic Gangs and Organized Crime." 1988. *U.S. News and World Report* 104:29-37.

Faris, Robert E. L. [1967] 1970. *Chicago Sociology, 1920-1932.* Chicago: University of Chicago Press.

Farley, John E. 1990. *Sociology.* NJ: Prentice-Hall.

"Finds Environment The Cause of Crime." 1929, February 24. *The New York Times*, p. 28.

Fish, Virginia Kemp. 1991, April 29. Letter to Marylee Reynolds.

Foster, Thomas W. 1977. "Why Don't We Know More About Organized Crime?" Paper presented at the Annual Meeting of the North Central Sociological Association, Pittsburgh, PA, May.

"Found Dead in A Sack." 1890, October 25. *The New York Times*, p. 1.

Fox, Stephen. 1989. *Blood and Power: Organized Crime in Twentieth-Century America.* NY: William Morrow and Company.

Frazier, E. Franklin. 1932. *The Negro Family in Chicago.* Chicago: University of Chicago Press.

_____. 1964. "The Negro Family In Chicago." Pp. 404-418 in *Contributions to Urban Sociology*, edited by Ernest W. Burgess and Donald J. Bogue. Chicago: University of Chicago Press.

Galliher, John F. and James A. Cain. 1974. "Citation Support for the Mafia Myth in Criminology Textbooks." *American Sociologist*, 9:68-74.

Gaylord, Mark Stratton. 1984. "Edwin Sutherland and the Origins of Differential Association." Unpublished doctoral dissertation, Department of Sociology, The University of Missouri-Columbia, Columbia, Missouri.

Gibbons, Don C. 1992. *Society, Crime, and Criminal Behavior* (6th ed.). NJ: Prentice-Hall.

Glaser, Daniel. 1992, January 24. Letter to Marylee Reynolds.

Glazer, Nathaniel. 1966. "Forward." Pp. vii-xviii in *The Negro Family in the United States*, by E. Franklin Frazier. Chicago: University of Chicago Press.

Golden, Daniel Stembroff. 1980. "The Fate of La Famiglia: Italian Images in American Film." Pp. 73-97 in *The* Kaleidoscopic Lens How Hollywood Views Ethnic Groups, edited by Randall M. Miller. Jerome S. Ozer, Publisher.

Goode, Erich. 1990. *Deviant Behavior* (3rd ed.). NJ: Prentice-Hall.

"Gotti Deputy Turned Informant Testifies on the Castellano 'hit'." 1992, March 3. *The Star Ledger*, p. 1, 7.

"Gotti Guilty on All Counts, Faces A Life Prison Sentence." 1992, April 3. *The Star Ledger*, p. 1, 8.

"Gotti, Judge Clash in Court." 1992, March 21. *The Star Ledger*, p. 2.

Gouldner, Alvin W. 1970. *The Coming Crisis of Western Sociology.* NY: Avon Books.

Greenberg, David F. (ed). 1981. *Crime and Capitalism.* California: Mayfield Publishing Company.

Griswold, Glenn. 1927, November 20. "Mid-West Is Taking Politics Seriously." *New York Times*, Section III, p. E2.

Gurfein, Murray I. 1962. "The Racket Defined." Pp. 181-182 in *Organized Crime In America*, edited by Gus Tyler. Michigan: University of Michigan Press.

Gusfield, Joseph. 1963. *Symbolic Crusade: Status Politics and the American Temperance Movement*. Urbana, IL: University of Illinois Press.

Hall, Jerome. 1950. "Edwin H. Sutherland: 1883-1950." *Journal of Criminal Law and Criminology* 41:393-396.

Haller, Mark H. N.d.a. "The Illinois Crime Survey." Unpublished manuscript.

_____. N.d.b. "Formation of the Illinois Association For Criminal Justice." Unpublished Manuscript.

_____. 1968. "Introduction." Pp. vii-xviii in *Organized Crime in Chicago*, by John Landesco. Chicago: University of Chicago Press.

_____. 1970. "Urban Crime and Criminal Justice: The Chicago Case." *Journal of American History* 57:619-635.

_____. 1971-72. "Organized Crime in Urban Society: Chicago in the Twentieth Century." *Journal of Social History* 5:210-233.

_____. 1989, September 5. Letter to Marylee Reynolds.

Haskell, Martin R. and Lewis Yablonsky. 1974. *Criminology: Crime and Criminality*. Chicago: Rand McNally Publishing Company.

Hawkins, Gordon. 1969. "God and the Mafia." *The Public Interest* 14:24-51.

Hayner, Norman. 1936. *Hotel Life*. North Carolina: University of North Carolina Press.

_____. 1964. "Hotel Life: Physical Proxmity and Social Distance." Pp. 314-323 in *Contributions to Urban Sociology*, edited by Ernest W. Burgess and Donald J. Bogue. Chicago: University of Chicago Press.

Higham, John. [1955] 1963. *Strangers in the Land: Patterns of American Nativism 1860-1925*. NY: Atheneum.

Homer, Frederick D. 1974. *Guns and Garlic: Myths and Realities of Organized Crime*. Indiana: Purdue University Studies.

Hunter, Albert. 1980. "Why Chicago? The Rise of the Chicago School of Urban Social Science." *American Behavioral Scientist* 24:215-227.

Ianni, Francis A.J. and Elizabeth Reuss-Ianni. 1972. *A Family Business: Kinship and Social Control in Organized* Crime. NY: Russell Sage Foundation.

_____. 1983. "Organized Crime: Overview." Pp. 1095-1106 in *Encyclopedia of Crime and Justice*, vol. 3, edited by Stanford H. Kadish. NY: The Free Press.

"In the Jungle." [Review of *Organized Crime In Chicago*] *Times Literary Supplement*, p. 386.

Inciardi, James A., Alan A. Block, and Lyle A. Hallowell. 1977. *Historical Approaches to Crime: Research Strategies and Issues*. Vol. 57, California: Sage Publications.

Jaehne, Karen. 1991. [Review of *Goodfellas*]. *Film Quarterly* 44:33-50.

Janowitz, Morris. 1966. "Introduction." Pp. vii-iviii in *W. I. Thomas, On Social Organization and Social Personality*, Selected Papers, edited by Morris Janowitz. Chicago: University of Chicago Press.

_____. 1967. "Introduction." Pp. vii-x in *The City*, edited by Robert E. Park and Ernest W. Burgess. Chicago: University of Chicago Press.

Jarvie, I. C. 1970. *Movies and Society*. NY: Garland Publishing.

Jedel, Celeste. 1931, March 8. "From Troy to Chicago the Racket Runs." *The New York Times*, Section V, pp. 6, 22.

Jeffery, Clarence Ray. 1972. "The Historical Development of Criminology." Pp. 458-498 in

Pioneers in Criminology (2nd ed.), edited by Herman Mannheim. Montclair, NJ: Patterson Smith.

Jowett, Garth. 1979. "Bullets, Beer and the Hays Office: Public Enemy (1931)." pP. 57-75 In *American History/ American Film: Interpreting the Hollywood Image*, edited by John E. O' Conner and Martin A. Jackson. NY: Frederick Unger Publishing Company.

Kobler, John. 1971. *Capone: The Life and World of Al Capone*. NY: G. P. Putnam's Sons.

Kobrin, Solomon. 1991, June 1. Letter to Marylee Reynolds.

Kooistra, Paul. 1989. *Criminals as Heroes: Structure, Power and Identity*. Bowling Green, Ohio: Bowling Green State University Popular Press.

Kornhauser, Ruth. 1978. *Social Sources of Delinquency: An Appraisal of Analytical Models*. Chicago: University of Chicago Press.

Kurtz, Lester. 1984. *Evaluating Chicago Sociology: A Guide to the Literature, With An Annotated Bibliography*. Chicago: University of Chicago Press.

Kyving, David E. 1979. *Repealing National Prohibition*. Chicago: University of Chicago Press.

Landesco, John. [1929] 1968. *Organized Crime In Chicago, Part III of the Illinois Crime Survey 1929*. Chicago: University of Chicago Press.

_____. 1932. "Prohibition and Crime." *The Annals of the American Academy of Political and Social Sciences* CLXIII:120-129.

_____. 1933. "Life History of A Member of the Forty-two Gang." *Journal of Criminal Law and Criminology* 24: 928-940.

_____. 1934. "The Criminal Underworld of Chicago in the '80's and '90's. *Journal of Criminal Law and* Criminology 25:341-357.

Lashley, Arthur. 1930. "Report of the Illinois Crime Survey." *Journal of Criminal Law, Criminology and Police Science* 20:588-605.

Lerner, Max. 1957. *America As A Civilization: Life and Thought in the United States Today*. NY: Simon and Schuster.

Lewis, D. J. and R. L. Smith. 1980. *American Sociology and Pragmatism: Mead, Chicago Sociology and Symbolic Interactionism*. Chicago: University of Chicago Press.

Liazos, Alexander. 1972. "The Poverty of the Sociology of Deviance: Nuts, Sluts and Preverts." *Social Problems* 20:103-120.

_____. 1975. "The Poverty of the Sociology of Deviance: Nuts, Sluts and Preverts." Pp. 250-272 in *Theories of Deviance*, edited by Stuart H. Traub and Craig B. Little. Illinois: F. E. Peacock Publishers.

Lupsha, Peter. 1981. "Individual Choice, Material Culture and Organized Crime." *Criminology* 19:3-24.

Martens, Frederick T. and Michelle Cunningham-Niederer. 1985. "Media Magic, Mafia Mania." *Federal Probation* 49:60-68.

Martin, John. 1991, April 23. Personal Interview.

Martin, John M. and Anne T. Romano. 1992. *Multinational Crime: The Challenges of Terrorism, Espionage, Drug and Arms Trafficking*. California: Sage Publications.

Martindale, Don. 1957. "Social Disorganizations: The Conflict of Normative and Empirical Approaches." Pp. 340-367 in *Modern Sociological Theory in Continuity and Change*, edited by H. Becker and A. Boskoff. NY: Dryden Press.

Masters, Ruth and Cliff Robinson. 1990. *Inside Criminology*. NJ: Prentice-Hall.

Matthews, F. H. 1977. *Quest for An American Sociology: Robert Park and the Chicago School*. London: McGill-Queen's University Press.

McLaughlin, John. 1992, February 20. "A Don Behind the Times." *The Star Ledger*, p. 17.

Merton, Robert. 1968. *Social Theory and Social Structure*. NY: The Free Press.

Mills, C. Wright. 1943. "The Professional Ideology of Social Pathologists." *The American Journal of Sociology*, 49:165-180.

Milne, David S. 1969. [Review of *Organized Crime in Chicago*]. *Sociology and Social Research* 53:407-410.

Mitchell, Duncan G. 1968. *A 100 Years of Sociology*. London: Duckworth.

Moley, Raymond. 1931, August 9. "The Racket: The Most Elusive of Crimes." *The New York Times*, Section IX, p. 1.

Moore, William H. 1974. *The Kefauver Committee and the Politics of Crime, 1950-1952*. Columbia, Missouri: University of Missouri Press.

Moquin, Wayne and Charles Van Doren (eds.). 1976. *The American Way of Crime: A Documentary History*. NY: Praeger Publishers.

Morris, Terrence. 1958. *The Criminal Area*. London: Routledge and Keegan Paul.

Mowrer, Ernest R. 1927. *Family Disorganization*. Chicago: University of Chicago Press.

_____. 1964. "Family Disorganization." Pp. 493-511 in *Contributions to Urban Sociology*, edited by Ernest W. Burgess and Donald J. Bogue. Chicago: University of Chicago Press.

Mueller, John J. 1950. "Edwin Hardin Sutherland, 1883-1950." *ASR* 801-803.

"Murder Trial Scratches the Surface of the Teflon Don's Many Faces." 1992, April 3. *The Star Ledger*, p. 8.

Murray, Lawrence L. 1979. "Hollywood, Nihilism, and the Youth Culture of the Sixties: Bonnie and Clyde (1967)." Pp. 237-256 in *American History/American Film: Interpreting the Hollywood Image*. NY: Frederick Unger Publishing Company.

Nelli, Hubert S. 1969. "Italians and Crime in Chicago: The Formative Years, 1890-1920." *The American Journal of Sociology*, 74:273-339.

_____. 1976. *The Business of Crime: Italians and Syndicate Crime in the United States*. NY: Oxford University Press.

Norland, Rod. 1992, April 13. "The 'Velcro Don': Wiseguys Finish Last." *Newsweek*, pp. 34-35.

O' Kane, James M. *The Crooked Ladder Gangsters, Ethnicity and the American Dream*. New Brunswick, NJ: Transaction Books.

Pearce, Frank. 1976. *Crimes of the Powerful: Marxism, Crime and Deviance*. London: Pluto Press.

_____. 1981. "Organized Crime and Class Politics." Pp. 157-181 in *Crime and Capitalism*, edited by David Greenberg. California: Mayfield Publishing Company.

Perlmutter, Emanuel. 1963, September 28. "Valachi Accuses Mafia Leaders at Senate Inquiry." *The New York Times*, p. 1.

_____. 1963, October 2. "Valachi Names 5 As Crime Chiefs in New York Area." *The New York Times*, p. 1.

Peterson, Virgil. 1952. *Barbarians in Our Midst: A History of Chicago Crime and Politics*. Massachusetts: Little, Brown and Company.

_____. 1963. "Chicago: Shades of Capone." *The Annals of the American Academy of Political and Social Science* 347:30-39.

Pfohl, Stephen J. 1985. *Images of Deviance and Social Control*. NY: McGraw-Hill.

Platt, Anthony M. [1969] 1977. *The Child Savers: The Invention of Delinquency* (2nd ed.). Chicago: University of Chicago Press.

_____. 1975. "Prospects For A Radical Criminology in the USA." Pp. 95-112 in *Critical Criminology*, edited by I. Taylor, P. Walton, and J. Young. London: Routledge and Keegan Paul.

Polsky, Ned. 1967. *Hustlers, Beats and Others*. Garden City, NY: Doubleday-Anchor.

Potter, Gary W. 1994. *Criminal Organizations Vice, Racketeering and Politics In An American City*.

Prospect Heights, Illinois: Waveland Press, Inc.

Powers, Richard G. 1983. *G-Men: Hoover's FBI In American Popular Culture.* Illinois: Southern Illinois University Press.

"Prosecutor Accuses Gotti of Shooting His Way to Top of Gambino Family." 1992, February 13. *The Star Ledger,* p. 20.

Quinney, Richard. 1970. *The Social Reality of Crime.* Boston, MA: Little, Brown and Company.

_____. 1974. *Critique of Legal Order: Crime Control in Capitalist Society.* Boston, MA: Little, Brown and Company.

_____. 1975. *Criminology: Analysis and Critique of Crime in America.* Boston, MA: Little, Brown and Company.

_____. 1977. *Class, State and Crime: On the Theory and Practice of Criminal Justice.* NY: Longman Incorporated.

"'Racket' is Defined by Loesh; 'Return to Faith' Held Remedy." 1932, April 11. *The New York Times,* p. 6.

Rae, Bruce. 1929, August 8. "The Will-O-The-Wisps of the Underworld." *The New York Times,* Section V, pp. 6, 7.

Raeburn, John. 1988. "The Gangster Film." Pp. 47-63 in *Handbook of American Film Genres,* edited by Wes D. Gehring. Connecticut: Greenwood Press.

Raushenbush, Winifred. 1979. *Robert E. Park: Biography of A Sociologist.* North Carolina: Duke University Press.

Reckless, Walter. 1933. *Vice In Chicago.* Chicago: University of Chicago Press.

_____. 1971. "The Distribution of Commercialized Vice in the City: A Sociological Analysis." Pp. 239-251 in *The Social Fabric of the Metropolis: Contributions to the Chicago School of Urban Sociology,* edited by James F. Short, Jr. Chicago: University of Chicago Press.

_____. 1973. *The Crime Problem* (5th ed.). NJ: Prentice-Hall.

Reed, Rex. 1986. [Review of *Prizzi's Honor*]. Pp. 1002-1003 in *Film Review Annual,* edited by Jerome S. Ozer. Englewood, NJ: Jerome S. Ozer, Publisher.

Reid, Sue Titus. 1991. *Crime and Criminology* (6th ed.). NY: Holt, Rinehart and Winston.

Reiman, Jeffrey H. [1979] 1984. *The Rich Get Richer and the Poor Get Poorer* (2nd ed.). NY: MacMillan Publishing Company.

Reynolds, Stanley. 1969. "The Chicago Mob-Then and Now." [Review of *Organized Crime in Chicago*]. *Manchester* Guardian Weekly 100:14.

Ruth, Henry S., Jr. 1969. [Review of *Organized Crime In Chicago*]. *American Sociological Review* 34:804-805.

Schmidt, William E. 1987, September 20. "Chicago Still Haunted by the Ghost of Capone." *The New York Times,* p. L26.

Schuessler, Karl. 1973. "Introduction." Pp. ix-xxxvi in *Edwin H. Sutherland: On Analyzing Crime,* edited by Karl Schuessler. Chicago: University of Chicago Press.

Schwendinger, Julia and Herman Schwendinger. 1974. *The Sociologists of the Chair: A Radical Analysis of the Formative Years of North American Sociology (1883-1922).* NY: Basic Books.

_____. 1975. "Defenders of Order or Guardians of Human Rights?" Pp. 113-146 in *Critical Criminology,* edited by I. Taylor, P. Walton, and J. Young. London: Routledge and Keegan Paul.

_____. 26, July 1989. Letter to Marylee Reynolds.

Sellin, Thorsten. 1938. *Culture Conflict and Crime.* NY: Social Science Research Council.

Sellin, Thorsten and Ralph W. England, Jr. 1956. "Criminology, 1945-1955." p. 120 in *Sociology in the United States of America,* edited by Hans L. Zetterberg. UNESCO.

Shadoian, Jack. 1977. *Dreams and Dead Ends: The American Gangster/Crime Film*. Massachusetts: MIT Press.

Shaw, Clifford R. 1930. *The Jack-Roller*. Chicago: University of Chicago Press.

Shaw, Clifford R. and Maurice E. Moore. 1931. *The Natural History of A Delinquent Career*. Chicago: University of Chicago Press.

Shaw, Clifford R. and Henry D. McKay. 1931. *Social Factors in Juvenile Delinquency*. Chicago: University of Chicago Press.

Shaw, Clifford R., Harvey Zorbaugh, and Henry D. McKay. 1929.*Delinquency Areas*. Chicago: University of Chicago Press.

Shils, Edward. 1945. *The Present State of American Sociology*. Glencoe, IL: The Free Press.

_____. 1970. "Tradition, Ecology, and Institution in the History of Sociology." *Daedalus*. 9:760-826.

Short, James F., Jr. 1971. "Introduction." Pp. xi-xlvi in *The Social Fabric of the Metropolis: Contributions to the Chicago School of Urban Sociology*, edited by James F. Short, Jr. Chicago: University of Chicago Press.

"Shot Down at His Door." 1890, October 17. *The New York Times*, p. 1.

Siegel, Larry J. 1989. *Criminology* (3rd ed.). Minnesota: West Publishing Company.

_____ . 1992. *Criminology* (4th ed.). Minnesota: West Publishing Company.

Silver, Isidore. 1980. "All in the Mafia Family: The Godfather." Pp. 51-58 in *Film in Society* edited by Arthur Asa Berger. NJ: Transaction Incorporated.

Smith, Dennis. 1988.*The Chicago School: A Liberal Critique of Capitalism*. NY: St. Martin's Press.

Smith, Dwight C. 1975. *The Mafia Mystique*. NY: Basic Books.

Smith, Dwight C. and Richard Alba. 1979. "Organized Crime and American Life." *Society* 16:32-38.

Snodgrass, Jon D. 1972. "The American Criminological Tradition: Portraits of the Men and Ideology In A Discipline." Unpublished doctoral dissertation, Department of Sociology, The University of Pennsylvania, Philadelphia, PA.

_____. 1976. "Clifford R. Shaw and Henry D. McKay: Chicago Criminologists." *The British Journal of Sociology* 16:1-19.

Sterritt, David. 1985. [Review of *Once Upon A Time In America*]. Pp. 1004-1005 in *Film Review Annual*, edited by Jerome S. Ozer. Englewood Cliffs, NJ: Jerome S. Ozer, Publisher.

Surrette, Ray. 1992. *Media, Crime and Criminal Justice*. Belmont, CA: Brooks/Cole.

Sutherland, Edwin H. 1937. *The Professional Thief*. Chicago: University of Chicago Press.

_____ . 1949. *White Collar Crime*. NY: Dryden Press.

Sutherland, Edwin H. and Harvey J. Locke. 1936. *Twenty Thousand Homeless Men: A Study of Unemployed Men in the Chicago Shelters*. Philadelphia, PA: J. B. Lippincott.

Sutherland, Edwin H. and Donald R. Cressey. 1978.*Criminology* (10th ed.). Philadelphia, PA: J. B. Lippincott.

Sykes, Gresham M. 1978. *Criminology*. NY: Harcourt, Brace, Jovanovich Incorporated.

Taft, Donald R. and Ralph W. England. 1964. *Criminology* (4th ed.). NY: MacMillan.

Taylor, Ian, Paul Walton and Jock Young. 1973. *The New Criminology: For A Social Theory of Deviance*. NY: Harper and Row.

_____. 1975. *Critical Criminology*. London: Routledge and Keegan Paul.

"The Murder of the Chief." 1890, October 18. *The New York Times*, p. 1.

Thio, Alex. 1973. "Class Bias in the Sociology of Deviance." *The American Sociologist*. 8:1-12.

_____. 1988. *Deviant Behavior*. NY: Harper and Row.

Thomas, Jim. 1983. "Chicago Sociology: An Introduction." *Urban Life* 11:387-395.

_____. 1983. "Toward A Critical Ethnography: A Re-Examination of the Chicago Legacy."

Urban Life 11:477-489.

Thomas, William I. 1966. *On Social Organization and Social Personality.* Chicago: University of Chicago Press.

Thomas, William I. and Florian Znaniecki. [1918-1919] 1927. *The Polish Peasant in Europe and America,* Vols. 1-2, NY: Knopf.

_____. 1975. "The Concept of Social Disorganization." Pp. 34-37 in *Theories of Deviance,* edited by Stuart H. Traub and Craig B. Little. Itasca, IL: F. E. Peacock Publishers.

Thrasher, Frederic. [1927] 1963. *The Gang: A Study of 1,313 Gangs In Chicago* (Abridged ed.). Chicago: University of Chicago Press.

"To Hunt the Assasins." 1890, October 19. *The New York Times,* p. 1.

Traub, Stuart H. and Craig B. Little (eds.). 1975. *Theories of Deviance.* Itasca, IL: F. E. Peacock Publishers.

"Trial Shows Gotti Broke Underworld's Basic Rules." 1992, March 23. *The Star Ledger,* p. 11.

Turk, Austin. 1969. *Criminality and Legal Order.* Chicago: Rand McNally.

Tyler, Gus. 1962. *Organized In America.* Michigan: University of Michigan Press.

Vetter, Harold J. and Ira J. Silverman. 1986. *Criminology and Crime: An Introduction.* NY: Harper and Row.

Vold, George. 1951. "Edwin Hardin Sutherland: Sociological Criminologist." *ASR* 16:3-9.

Vold, George and Thomas Bernard. 1986. *Theoretical Criminology* (3rd ed.). NY: Oxford University Press.

Walsh, Marilyn E. 1992. "Organized Crime." Pp. 1404-1409 in *Encyclopedia of Sociology,* Vol. 3, edited by Edgar F. Borgatta and Marie L. Borgatta. NY: MacMillan.

Weir, Eligius O.F.M. 1941. *Criminology.* Indiana: The Abbey Press.

Wirth, Louis. 1928. *The Ghetto.* Chicago: University of Chicago Press.

Woodiwiss, Michael. 1987. "Capone to Kefauver: Organised Crime in America." *History Today,* pp. 8-15.

Young, Pauline. 1932. *The Pilgrims of Russian-Town.* Chicago: University of Chicago Press.

_____. 1939. *Scientific Social Surveys and Research An Introduction to the Background, Content, Methods, and Analysis of Social Studies.* NY: Prentice-Hall.

Zorbaugh, Harvey W. 1929. *The Gold Coast and the Slum: A Sociological Study of Chicago's Near North Side.* Chicago: University of Chicago Press.

Index